Shinners, Dissos and Dissenters

D1330592

MANCHESTER
1824

Manchester University Press

Shinners, Dissos and Dissenters

Irish republican media activism since the Good Friday Agreement

Paddy Hoey

Manchester University Press

The right of Paddy Hoey to be identified as the author of this work has been asserted by him in accordance with the Copyright, Designs and Patents Act 1988.

Published by Manchester University Press
Altrincham Street, Manchester M1 7JA, UK
www.manchesteruniversitypress.co.uk

British Library Cataloguing-in-Publication Data is available

ISBN 978 1 5261 1424 2 *hardback*
ISBN 978 1 5261 1425 9 *paperback*

First published by Manchester University Press in hardback 2018

This edition published 2020

The publisher has no responsibility for the persistence or accuracy of URLs for any external or third-party internet websites referred to in this book, and does not guarantee that any content on such websites is, or will remain, accurate or appropriate.

Typeset by Toppan Best-set Premedia Limited

For Pamela and Ella

Contents

Acknowledgements

My gratitude to Professor Peter Shirlow, Dr Diane Urquhart and Professor Frank Shovlin of the Institute of Irish Studies at the University of Liverpool, for advice and support. Thanks also to Dr Stephen Baker, Dr Aaron Edwards, Dr Ultán Gillen, Dr Deaglán Ó'Donghaile, Dr Ciarán O'Neill, Dr Ciarán Swan, Professor Jonathan Tonge, Dr Jason Walsh, Mick Fealty, Carrie McIntyre and Dr Malachi O'Doherty for being invaluable sounding boards. I would like to thank former colleagues at Liverpool Hope University, in particular the Irish Studies Research Group, including Dr Michael Holmes and Dr Terry Phillips. Dr Sue Cronshaw, Dr Gary Morrisroe and Andy Catterall of Liverpool Hope are also offered my gratitude. Professor Owen Evans, Professor Claire Molloy and Professor Victor Merriman of Edge Hill University were also of enormous help. More thanks to Dr Niall Carson and Dr Robert Busby, close friends with whom I hope to work again.

Very special thanks to Dr Kevin Bean, who was a major inspiration for starting the project and was a supportive guide throughout. As my mother says, 'You were well met!'

Ma, Da, Brona, Martin, Simon, Ciara, Cillian and Cormac, and the Flemings, assorted Hoeys and McCanns. Jane and Rob Murdoch are also thanked for this being one of the best-travelled books and perhaps the only one partly written in a tent in northern France.

Glossary

32CSM	32 County Sovereignty Movement. Organization which split from Sinn Féin in 1997, linked to Real IRA
AGFAR	Anti-Good Friday Agreement Republican. Republicans who dissented from Sinn Féin's and the Provisional movement's support for the 1998 Belfast peace agreement
An Glór Gafa	Journal written by republican prisoners. Means 'captive voice' in Irish
AP/RN	*An Phoblacht/Republican News*. Sinn Féin newspapers established in 1970 which merged in 1979
Ard comhairle	National party executive
Ard fheis	Annual party conference
CFAD	Concerned Families Against Drugs. North Belfast vigilante organization that targeted drug dealers with links to dissident armed groups. Similar to Derry-based Republican Action Against Drugs (RAAD)
CIRA	Continuity IRA, linked to Republican Sinn Féin. Armed organization which split from PIRA in 1986. However, it did not become active until 1994
Colour party	Uniformed and often armed guard that flanked coffins and graves at paramilitary funerals
Cumann	Local branch of Sinn Féin and Republican Sinn Féin parties
Dáil Éireann	The lower house of the Irish Parliament
DUP	Democratic Unionist Party. Dominant unionist party in Northern Ireland since 2003. Established by Rev. Ian Paisley in 1971 with strong links to the evangelical Protestant Free Presbyterian Church

Fianna Fáil	Republic of Ireland centre-right political party with revolutionary connections to the 1916 Rising, War of Independence, Civil War and anti-Anglo Irish Treaty position. Split from early incarnation of Sinn Féin in 1926
Fine Gael	Centre-right Irish political party emanating from pro-Anglo Irish Treaty forces
GFA	Good Friday/Belfast Agreement. Peace agreement signed on 10 April 1998 which effectively ended the armed conflict known as the Troubles
grá	Irish word for love/affection
INLA	Irish National Liberation Army. Left-wing republican armed organization which split from the Provisional movement in 1974. Linked to IRSP
IRIS	Irish Republican Information Service. Early Internet republican newsletter. Also name of Sinn Féin's republican magazine which appeared irregularly between 2006 and 2012
IRSP	Irish Republican Socialist Party. Left-wing republican party which split from the Provisional movement in 1974
IRWG	Irish Republican Writers Group. Small group of AGFARs responsible for the first wave of countercultural writing beginning in 1999
MLA	Member of the Legislative Assembly in Northern Ireland Parliament at Stormont
Mosquito press	Small countercultural journals and newspapers which buzz around mainstream political media causing an annoyance
Nama	National Asset Management Agency. Body created by the Irish government to manage the billions of pounds of bad debts resulting from the Irish financial crisis
NORAID	Irish Northern Aid Committee. American body which raised funds for republicans during the Troubles
Officials	Official IRA/Official Sinn Féin. Group from which Provisionals split in 1969/ 70
ONH	Óglaigh na hÉireann. Irish-language name for the IRA. Also the name of a Real IRA splinter group
PDs	Progressive Democrats. Former centre-right party in Republic of Ireland

PIRA	Provisional IRA. Military wing of the Provisional republican movement which split from the Official IRA in 1969
PSNI	Police Service of Northern Ireland. Policing service that replaced the RUC in 2001
RHI	Renewable Heat Incentive. Scheme established by the Northern Ireland Executive to help to increase consumption of heat from renewable sources
RIRA	Real Irish Republican Army. Armed group linked to 32CSM
RNU	Republican Network for Unity. Dissenting republican group established in 2007, initially known as Ex-POWs and Concerned Republicans against RUC/PSNI & MI5. Registered as a political party in 2013
RSF	Republican Sinn Féin. Republican traditionalist party which split from Sinn Féin in 1986
RUC	Royal Ulster Constabulary. Northern Irish police force 1922–2001
Saoradh	Dissident republican organization established in 2016. Means 'freedom' in Irish
SDLP	Social Democratic and Labour Party. Centre-left nationalist party in Northern Ireland linked to the civil rights movement. Was the dominant force in northern nationalist Catholic politics from the 1970s to 2003
Sinn Féin	Political wing of PIRA. Split from the Officials in 1970
TD	Teachta Dála. An elective representative of the Dáil
UVF	Ulster Volunteer Force. Armed loyalist group with links to the Progressive Unionist Party
White line picket	Protests in the middle of roads, traditionally used by republicans in Belfast to raise awareness of specific campaigns

Till Homer's ghost came whispering to my mind.
He said: I made the Iliad from such
A local row. Gods make their own importance.
Patrick Kavanagh, 'Epic'

1

Northern Ireland, the public sphere and activist media

The appearance of a political journal and its survival was equivalent to involvement in the struggle over the range of freedom to be granted to public opinion and over publicity as a principle.[1]

In May 2013 a tweet sent by the author of this book contributed to a minor controversy involving Sinn Féin and the BBC. A picture taken at a recording of the BBC's flagship debate programme, *Question Time*, that week being hosted in Belfast, showed a floor plan for the panel of guests that appeared to link Sinn Féin to the IRA.[2] The plan, drawn up to identify guests to camera operators from outside Northern Ireland, said 'SF IRA!' while the Democratic Unionist Party (DUP) was 'the goodies'. Although an apparently throwaway example of trench humour, commonplace for many working in news and current affairs, its potential to embarrass the BBC was manifest in the age of smart phones enabled with Internet access. When the author resized the picture sent by a member of the audience, and re-tweeted it, it was, in turn, to be re-tweeted by thousands of accounts, including that of Sinn Féin's then Northern Ireland Deputy First Minister, the late Martin McGuinness, and several Members of the Legislative Assembly (MLAs). The spread of the tweet was explained by the fact that it had been picked up and re-tweeted by a member of the Northern Irish political journalism community who was followed by many senior Sinn Féin activists. When Sinn Féin put out a press release demanding an apology, it was picked up by the Press Association news agency, and the story ran in most major daily newspapers in Ireland the following day.[3] By the middle of the following morning, the BBC had issued its apology and Sinn Féin had won a minor battle against a media institution that it believed to have been central to the party's marginalization through the years of the Provisional IRA's (PIRA's) armed campaign during the Troubles. Superficially, at least, it demonstrated the power of social media to hold major media institutions to account and offer a means of protest in the face of the institutional power of mass media organizations.

The incident captures the essence of the intersection between new media and political environments globally in the early period of the twenty-first century. An independent data consultant analysed the picture's rapid spread on social networks, showing a large-scale mobilization of social media accounts held by Irish republicans and significant use by unionists and loyalists. It has since been re-tweeted more than 10,000 times, from multiple accounts in locations across the world.[4] This constructive use of Twitter by Sinn Féin and its supporters was a microcosm of the potential of new many-to-many models of communication and how activist groups using new technology can subvert former gatekeepers in the mass media and political elite.

If this episode was a minor expression of changed media times, then it was a perfect encapsulation of the superficial and depthless arguments produced in the West for the power of social media, because, although it evidenced a large mobilization of activists and the politically engaged online, it produced few deliberative results. Social media, like Twitter or Facebook, as opposed to mainstream print or broadcast media, provided a form of political participation that was illusory – their deliberative effects were depthless. Sinn Féin, in receiving an apology from the BBC for a minor slur, displayed its savvy and active 'always-on' media strategy, but the episode represented nothing more than a minor set-to between political and media actors in the Northern Irish political sphere. It does, however, capture the debates between the purported immense power of activist media situated on the Internet to mobilize people supported by Internet evangelists, and the more circumspect analyses of the online world as a space for definitive political change. It is a cautionary tale that helps us understand claims for universalizing the political power of the Internet across the globe without first analysing the specific factors underpinning activism, and in seeking to infer its effects beyond simply demonstrating that online activism has some inherent power.

The Internet may be implicated in the battle to speak truth to power that has influenced mass mobilizations of people across the globe, but its uses cannot be universalized, certainly not in the Northern Irish or Irish context. The Internet and its activist media must be addressed from specific 'generic' forms and from within the geographical and ideological contexts from which they emerge. Activist media and the Internet are ascribed enormous influence because of their potential global reach, while older offline forms are dismissed because of limited spread. However, as the experience of Irish republicans since 1998 shows, the context of political activism and its immediate impetuses are more important starting points for analysis than the technology or platforms on which they appear.

Republican newspapers remain important for specific groups, and, as a genre, the republican publication has simply moved online.

The use of social media sites like Facebook and Twitter are not the specific focus of this book, although many of the issues surrounding their use run parallel to its central concerns. This book is largely interested in the development of traditional forms of activist media as they have manifested themselves in the age of the Internet. Chapters two and three use activist materials from party newspapers, online magazines, websites, blogs and interviews to establish the restructuring of Irish republicanism since the signing of the Good Friday/Belfast Agreement (GFA) in 1998. As this restructuring happens concurrently with the development of the mass Internet, it is also therefore concerned with the life and apparently slow death of the Irish republican newspaper or journal – perhaps the most enduring example of republican media activism for more than 200 years – in hard-copy format, and how it has developed in the Internet age. As a result it is also primarily concerned with the movement of older print journals to the Internet. Chapters four and five look at *An Phoblacht/ Republican News (AP/RN), Daily Ireland, Fourthwrite* and the *Blanket*, newspapers and magazines that illustrate the evolution of the republican publication in the Internet age. Chapter six addresses how resource-poor republican groups resorted to a return to established activist repertoires when online activism provided little opportunity for success, including those traditional expressions of republican dissent. The Internet was thus a platform upon which marginalized republican groups could publicize their protests against the Good Friday Agreement and the financial crisis that was affecting both Northern Ireland and the Republic of Ireland, but it was an adjunct tool.

Chapter two notes that the primary impetus for this changing landscape was located in the post-GFA political environment, and the effects of the agreement on the historically rooted dialectical struggles of republicanism in periods of dynamic reform. Sinn Féin's establishment republican reformism in the current period largely emerged through the party's own long-term acknowledgement that armed struggle could not deliver the aspiration of a united Ireland, and in reaction to the longer-term counter insurgency and diplomatic strategies of the British and Irish governments, which primarily sought an end to the Troubles. Neither of these strategies had any root in the expanded horizons of globalized media communication. Republicanism's internal power battles also originated in the offline world and simply manifested themselves online because of a wider shift in media consumption habits in the Western world. That Irish republican activists would express themselves online was not an off-shoot of the blogosphere or the so-called Facebook or Twitter revolutions in the

Middle East, or Western countercultural movements like Occupy, although there are some parallels and influences from them. As Ó'Broin notes in chapter four, republicans had utilized activist media platforms since the United Irishmen in 1798 and their pamphleteering was a means of contesting marginalization and criminalization. To paraphrase Morozov, another author cited herein, for republicans the Internet was just an additional space where activists went to make public their positions.

The Troubles and the news media

The journey that Sinn Féin had completed can be captured in two phases of academic writing about the news media and its role in reporting the Troubles in Northern Ireland. The first phase identified the structural bias of the mainstream media and British state authorities against republicans and other subaltern groups. From the start of the Troubles through to the signing of the Good Friday Agreement, the major academic narratives of the media suggested systematic bias against republican groups and an implicit reflection of the dominant ideological position of the British government. Schlesinger identified state censorship and the self-censorship of news media organizations that, 'in general, failed to give much more than a one-dimensional picture of the current conflict in Northern Ireland'.[5] Spencer illustrated systemic anti-Irish propaganda in the media that was a direct result of the agenda-setting power of the government: 'analysis of the media's role in the Northern Ireland conflict demonstrates only too well how the news media have traditionally followed the British government agenda in demonising the republican cause'.[6]

Sinn Féin's movement from the political margins to the mainstream was in part born of an almost quixotic resistance to the effects of censorship and demonization. In the face of state counter insurgency and mass media resistance, the party embarked on a concerted media activist campaign aimed at gaining as much public attention as possible while marginalized. Its production of the newspaper *An Phoblacht/Republican News*, as well as a raft of other propaganda products, was aimed at spreading its message in times of censorship and broadcasting bans. Its far-reaching attitude towards combating negative mainstream media coverage was to engage with journalists across the world and use emerging technologies like telex machines, photocopiers, faxes and the developing Internet to build understanding of the party and its cause, even in the face of overwhelming opposition.[7] The tradition of using wall murals and street art in Northern Ireland as alternative sites of political information began in the 1980s and has become something of a cultural phenomenon, as well as a tourist attraction.[8]

The development of the Peace Process, dated to the early 1990s, saw the gradual need for Sinn Féin to become integrated into the mainstream media sphere. To create the space in which Sinn Féin could be viewed as a credible partner in the peace negotiations, the media's previous emphasis on violence evolved 'towards a process of dialogue and discussion which enabled Sinn Fein to more openly articulate its position, exert pressure on the British government and forcefully promote its own agenda'.[9]

This period has seen a second phase of scholarship surrounding the news media and Northern Ireland. As the Peace Process redrew the political landscape of Northern Ireland and facilitated the cessation of PIRA violence (and vice versa), the media gradually began to accommodate the constitutional Sinn Féin, and the censorship of the past slowly eroded. Key texts in this second period of academic analysis investigated the media spaces in which this occurred. As Sinn Féin moved further from the politically marginalized space during the conflict, 'mainstream media were instrumental in facilitating indirect dialogue between their governments and the Irish republican movement about the terms on which Sinn Féin could be admitted to the talks'.[10] The party was also interviewed more often and with much less hostility than it had been in the past.[11] Rather than simply being seen through the filter of a terrorist organization, Sinn Féin was now being approached by journalists as a legitimated actor in the Peace Process.[12] There was also a wider commitment from journalists to support the process, with many becoming politically and emotionally engaged in using their publications or programmes as a site upon which to maintain the developing peace and as a space in which the actors could negotiate safely.[13] Ed Moloney, author of the definitive book on the PIRA, disparagingly suggested that both himself, and those fellow writers who also chose to retain a degree of critical detachment from the gospel of peace, were known as JAPPs, 'Journalists Against the Peace Process'.[14]

This period also saw a developing realization of the media being used as a primary space where the Peace Process could be fostered and developed. Dixon noted the political choreography of the Peace Process and how it was performed and moulded in the media space.[15] Television news was 'central in shaping public perceptions about the possibilities of peace and became especially potent as a force of influence because of its ability to reach all audiences simultaneously'.[16] The academy correctly identified how the media sought to facilitate peace negotiations, with Butler noting that the broadcast media performed a mediating role facilitating the discussions of opposing voices in a 'balanced sectarianism'.[17] The second phase of analysis therefore illustrated the primacy of media commitment to capturing and developing public zeitgeist for building and maintaining peace.

The most recent, third phase of analysis has addressed the growing influence of online and social media, not just in the maintenance of the Peace Process, but also in the organization and interaction of political organizations in Northern Ireland. Some, in the post-9/11 period, have fallen within the ambit of the orthodoxies of International Relations or Terrorism Studies and see the Internet and non-mainstream media in the same way as radical Islamic online spaces are used – as potential breeding grounds of radicalization among dissident republicans.[18] It is also a space in which the academy has sought to elevate a growing degree of public interaction beyond the confines of narrow political and cultural identities in Northern Ireland.[19] The development of the Internet as a mass communications platform in the mid 1990s coincides with the major landmarks in the Peace Process, and cyberspace has been addressed as another terrain in which the journey to peace was discussed publicly and contributed to the construction of the post-GFA political landscape.[20] Perhaps a more circumspect and nuanced aspect of analysis of the contribution of the Internet to the development of republican politics is that it has, in some cases, contributed to a greater degree of intra-group isolation, with various groups across the Northern Irish political Internet actually using it as an inward-looking space that diminished interaction with opponents.[21]

Irish republican media activism within the changed environment of the post-Good Friday Agreement period, and from the context of the developing spaces and activist media in the online and offline worlds, can be read as a multiplicity of public spheres of individual and organizational concerns which have the capacity to overlap at junctures of common political concerns. Although, as chapter two points out, most republican groups are defined by common republicanisms, they are often divided on individual issues relating to group interpretation of ideological dogma.

Activist journalism, popular culture, contesting hegemony and counterpublics

Irish republican activist media and journalism stand in a lineage of popular culture as active resistance paradigm pioneered by British scholars Hall, Fiske and Hebdige, who interpreted the use of popular cultural products and the media as active and autonomous and separated them from the enslaving power of the culture industries. For example, those involved in committed musical and popular cultural subcultures like those in fan communities demonstrate a great deal of active participation as opposed to simple passive consumption. By definition, highly engaged Irish republican activists cannot be seen as passive viewers of the spectacle of modern political culture; their production of activist materials demonstrates commitment and labour, whether they achieve a degree of power or not. Activist media should be situated within other popular cultural forms of journalism because it becomes derived of lived experience and is not merely something that is either passively created or consumed. Irish republican activists do not get involved in the often long-term production of newspapers, online magazines or other forms of political communication because they feel the need to be popular; they do so because the activity, in and of itself, is both active and activism. For Hall, the use of popular media forms, either by mass media or individuals, is an active contestation of power. 'Popular culture is one of the sites where this struggle for and against a culture of the powerful is engaged; it is also the stake to be won or lost in that struggle. It is the arena of consent and resistance.'[22] In this sense, social media used by republican groups becomes another site of struggle. It is also the central contention of activist media and Internet evangelists who have noted that the online world is a place of media production, of the people and for the people.[23]

This reading of popular culture, in which we situate activist journalism and activist media, allows us to see them as expressions of both autonomy and resistance. Rather than seeing popular cultural life within the environs of simple consumption of 'texts', the often inventive reinterpretation of popular cultural artefacts like newspapers, magazines, pamphlets and films by republican groups is a reflection of Fiske's assertion that

> it is culture – the active process of generating and circulating meanings and pleasures within a social system: culture, however industrialised, can never adequately be described in terms of selling commodities. Culture is a living active process, it can only be developed from within, it cannot be imposed from without or above.[24]

Republican activist media projects that utilize all these forms are an expression of autonomous lived culture that emerged as a result of the complex contestation of the concomitant interests of the state, the private interests of the mass media, the internal ideological power structures of the republican sphere itself, and the narratives of the Peace Process. They are also living, autonomous cultural contestations of power and representative of Carey's conclusion of 'communication as culture'.[25] In this battle for political and cultural hegemony, activist media projects also represent the 'notion of culture as a key to understanding specific features of a particular historical situation'.[26] Dissenting republican Tommy McKearney's evocation of writing simply being a part of the activist's repertoire fits with the notion of its centrality in a cultural repertoire for contesting power.[27] *Blanket* correspondent, Aine Fox put it more simply: 'writing is a simple straightforward task that involves a complex challenge if you have a dissenting voice'.[28]

The definition of activist journalism, as a subgenre of journalism, could be seen as popular culture using Williams's definition that 'popular was being seen from the point of view of the people rather than from those seeking favour or power from them'.[29] Unlike popular cultural forms of art, such as pop music, film or mainstream journalism, that can exist on a global plane of simple consumption, with few effects on local or individual polities or contested space, the battle for hegemony within the Irish republican sphere has a specific set of actors that are engaged in a mutual battle for hegemony, including the state, mass media and other activist media projects.

In the case of Northern Ireland, with a multiplicity of local and national newspapers, radio and television broadcasting outlets, and a large number of political parties split down ethno-religious lines, the contest for hegemony is already highly developed and the political public sphere a crowded space. The dynamics of these power relations are simply expressed online as further space of interaction. All are involved in a propaganda battle, for control of the dominant narrative of the Northern Ireland conflict and the Peace Process.[30] In this sense, the space itself is not simply a 'space' or vacuum, but a constantly contested terrain of negotiation inhabited by key actors of the Peace Process and their opponents.[31] This terrain, which emerged as an effect of the competing interests of the Peace Process, was one in which the dominant supporters of the process – the mass media, the British and Irish states, and the popular culture industries – developed support for peace, and republican dissidents and dissenters remained essentially marginalized.[32]

The domination of this space by the mass media and the state is central in our understandings of the development of republican activist media. Politics has become mediated due to the centrality of the media as a means by which politicians convey information to the public(s), and as a means by which public opinion is communicated back to political organizations.[33] The mass media in this model is the primary definer of the 'reality' of modern politics, and the active agent in any political process.[34] Developing from this is the deeper sense that politics has become 'mediatized', in that the narratives and strategies of political organizations have become primarily predicated upon gaining access to the media output and support from mass media organizations to manufacture public opinion rather than developing cogent policy. 'Media logic' and not 'political logic' is the most active definer of public political discourse. The media, as an active agency in this process, is also able to define not just the parameters of the debate but also to select those actors allowed to play a part in the debates. What results is a politics that is defined by a relatively small number of elite actors, with other groups, such as republican dissidents, actively marginalized and branded either as irrelevant actors or as dangerous and transgressive threats to the process. The 'staging' of politics for the media sphere ultimately resulted in the development of marginalized publics that lost their autonomy and became subaltern.[35] The media activism of these groups is therefore a reaction against marginalization politically and an expression of protest against the coterminous control of the narrative produced by the state, mass media and dominant political voices.

In this sense republican activist media space and its writing comes to represent a Gramscian idea of contesting hegemony, or the battle for control or dominance of the space politically and culturally. Gramsci argues that dominant groups in society achieve hegemony through both coercion and cultural consent. Hegemony is achieved when 'intellectual, moral and political leadership secures the consent of the majority'.[36] However, as the terrain on which these groups exist is constantly shifting ideologically, it becomes a contested space, and the increased role of the media, both mass and activist, is central to the contest. The shifting ideological terrain of the Peace Process, evidenced by evolving dissident and dissenting condemnations of Sinn Féin's reformism, illustrates the hegemonic battle for Anti-Good Friday Agreement republicans.[37] Fiske captures the hegemonic struggle in a wider sense: 'consent must be constantly won and re-won, for people's material social experience constantly reminds them of the disadvantages of subordination and this poses a threat to the dominant class'.[38] Hegemony is a sphere in itself, 'the terrain of power exercised by one group or grouping over others'.[39] This 'popular culture as resistance paradigm' has been integrated into Internet utopian readings of the power of the virtual sphere of public communication to empower the public, especially within the analysis of the effects and power of new activist media and that of citizen and public journalism. Cyber utopians grasped the development of the Internet as a means of empowering the individuals and the masses, with citizen and activist media centrally implicated in the process.[40] This was a further step in the Westernizing of the media space, where technologies would spread liberal democracy and challenge dictatorships. This interpretation of the Internet means it is also potentially a space in which new 'publicness' is created, a space of freedom and co-operation.[41] The conclusion to be drawn from this standpoint is that the Internet and new online technologies are those that favour the oppressed, rather than the oppressor.[42]

Hegemony is constantly being contested by the participants. In this space we see a restructuring of the public sphere in microcosm. The multiple competing publics surrounding political parties, political organizations and political publications are active in contestations of power that only a small number can actually achieve. Those that remained resistance publics in republicanism, like the mosaic of dissident and dissenting groups in the Irish republican sphere, became defined by their opposition to the mainstream, whether it was the domination of the republican space by Sinn Féin or the elite actors within the state. If we see their activism as a constant process of counter hegemonic resistance then they become recognized as counterpublics, that is, subaltern publics that become visible in the space specifically because of their oppositional status.

The terrain on which the battle for hegemony takes place in republican activist journalism reveals the physical, ideological and psychological spaces from which it emerges. Unlike many modern decentralized and diffuse globalized social movements, republicanism has a specific set of social contexts that influence its activism. In many modern activist movements, activism can develop despite relatively weak social ties between activists, particularly since the development and mass adoption of social media. However, republican activist journalism remains rooted in physical communities that are produced from shared subjective concerns on ideological issues. The close bonds of family and close-knit community lead to these concerns becoming intertwined with wider contested collective issues of nationalism.[43] Traditional nationalist narratives of people and territory can be mapped on to the republican sphere, with media activity connected to local community activism. This activism competes for a space both within the Irish republican sphere and the wider activist and mainstream media spheres. From a New Social Movement perspective, struggles are over 'cultural, economic and political meanings, differences and identities that are place-specific, articulated in opposition to state centred and defined meanings values'.[44] Each of the actors in the republican sphere interacts in nationalist civil society, that is, the 'sphere of social interaction between the economy and state, composed above all of the intimate sphere'.[45]

Fraser notes that marginalized groups have always found a means of mobilizing and making their presence felt in the discursive arena. Fraser, developing this view, contends that 'members of subordinated groups – women, workers, peoples of colour, and gays and lesbians – have repeatedly found it advantageous to constitute alternative publics', and that the 'proliferation of these counterpublics means a widening discursive contestation, and that is a good thing in stratified societies'.[46] Castells sees these groups wielding counterpower, through what he defines as 'the capacity by social actors to challenge and eventually change the power relations institutionalized in society'.[47] As a means of conceptualizing a Northern Irish public sphere, and its constituent republican components, multiple overlayered counterpublics and smaller subdivided public sphericules begin to explain the fractured structure of republican activist communication and its discourses.[48]

Counterpublics, marginalized by social, political or cultural otherness, can however be hidden from the public gaze and may only become visible thanks to the production of texts and their circulation.[49] Warner asserts that this is a 'social space of discourse organized by nothing other than discourse itself'. In this, the space is autotelic, a space where discourse happens publicly, perhaps through activist publications, and it exists simply 'by virtue of being addressed'.[50] Warner's publics, like those of Fraser and Benhabib, are self-organized and can be hidden from view due to the nature of modern society, but they do constitute counterpublics because they are aware of their subordinate status:[51]

> A public in practice appears as *the* public. It is easy to be misled by this appearance. Even in the blurred usage of the public sphere, a public is never just a congeries of people, never just a sum of persons who happen to exist. It must first have some way of organizing itself as a body and being addressed in discourse.[52]

Furthermore, Warner suggests that it can only be created by reflexive circulation of discourse and that this has to be constituted through regular publication.[53] Ganter notes, 'in Warner's formulation, counterpublics are simply publics aware of their subordinate status'.[54] His belief is that no single text can create a public; nor can a single voice, genre or medium. However, sections of the republican activist media are clearly counterpublics, especially those marginalized dissenters and dissidents. These become visible as a result of the contestation in which they are involved: 'counterpublics are, by definition, formed by their conflict with the norms and contexts of their cultural environment, and this context of domination inevitably entails distortion'.[55]

In the Irish republican sense, for example, there were few publics more marginalized than the jail community, but it still played a significant role in the production of texts that circulated in the republican sphere and provided a template for understanding how dissenting tracts can map on to the space. It was through their activist journalism that this public revealed itself, despite the restraints of the state apparatus. Post-colonialists such as Lloyd have noted how the blanket and dirty protests and Hunger Strikes were attempts at using elements of the state apparatus against the state in the republican struggle; prison writing performed a similar role.[56] However, they were also central to a strategy that recognized the mediated nature of the struggle and which revealed them as a public with a degree of power. Just as the jail became a republican counter or surrogate state of spheres within the wider British state apparatus which republicans sought to subvert and re-mould, then the regular stories in *An Phoblacht* and the writing in the prison journal *An Glór Gafa* saw this subaltern community or counterpublic both reveal itself and produce narratives which sought to have a deliberative effect on the movement as a whole. The famously eclectic library in the republican H-Blocks, and the writing that emerged from the jail, was 'an evocation of a particular episode in republican thinking where there was a strong commitment to embrace the left after the Hunger Strikes'.[57] The prison counterpublic's leftism was expressed in the journals, with this most subaltern of publics using activist media to bear on the movement on the outside. The writing and journals were also forms of communicating powerfully to both internal republican audiences and external publics. *An Glór Gafa*, which emerged from prison education programmes which started after the Hunger Strikes, was also intended not just as a propaganda tool but also to make a significant contribution to dialogues within the republican sphere.[58] It should be noted that two authors addressed at some length in this book, Anthony McIntyre and Tommy McKearney, were highly active prison writers. This impulse to produce high-quality analysis evidenced a self-actualized Do-It-Yourself activist media that is central to our understandings of their work discussed in chapter five.

What the prison journals illustrate was that, although counterpublics can reveal themselves through production of media materials, it doesn't necessarily mean that anyone beyond their own ambit is paying any attention. Counterpublics might struggle to make a deliberative contribution to the zones of discourse because they 'are often not exposed to competing positions and tend to construct straw man positions that show their positions to be good and true'.[59] Counterpublics, therefore, can be talking to themselves. Updating this to the Internet age, where digital isolation can often be necessity dressed up as a virtue, Sunstein warns of people of like mind gathering in ideological echo chambers where the deliberative rational critical dialogue, which he sees as vital for democracy, erodes in the face of partisanism.[60] He argues there 'is an omnipresent risk of information overload – too many options, too many topics, too many opinions, a cacophony of voices'.[61] The pragmatic issue is, 'Counterpublics, if they are going to contribute to bringing about emancipatory social change, they need to win recruits. Social process of recruitment becomes even more difficult in a fragmented public sphere characterized by diverging communities of interest.'[62]

Alternative activist media, the Internet and democratized modes of production

The activist journalism of these counterpublics is primarily in sites marginal to the mainstream and is thus alternative media, created in spaces that conjoin to create a surrogate public sphere in which is forged new spaces of belonging through activist practice. These have the potential to influence deliberative political change as a cumulative effect of multiple, ideologically congruent interventions. Atton asserts that this activity develops 'a conception of the public sphere as an arena for dialogic praxis ... and arena for radical inclusivity'.[63] Atton's focus on *Indymedia*, the global collective of alternative movement media activism online, is hugely relevant for the analysis of Irish republican groups, particularly dissenters. Established to disseminate information on protests against the World Trade Organization meeting in Seattle in November 1999, *Indymedia* has become a portal for a global network of activists, largely working in the leftist anti-globalization space, which utilizes online technologies as an alternative media source and a counterbalance to the mainstream media. Atton notes that 'such independent accounts provide a powerful counter to the enduring frames of social movement coverage in the media'.[64] His contention that alternative media has privileged amateur journalists 'who are writing from a position of engagement with the event or process that is their subject' is an almost perfect summation of the commitment and intent of the radical republican magazines, *Fourthwrite* and the *Blanket*.[65] Atton presents *Indymedia* as an example of alternative journalism and 'communicative democracy'.[66] Developing the idea that 'it is the right of citizens to communicate what they like ..., however hideous', the Internet provides a space to destabilize old modes of top-down mainstream media communication and has 'the capacity to transform the practice of journalism'.[67] This democratizes public writing and encapsulates the concept of citizens' journalism.[68]

However, Atton rightly counsels that this type of media activism does not necessarily mean there has been a greater deliberative effect on the political system. While he notes that new technologies have helped the development of such diverse pursuits as online radio and the production of fanzines, 'such attempts have done little to break with this history of marginality ... the history of such media is replete with such marginality: economic, cultural and political'.[69] Castells also notes that there were alternative political practices long before the development of modern technologies; 'other communication processes and media, both wired and unwired, were also important in these processes. And, of course, revolutionary political mobilizations have occurred in countries where wireless communication was lacking.'[70]

The liberal Western belief in the power of new technologically connected resistance publics relies on an erroneous binary: dissidence emerges as a result of new technologies and these technologies are therefore liberating. In the West, new narratives saw the web being a space which

decentralized collaboration between publics and which destabilized hierarchical modes of communication while empowering 'the people'. The web
was 'a new cultural force based on mass collaboration. Blogs, *Wikipedia*,
open source, peer-to-peer – behold the power of the people.'[71] Of course
within the Irish context, this utopian optimism would have to be tempered
when considered within the paradigm of radicalization – empowering
people is OK, just not dissidents.

Nowhere can you better see the cleavage between the digital realists
and the utopians than in the almost naïve belief that the latter had in the
power of the net as a radical force for optimism. In the Middle East it was
a means of destabilizing tyrannical regimes; in the West it was a space for
reproducing the freedoms once advocated by the counterculture. A substantial tranche of writing about the Internet and new media elevated
these spaces of public communication to a status of utopian dynamic
effectiveness. The blogosphere, on which many of the first Irish republican
blogs were written, was accorded the status of a dynamic political public
sphere based not only on a number of high-profile examples of how it had
scooped established mainstream media, but also on the almost quaint
utopianism of those who saw it as a replacement for the old top-down
mainstream media model. Unshackled from the constraints of the mainstream media, and with a potentially global audience of billions, Internet
utopians shouted that 'we're all journalists now', and that the boundary
between established journalism and activism was going to blur significantly, or be eroded completely.[72] Papacharissi, writing in 2002, said:

> Proponents of cyberspace promise online discourse will increase political
> participation and pave the way for a democratic utopia. According to them,
> the alleged decline of the public sphere lamented by academics, politicos
> and several members of the public will be halted by the democratizing
> effects of the internet and surrounding technologies.[73]

Morozov, a critic of the gospel of cyber idealism writing nine years later,
was more scathing of the claims made for Internet activism:

> It stems from the starry-eyed digital fervor of the 1990s, when former
> hippies, by this time ensconced in some of the most prestigious universities
> in the world, went on an argumentative spree to prove that the Internet
> could deliver what the 1960s couldn't: boost democratic participation,
> trigger a renaissance of moribund communities, strengthen associational
> life, and serve as a bridge from bowling alone to blogging together. And if
> it works in Seattle, it must also work in Shanghai.[74]

As the narrative of the new political commons of the Internet has emerged,
the story has often been about technology, and of its potential, but not of
measuring the extent to which new technologies have been responsible

for real political change in emerging democracies. Curran noted: 'The Internet has energised activism. But in the context of political disaffection, increasing political manipulation at the centre, an unaccountable global order and the weakening of electoral power, the Internet has not revitalised democracy.'[75]

As a place to gather and mobilize, the Internet undoubtedly allows opportunities for protest and for street-level pressure groups to meet and distribute information and news. The result is a newer, more nuanced political sphere which developed in some instances, particularly that of *Indymedia*. The myriad influences of the anti-corporate campaigns which morphed into the Occupy movement can also be seen in some of the activities of dissenting Irish republican groups. However, the Internet was merely a supporting space in which this activism took place. When éirígí occupied banks, they did so in a physical sense, with the virtual world as the secondary space of public visibility. Morozov has argued that the Internet is merely somewhere that activists have gone to organize, and that the ideological base and nature of their activism do not really change, but merely the channels in which it is dispersed.[76]

Narratives of the Arab Spring of 2010–2011 became the apotheosis of the Westernized, libertarian potential of the Internet and alternative media to democratize the world and destabilize despotic regimes. They represented the conclusion of twenty years of Internet utopianism that presented the open and 'democratizing' spaces of cyberspace where the disenfranchised from the 'broken' political apparatuses of both the dictatorships and Western democracy could flourish. British centre-left commentators like the BBC's Paul Mason noted, 'digital communications and social networks are the two big things facilitating revolutions and uprisings'.[77]

It is true that Facebook, Twitter and other social media had a powerful influence in allowing people to inform each other of developments and mobilize more quickly and effectively, but they did not democratize any Arab Spring governments. In this case, two points are important to note in relation to the role that social and activist media has played in the development of modern Irish republican activism. First, what was lost in much of the discourse of the Arab Spring was the context within which political protest and insurrection takes place. The deep political and social divisions that had festered in the individual polities of Tunisia, Libya and Egypt were the catalyst for the uprisings. To universalize the effects of social media was to overestimate its power elsewhere, certainly in the Irish and Northern Irish context. Secondly, many commentators, both within and outside of the academy, problematically defined any use of social media within a political space as an act of activism. This is problematic in the context of

Northern Ireland. While recording and circulating videos of riots in Egypt or Tunisia could, to some extent, be decreed an act of activism (but surely a secondary activism to protesting), can the same be said of Northern Ireland and of someone with the *YouTube* channel named upthera99 or Mr32CSM? Equally, could what happened in Seattle or Shanghai really also happen in Shantallow or South Armagh?

Notes

1 Habermas, Jürgen, *Structural Transformation of the Public Sphere* (London: Polity, 1989), p. 184.

2 'BBC apologises over Question Time Sinn Fein "IRA" label', *BBC News Online*, 24 May 2013. Available at: http://www.bbc.co.uk/news/uk-northern-ireland-22652433. Accessed 24 May 2013.

3 See: 'BBC "very sorry" after John O'Dowd labelled "SF/IRA!" on Question Time', *Belfast Telegraph*, 24 May 2013. Available at: www.belfasttelegraph.co.uk/news/politics/bbc-very-sorry-after-john-odowd-labelled-sfira-on-question-time-29293287.html. Accessed 24 May 2013.

   See also: Young, D., 'BBC apologise over "Sinn Fein/IRA" tag for Minister', *Irish Independent*, 24 May 2013. Available at: www.independent.ie/irish-news/bbc-apologise-over-sinn-feinira-tag-for-minister-29294102.html. The copy appears to have been culled straight from the PA wire service. Accessed 24 May 2013.

4 Information from private data consultant, 28 May 2013.

5 Schlesinger, P., *The British Media and Ireland. Truth: The First Casualty*. Pamphlet produced by the Campaign for Free Speech on Ireland. Available at: www.cain.ulst.ac.uk/othelem/media/docs/freespeech.htm. Accessed 20 September 2010. Also available in Rolston, Bill, and Miller, David, *War and Words: The Northern Ireland Media Reader* (Belfast: Beyond the Pale Publications, 1996).

6 Spencer, Graham, 'Sinn Féin and the media in Northern Ireland: the new terrain of policy articulation', *Irish Political Studies* vol. 21, no. 3, 2006, p. 359.

7 Hartley, Tom, interview, 3 May 2012.

8 Hartley interview. See also: Rolston, Bill, 'Changing the political landscape: murals and transition in Northern Ireland', *Irish Studies Review* vol. 11, no. 1, 2003, pp. 3–16.

9 Hartley interview.

10 Sparre, Kirsten, 'Megaphone diplomacy in the Northern Irish Peace Process: squaring the circle by talking to terrorists through journalists', *Press/Politics* vol. 6, no. 1, 2001, p. 88.

11 Lago, Rita, 'Interviewing Sinn Féin under the new political environment: a comparative analysis of interviews with Sinn Féin on British television', *Media, Culture and Society* vol. 20, no. 4, 1998, p. 680.

12 Lago, 'Interviewing Sinn Fein'.

13 Sparre, 'Megaphone diplomacy'.

14 Moloney, Ed, 'The Peace Process and journalism', *Britain and Ireland: Lives Entwined II* (London: British Council, 2006), p. 77.
15 Dixon, Paul, 'Political skills or lying and manipulation? The choreography of the Northern Ireland Peace Process', *Political Studies* vol. 50, no. 4, 2002, 725–741. See also: Dixon, P., 'Performing the Northern Ireland Peace Process on the world stage', *Political Science Quarterly* vol. 121, no. 1, 2006, 61–91.
16 Spencer, Graham, *The Media and Peace: From Vietnam to the 'War on Terror'* (London: Palgrave Macmillan, 2005), p. 127.
17 Butler, David, *The Trouble With Reporting Northern Ireland* (Aldershot: Avebury, 1995).
18 Bowman-Grieve, Loraine, and Conway, Maura, 'Exploring the form and function of dissident Irish Republican online discourses', *Media, War and Conflict* vol. 5, no. 1, 2012, pp. 71–85.
19 Reilly, Paul, 'Ourselves alone (but making connections): the social media strategies of Sinn Fein', in Nixon, Paul, Rawal, Rajash, and Mercea, Dan (eds), *Politics and the Internet in Comparative Context: Views from the Cloud* (London: Routledge, 2013).
20 Fealty, Mick, '"Slugger O'Toole": the new media as track two diplomacy', in Popiolkowski, Joseph J., and Cull, Nicholas J. (eds), *Public Diplomacy, Cultural Interventions and the Peace Process in Northern Ireland: Track Two to Peace?* (Los Angeles: Figueroa Press, 2009).
21 See: Ó'Dochartaigh, Niall, 'Conflict, territory and new technologies: online interaction at a Belfast interface', *Political Geography* vol. 26, no. 4, 2007, pp. 474–491.
22 Hall, Stuart, 'Notes on deconstructing "the popular"', in Story, John (ed.), *Cultural Theory and Popular Culture: A Reader* (Harlow: Pearson, 1998), p. 453.
23 Gilmor, Dan, *We the Media* (Sebastopol: O'Reilly Media, 2004).
24 Fiske, John, *Understanding Popular Culture* (Abingdon: Routledge, 2011), p. 20.
25 Carey, James W., *Communication as Culture* (London: Routledge, 1992).
26 Atton, Chris, *An Alternative Internet* (Edinburgh: Edinburgh University Press, 2004), p. 3.
27 McKearney, Tommy, interview, 20 November 2009.
28 Fox, Aine, 'Writing as activism', *Blanket*, 10 January 2002. Available at: www.indiamond6.ulib.iupui.edu:81/writing.html. Accessed 9 December 2010.
29 Williams, Raymond, *Keywords: A Vocabulary of Culture and Society* (Oxford: Oxford University Press, 1983), p. 111.
30 Rolston and Miller, *War and Words*.
31 Wolfsfeld, Gadi, *Media and the Path to Peace* (Cambridge: Cambridge University Press, 2004).
32 McLaughlin, Greg, and Baker, Stephen J., *The Propaganda of Peace: The Role of Media and Culture in the Northern Ireland Peace Process* (Bristol: Intellect Books, 2010).
33 Mazzoleni, Gianpietro, and Schulz, Winifried, '"Mediatization" of politics: a challenge for democracy?', *Political Communication* vol. 16, no. 3, 1999, 247–261.
34 Strömbäck, Jesper, 'Four phases of mediatization: an analysis of the mediatization of politics', *Press/Politics* vol. 13, no. 3, 2008, pp. 228–246.

35 Krotz, Friedrich, 'Mediatization: a concept with which to grasp media and societal change', in Lundby, Knut (ed.), *Mediatization: Concept, Changes, Consequences* (Oxford: Peter Lang Publishing, 2009).

36 Quoted in Routledge, Paul, 'Critical geopolitics and terrains of resistance', *Political Geography* vol. 15, nos. 6–7, 1996, p. 521.

37 'Anti-Good Friday Agreement Republicans' (AGFAR) was a term coined by Gerry Ruddy of the Irish Republican Socialist Party (IRSP). See: 'Is there a Republican alternative to the Good Friday Agreement?', *Blanket*, 8 April 2004. Available at: www.indiamond6.ulib.iupui.edu:81/ruddyalt.html. Accessed 9 December 2010.

38 Fiske, John, 'British cultural studies and television', in Allen, Robert C. (ed.), *Channels of Discourse, Reassembled: Television and Contemporary Criticism* (Abingdon: Routledge, 1992), p. 219.

39 Buttigieg, Joseph A., 'Gramsci on civil society', *Boundary 2* vol. 22, no. 3, 1995, p. 31.

40 Morozov, Evgeny, *The Net Delusion: How Not to Liberate the World* (London: Penguin, 2011).

41 Jarvis, Jeff, *Public Parts* (New York: Simon & Schuster, 2011).

42 Jarvis, *Public Parts*.

43 English, Richard, *Irish Freedom: The History of the IRA* (London: Macmillan, 2006).

44 Routledge, 'Critical geopolitics and terrains of resistance'.

45 Cohen, Jean L., and Arato, Andrew, *Civil Society and Political Theory* (Cambridge, MA: MIT Press, 1994), p. ix.

46 Fraser, Nancy, 'Rethinking the public sphere: a contribution to the critique of actually existing democracy,' in Calhoun, Craig (ed.), *Habermas and the Public Sphere* (Cambridge, MA: MIT Press, 1993), pp. 123–124.

47 Castells, Manuel, 'Communication, power and counter-power in the network society', *International Journal of Communication* vol. 1, no. 1, 2007, p. 258.

48 Gitlin, Todd, 'Public sphere or public sphericules?', in Curran, James, and Liebes, Tamar (eds), *Media, Ritual and Identity* (London: Routledge, 1998).

49 Warner, Michael, *Publics and Counter Publics* (Cambridge, MA: MIT Press, 2002), p. 50.

50 Warner, *Publics and Counter Publics*, p. 66.

51 Warner, *Publics and Counter Publics*, pp. 49–50.

52 Warner, *Publics and Counter Publics*, p. 68.

53 Warner works primarily within Queer theory and has a wide breadth of reference from sexual discourses of the nineteenth century to modern drag entertainers. He notes how subordinated queer groups co-opted mainstream communication tools and techniques to create counterpublics.

54 Ganter, Granville, 'Counterpublics, book review', *St. John's University Humanities Review* vol. 1, no. 1, March 2003. Available at: http://facpub.stjohns.edu/~ganterg/sjureview/vol1–1/publics.html. Accessed 23 August 2013.

55 Warner, *Publics and Counter Publics*, p. 63.

56 Lloyd, David, 'Regarding Ireland in a post-colonial frame', *Cultural Studies* vol. 15, no. 1, 2001, pp. 12–32.

57 Scott, Kirsty, 'Men of letters, men of arms', *Guardian*, 2 December 2000.
58 McKeown, Laurence, *Out of Time: Irish Republican Prisoners, 1970–2000* (Belfast: Beyond the Pale Publications, 2001), p. 183.
59 Downey, John, 'Participation and/or deliberation? The Internet as a tool for achieving radical democratic aims', in Dahlberg, Lincoln, and Siapera, Eugenia (eds), *Radical Democracy and the Internet* (Basingstoke: Palgrave Macmillan, 2007), p. 123.
60 Sunstein, Cass, *Republic 2.0* (Princeton, NJ: Princeton University Press, 2009), p. 44.
61 Sunstein, *Republic 2.0*, p. 51.
62 Downey, 'Participation and/or deliberation?', p. 123.
63 Atton, *An Alternative Internet*, p. 30.
64 Atton, *An Alternative Internet*, p. 30. See also: Platon, Sarah, and Deuze, Mark, 'Indymedia journalism: a radical way of making, selecting and sharing news?', *Journalism* vol. 4, no. 3, 2003, 336–355.
65 Atton, *An Alternative Internet*, p. 31.
66 Atton, *An Alternative Internet*, p. 36.
67 Atton, *An Alternative Internet*, p. 37.
68 Atton, *An Alternative Internet*, p. 37.
69 Atton, *An Alternative Internet*, p. xi.
70 Castells, M., Fernandez-Ardevol, M., Qiu, J.L., and Sey, A. *Mobile Communication and Society: A Global Perspective* (Cambridge, MA: MIT Press, 2009), p. 212.
71 Kelly, Kevin, 'We are the web', Wired.com, August 2005. Available at: http://www.wired.com/wired/archive/13.08/tech.html?pg=1&topic=tech&topic_set=. Accessed 20 September 2013.
72 Dan Gilmor's phrase became somewhat of a rallying cry for Internet utopians who saw the participatory nature of Internet interaction as presaging a new era of democratic participation, where, as bloggers were freed of the constrictions of mainstream media, activism and journalism would become more closely related.
73 Papacharissi, Zizi, 'The virtual sphere: the Internet as a public sphere', *New Media and Society* vol. 4, no. 1, 2002, p. 10.
74 Morozov, *The Net Delusion*, p. xiii.
75 Curran, James, Fenton, Natalie, and Freedman, Des, *Misunderstanding the Internet* (Abingdon: Routledge, 2012), p. 17.
76 Morozov, Evgeny, '*Facebook* and *Twitter* are just places revolutionaries go', the *Guardian*, 7 March 2011. Available at: www.theguardian.com/commentisfree/2011/mar/07/facebook-twitter-revolutionaries-cyber-utopians. Accessed 7 March 2011.
77 Else, Liz, 'The revolution will be tweeted', *New Scientist*, 1 February 2012. Available at: www.newscientist.com/article/mg21328500-400-the-revolution-will-be-tweeted/. Accessed 6 February 2012.

2

Contemporary Irish republicanism since 1998: the Shinners[1]

At present republican groups dissenting from the pro-Stormont 'Agreement' line include groups ranging from traditionalist Republican SF, to the supposedly Marxist IRSP, to the I'm not sure about the ideology beyond sovereignty 32CSM, to trendy leftist agitprop junkies éirígí, to the newest group Republican Network for Unity (RNU).[2]

The diverse spectrum of dissenting organizations represented in the quote that begins this chapter gives a sense of the fragmented and deeply contested space that is Irish republican politics at the start of the twenty-first century. The Irish republican sphere and its activist media outlets in the post-1998 period can be split into four ideologically overlapping blocs, to be examined in terms of their shared and divergent themes and in the timeframes in which they emerged and developed.

The four blocs emerged in three distinct timeframes: pre-1998; 2000–2006; and 2006 onwards. The first bloc is the establishment republicanism of Sinn Féin, while the second encompasses opposition groups like the Irish Republican Socialist Party (IRSP)/Irish National Liberation Army (INLA) which emerged in 1974, as well as the post-1986 dissidents of Republican Sinn Féin (RSF) and the 32 County Sovereignty Movement (32CSM) which originated in the post-1997 split. The last two organizations retain links to dissident armed groups.

The third bloc, post-2000, encompasses republican activist journalism projects and new grassroots dissenting republicanism seen in *Fourthwrite*, the *Blanket* and *New Republican Forum* magazines. This bloc was important because of the dissenting dialogical space that it cut and the opportunities that it presented for the fourth bloc that emerged in the final time period. The final bloc comprises dissenting groups like éirígí and Republican Network for Unity (RNU), the 1916 Committees and Saoradh, who entered the fray from 2006–2016 as a response to the further compromises to the Peace Process by Sinn Féin. This bloc sought, through deep engagement with disillusioned former Provisional activists and dissenting media space, to interrogate an alternative to both establishment republicanism, as represented by Sinn Féin, and to the simplistic traditions of armed dissidents.

It would be more accurate to describe these final two blocs as republican dissenters rather than dissidents, largely because the word 'dissident' connotes a direct link to armed groups still committed to armed struggle. While RNU has an ambiguous relationship with armed groups, it still argues that purely militarist strategy is doomed to failure and will not achieve lasting social change in republican communities. Saoradh, however, which emerged in late 2016, appears to be the latest home for unreconstructed physical force figures who remain concerned with seeking a vehicle that will investigate a means of building a wider platform for traditional physical force republicanism in the face of state counter insurgency and marginalization from the political mainstream.[3] It has also struggled to articulate a political platform, and the fact that there were striking similarities between its constitution and that of éirígí led it to be accused of, at best, plagiarizing its rival, and, at worst, relegating constitutional politics to a distant second place to finding a new platform for traditional armed force republicanism.[4] A republican activist, however, counselled that it was too early to evaluate the political potential of Saoradh: 'Like any political project, Saoradh will be judged by actions and ideology collectively – not the mistakes, failures (or successes) of others post-GFA. Anyone rushing to make judgement of Saoradh in their infancy would be incredibly harsh, but also politically naïve.'[5]

Regardless of semantics, all non-establishment groups remain, by definition, dissident, but all, however, argued that it was actually Sinn Féin that was dissenting from republicanism's ideological roots through its recalibration of the movement's immediate goals. The terminology within the parameters of traditional definitions was flawed, argued one commentator: 'The expression "dissident republicanism" to describe Republicans opposed to the Belfast Agreement is incorrect. Republicans opposed to the 1998 Belfast Agreement are no more "dissidents" than republicans opposed to the 1921 Treaty were "irregulars".'[6] He also noted that the traditional unionist newspaper, the *Newsletter* had correctly noted that it was 'Adams, McGuinness et al who are the real dissident republicans, because they are the ones who have reached an accommodation with unionists and the British Government. They are the ones who have abandoned the abstentionist policy. They are the ones who have legitimised partition.'[7]

There was therefore a more specific distinction to make – between dissidents, who were those that continued to support an armed struggle for Irish freedom, and the dissenters, who, in a more nuanced sense, opposed both the armed struggle and the changing focus of establishment republicanism. The dissidents, also defined as militants or militarists, were

those for whom physical force was a defining characteristic of republicanism. The word 'dissident' became charged with an emotive power, carrying
the underlying connotation of those who were threats to the Peace Process.
The dissenters were, however, those that could be described as opposing
not the peace, but the process.[8] The distinction between the two terms
was perhaps, unknowingly at the time, made clearer by one of those who
opposed a return to militarism. Former PIRA commander, turned Peace
Process dissenter, Brendan Hughes told the *Guardian*, 'I don't mind being
labelled a dissenter, I've been a dissenter all my life.'[9] The constitutional
development of Sinn Féin and establishment republicanism was charged
by dissidents as a betrayal of republican traditions of armed struggle and
resistance; underpinned by the corrosive influence of the British and Irish
states, and the constitutional politics that led to moderation and not the
republic.[10] For others, the goals and values had been eroded for the benefit
of the party. Carrie McIntyre, editor of the *Blanket* said:

> Are the goals of Sinn Féin to achieve, ultimately a united Ireland (note: no
> longer to achieve an Irish socialist republic)? Or is the goal of Sinn Féin to
> be the biggest party in Ireland, partitioned or not? Sinn Féin's strategy is
> the strategy of a Movement; it has not been such for a long time now. Sinn
> Féin's strategy is that of a political party, and as such everything it does is
> predicated on the notion of how to ensure success, both long and short term,
> for the party not the nation.[11]

For Sinn Féin, the abandonment of some tenets of traditional republicanism in the move towards constitutionalism represented the evolution of
the struggle which had begun as armed struggle but was now being taken
forward by other means.[12] Like Fianna Fáil and the Official movement in
previous generations, Sinn Féin had become both to define and to embody
republicanism by virtue of either its electoral or social hegemony.

In the contestation of this hegemony there continued to operate centripetal and centrifugal forces in the interaction of dissidents with Sinn
Féin. The interplay of these forces provided an important catalyst for the
republican activist media sphere. In a centripetal sense, all republicans
remain rooted in a central bank of political ideals, 'republicanisms', that
focus on nationalism and violence, national and ethno-religious identity,
aspirations of Irish self-determination, national and social liberation, class,
identity and communal politics which all intersect with a generalized core
identification with a socialist labour activism rooted in the tradition of
James Connolly.[13] However, centrifugally, all the significant anti-Good
Friday Agreement dissenting groups emerged through this time as a result
of resistance to the reformist centre-ground strategy of Sinn Féin. The
acceptance of partition, however temporary, its involvement in institutions

of the states that it had previously opposed and the suppression of those that highlighted these 'double standards', saw dissidents and dissenters pushed further to the margins.

Some dissenters were marginalized from the political process by adhering to a long-held republican policy of abstentionism, neither fighting elections nor recognizing the parliaments of Britain, the Republic of Ireland or the Northern Ireland state. Elections, articulated republican dissenters, 'have a corrupting influence on Irish national liberation',[14] while participation in the assemblies saps 'popular support away from the revolutionary structure and attempt[s] to pacify people within the confines of partition and British rule'.[15] They were also marginalized by their belief in the 'ultimate betrayal of the Irish people', the 'abject treachery' of the decommissioning of PIRA weapons, and the acceptance of policing and justice reforms in Northern Ireland which further entrenched republicanism within partition and the British state apparatus.[16] For the dissenters, the authoritarian nature of Sinn Féin's political and social power in republican communities in the North became a key impulse in their rejection of the party's attempts at silencing dissent. One writer noted, 'Sinn Féin members are among those who inhabit a culture where authoritarian power is virtually the centre of gravity.'[17] He also noted, 'the nature of the provisional relationship to the nationalist community has evolved from one of loosely defending it to a position of tightly controlling it.'[18] A primary impulse for those primarily activist media outlets, like *Fourthwrite* and the *Blanket*, was to highlight and obstruct establishment republicanism's attempts at policing dissent and closing of the republican sphere to alternative voices.

However, while the circumstances of their divergence from the establishment republican path are, in some cases, quite specifically rooted to the period 1998–2016, post-Good Friday Agreement, they are also equally emblematic of the historically highly brittle nature of republican collective identity and its tendency towards schism. The splits in republicanism, whether they have occurred in 1921, 1970 or 1986, have always been the expression of the conflict between modernizing reformism and traditionalism. The rapid and dynamic ideological restructuring of republicanism would in this period still evoke perennial battles of identity over 'assimilation vs. resistance, compromise vs. idealism, corruption vs. purity'.[19] Outside of the republican firmament, this battle was simplistically expressed in the mainstream media in the post-Good Friday era as being between Sinn Féin's 'historic step towards history' and the dissident standpoint of it being 'a sequence to surrender'.[20] Dissenters who had served often long jail sentences for their part in an armed campaign to smash the Stormont Parliament and British rule in Northern Ireland saw devolution as an unacceptable dénouement to their struggle. 'A revolutionary body that settles for and then seeks to legitimise the very terms it fought against simultaneously de-legitimises and arguably criminalizes its own existence.'[21] An activist questioned thirteen years after the agreement said, 'the Brits got everything they set out to achieve: normalisation, Ulsterisation and the criminalisation of the republican struggle.'[22] Much of the activist media writing of dissenters would be concerned with articulating the sense of outrage at the political settlement of the GFA and at articulating republicanism's future.

The pressures of constitutionalism and the crowded left space

There is nothing particularly exceptional about the fractured nature of the Irish republican sphere or the porous nature of the boundaries between groups which saw dissenters sometimes active in two or more projects: there was a historical precedent dating back at least to the Irish Civil War. Nor were the underlying causes of those fractures ultimately specific to the Peace Process; schism was a feature of the movement, if it can be described as such. Republican factionalism was not a series of dramatic and decisive splits over specific changes in ideology and strategy, but the gradual result of dialectical friction in the contemporary republican sphere. That is not to say that it does not have historical parallels or precedents that are instructive. The éirígí project, for instance, reflects the evolution of conflict in the interwar years between the radical republican left of Peadar O'Donnell and the more conservative republicanism of Frank Ryan, as well as similar ideological battles between the Officials, Provisionals and IRSP in the 1970s.

The contemporary period also reflects the difficulty of articulating One Nation Irish republicanism in a period of deepening partition made more complex by the establishment of the Northern Ireland Assembly and its cementing of partition in the medium to long term. In Northern Ireland, Sinn Féin was given no other option by the architecture of the Peace Process than to recognize the realities of partition and to work in an executive that had little financial or legislative independence to offer opportunity for radical social transformation for republican communities. Sinn Féin's Francie Molloy noted, 'republicans are prepared to work on an executive. We are really prepared to administer British rule in Ireland for the foreseeable future. The very principle of partition is accepted.'[23] While Sinn Féin was seen as operating within the parameters of the Belfast Assembly and administering Public Private Finance initiatives, in the Republic of Ireland and not in power it has strategically situated itself within the firmament of the radical Irish left. Acting with a degree of cognitive dissonance, it was deemed to be in acceptance of the status quo to strengthen its vote in the North while acting as a countercultural left in the South. It altered the base ideological assumptions of the structure of both left and left republican politics to redraw the absolute boundaries of traditional republican catechism. Marian Price, a former PIRA Hunger Striker, said:

> To suggest that those Republicans and indeed nationalists, who suffered, fought and died over the past three decades did so in order to walk through the doors of a revamped Stormont, abandon Articles 2 and 3 of the Southern Constitution, and establish a British-Irish Council which would extend British influence in the 26 Counties, is a blasphemy and fraudulent assertion.[24]

In the South, the recession and the revelations of deeply ingrained corruption in the government energized the left, but only resulted in increasing congestion in that space. One casualty of this congestion was One Nation republicanism, which became less important with the greater focus on developing the socialist, left interest.

The result of these specific differences in social and political culture saw parties having to operate in a Janusian fashion – as ideologically linked but separate entities on either side of the border – to garner support. While there were apparently universal republican socialist issues that were common to Northern Ireland and the Republic, the political reality meant that there were sometimes radically different platforms in each state. The flexibility of Sinn Féin to operate in this way, as an ideological construct, is also inherent in republican traditions and representative of an ideological promiscuity and political opportunism that underpinned the party's development, allowing it to appropriate elements of the constitutional nationalist left of the Social Democratic and Labour Party (SDLP) where it has seen necessary.[25] However, this opportunism was seen as lacking depth, particularly in the Republic of Ireland, where some critics questioned whether the predominantly Northern leadership understood the political landscape of the South. Political columnist Tom McGurk noted, 'Sinn Féin's embrace of secularism has disappointed traditionalists and cost it the chance to garner support from socially-conservative voters in the Republic. But beyond all this is the real suspicion that Sinn Féin's Northern leadership actually doesn't understand how the Republic ticks.'[26] Former Sinn Féin Dublin City councillor in Dublin, Louise Minihan, who defected to éirígí in the week previous to McGurk's column said:

> Sinn Féin has, over the course of the last twelve years, moved steadily away from the core values of Irish socialist republicanism and is no longer willing, or able, to challenge the British occupation of the Six Counties or the rotten capitalist system which is causing so much hardship to working families across Ireland today.[27]

In terms of countering these accusations of a cultural division in understanding between the two polities, Sinn Féin's media strategy incorporated the expanded horizons of growing integration into the political structures of the Republic of Ireland. *An Phoblacht* throughout this period became an ever more highly functioning thirty-two-county party publication and its predominantly Southern-born staff were more rooted in the realities of the Republic of Ireland.

Commonality and difference: republican eclecticism

Republicanism's contemporary era reflects a longer tradition of eclecticism which has provided a home for 'militant Nationalists, unreconstructed militarists, romantic Fenians, Gaelic Republicans, Catholic sectarians, Northern defenders, international marxists, socialists, libertarians and liberal Protestants'.[28] The current period of republican activist politics displays a similar eclecticism, and the range of political identities in the preceding quote almost perfectly reflects the range of standpoints on the contributors list of the *Blanket*, the most diverse dissenting project of the period.[29] In this period the umbrella term 'Irish republican' could encompass the unreconstructed militarists of the Real IRA (RIRA) and Continuity IRA (CIRA), militants of RSF and 32CSM, Catholic sectarians represented by the *Hibernian* magazine, international Marxists in éirígí and libertarians like Carrie McIntyre, the editor of the *Blanket*, who conceived its space as one that accommodated expression of all the viewpoints above.[30] The development of splits and schisms can also be put down to the ideological promiscuity of republicanism across the last hundred years, and in Provisionalism, in particular.[31] Republicanism and republican politics, although portrayed as being theocratic, could still embrace 'left-wing radicals, terrorists and right-wing fanatics'.[32] One writer noted:

> republicanism as a concept can be so embracing as to include virtually everyone opposed to monarchical rule. If Bertie Ahern can claim to be a socialist then almost anyone can claim to be a republican. In a post modernist world where all narratives are broken down into the free standing atoms that form them and are allowed to drift into other narratives which are in turn dispersed and fragmented, it is easy to see why such conceptual promiscuity is possible.[33]

Internationalism remains central to the republican identity and Sinn Féin has been successful in adapting to global ideological currents from liberation movements to New Social Movements: 'as a party fighting for self-determination, Sinn Féin supports what are perceived to be similar struggles throughout the world. As a socialist party, it establishes links with regimes that are considered revolutionary.'[34] Sinn Féin kinship with these causes is not simply out of ideological fealty, but through well-established links, particularly those in the Basque country, Palestine and Latin America. One dissenting writer noted: 'The foreign policies of Sinn Féin are intended to appear all things to all people. Sinn Féin will adopt "anti-imperialist" rhetoric on one occasion, and "conflict resolution" approach on another. Some of the current pressure groups and organizations such as éirígí and RNU have shown a similar instinct to embrace the geographically diverse to inform their struggle. It is a matter of rhetoric, not of ideological coherence.'[35] éirígí situated the republican cause globally, insisting that 'the struggle for an Ireland free of the twin fetters of capitalism and imperialism is integrally linked to the wider international struggle of the poor and oppressed against the rich and powerful.'[36] RSF also has manifest international influences, from European separatist movements to global liberation struggles; whether it is directly comparable to these movements remains moot. There is also much that republican groups agree on – in recent years there has been a unified front in opposition to a reform of the Republic of Ireland's continued membership of the European Union and support for a No vote in the two Lisbon Treaty referenda.[37] Republican eclecticism reveals clear ideological similarities and inheritances but it alone fails to illustrate the divisions that exist between republican groups, and those divisions usually occur as a result of differences in political principles.

The interplay between political principles and ideological structures has been at the heart of republicanism's divergent landscape. The Peace Process, built on expediency, ideological flexibility and political 'realism', has been one of the primary definers of Sinn Féin's development in the post-1998 period. The pressures of the agreement have seen the party re-contextualize ideological compromise within the framework of political realism. In assuming the position of political realism, it diverged from the catechism of republican purity that it followed during the 1970s split, and allowed it to accuse traditionalists of republican theocracy and being hamstrung by ideological inflexibility. However, in trying to mould the new position to fit the specific realities of the Peace Process, one writer noted that Sinn Féin, 'not without merit accused the 32 County Sovereignty Movement of engaging in theology,' but overlooked their own contribution, which amounted to 'codology'.[38] In the changed landscape of the post-Troubles period, ideological inflexibility has replaced revisionism as the greatest sin for establishment republicanism. 'Sinn Féin views ideology as a flexible and constantly evolving concept, whereas principles are often "fundamental truths" and therefore "don't change".'[39] At important junctures of the Peace Process, during the Downing Street Declaration negotiations of 1993 and policing reform debates at St Andrews, 2007, establishment republicanism was party to a collective recalibration of ideological standpoints in initiatives that diluted republicanism in a means primarily designed not to alienate unionists and derail the process.[40] Sinn Féin's approach to the Peace Process has been to situate the evolution of republican doctrine within the confines of compromises that are required to sustain the inclusiveness of the process. Fighting on two fronts, the party was able to deflect criticisms from dissident republicans by highlighting the social and political gains it had secured by being involved in the process, while being able to denounce any unionist intransigence in the face of its own flexibility and commitment to compromise:

> Through our peace strategy and the talks process, Sinn Féin has, like never before, succeeded in putting the republican analysis right at the heart of Irish politics. This has, in turn, changed the Irish political landscape. Never again can the question of partition be relegated to the sidelines of Irish political life.[41]

Despite these gains, dissidents and dissenters have emerged in protest against the erosion of republican tradition during the apparent 'normalization' of Sinn Féin and establishment republican ideals. In the same period the republican sphere expanded to include many newer activists who had no connection with Sinn Féin. Indeed, 'the fractured nature of radical republicanism' includes 'significant numbers of people who view themselves as non-establishment republicans and who were not part of the Provisional movement'.[42] With some degree of legitimacy, these activists could accuse the party of 'vampirising' Provisional republicanism of its original political heart.[43] Peripherally involved organizations, particularly those on the left, have accused Sinn Féin of a centrist urge that has stripped it of its social radicalism. The party was accused of acting in a contradictory fashion in the North and the South, administering cuts in the Northern Assembly and opposing them in the South: 'Sinn Féin does not represent any sort of alternative to working people in the south in the next election. They represent a serious dead end for anyone looking for a radical alternative to the corrupt politics of the southern establishment.'[44]

However, what none of the groups involved in the blocs of dissidence across this period can contest is that Sinn Féin's three decades of grassroots political organization built on sophisticated media activism has made it the most successful and politically agile republican party since the 1960s. It has rarely been given credit for being able to successfully articulate and manage enormous political transformation in the face of the external pressures of the Peace Process and the internal challenges of dissidents. The award-winning Irish political blogger Splintered Sunrise noted in the wake of the rise of dissident violence in 2009:

It's often said in dissident circles that the Provisionals have given up on the goal of the 32-county socialist republic. But, while you can make some rhetorical hay around them sitting in the Stormont executive, it's not true to say they've ditched the goal. It's on the first page of their programme, after all. You can talk about people being corrupted, or institutionalised by a process they thought was going in another direction, or simply worn down by war-weariness, but you're still, in the main, talking about people who want to be republicans on some level.[45]

The first bloc (part 1): Sinn Féin

Sinn Féin has developed an electoral and social hegemony that is unprecedented in Northern Irish republican history. Although its ideological and emotional roots were in the Provisional IRA campaign between 1970 and 1998, it became the dominant republican voice through thirty years' grassroots activism that strategically won it the right to instal itself as the arbiter of republican self-definition. More specifically, Sinn Féin in the period 1977–1981, and especially from 1981–1993, would slowly change the focus of the Provisional movement from junior partner to liberation army to political party. For senior activists, Sinn Féin is more than merely a political party – it is the modern encapsulation of republicanism. One senior activist said it was 'the voice of an idea': 'Sinn Féin does not claim to have a monopoly on Irish republicanism – far from it. But we do believe that we have woven together the strands of Irish republicanism in a unique tapestry and that we have made that political tradition vital and relevant to today's Ireland.'[46] The metaphor of tapestry is apposite, because Sinn Féin had tied together the dominant cultural legacies of history and militarism and reconciled them with electoralism, communitarianism, internationalism and socialism rooted in the democratic tradition. Sinn Féin's achievement in this period was, for senior activists, to unify politically and socially diverse strands of previously competing republican opinion, without necessarily eschewing the two key historic influences that were central to its development: republicanism and socialism. 'It is an idea, an idealism that is both republican and labour, the idea of a free Ireland and a sovereign people.'[47]

The voice of an idea, rooted in the writings of Patrick Pearse and referring to his appreciation of the United Irishman Robert Emmett, was a skilful and politically astute means of conflating more than 200 years of republican history at a time when the enormous effects of social, political, constitutional and global change were dynamically transforming the landscape of Northern Ireland and the Republic of Ireland.[48] The Peace Process, economic recession and the rapid restructuring of the Catholic/

nationalist/republican community, often through rapid social upward mobility, were key dynamics in influencing Sinn Féin's redefinition of the idea of republicanism, and allowed it to forge a party that could credibly compete in all the elections in which it would stand.[49] With strong electoral representation in the Dáil, the Stormont Assembly (in which it is in government with the DUP), Westminster (in which it historically refuses to take its seats), the European Parliament, and councils in both Northern Ireland and the Republic, it has built an active and confident activist base that has made significant political gains, particularly in the twenty-first century.[50] Sinn Féin's ideological and political standings offer a strong basis upon which to understand the changing modes of activism in the modern era. They do so particularly in understanding the power struggle between Sinn Féin as dominant ideological voice from which as a reaction dissident strands diverge. The party's twin aims have been to control the ideological agenda of republicanism, maintaining its key indicators of identity while attempting to modify them to fit with the changed political environment of post-Peace Process Northern Ireland and the post-Celtic Tiger Republic. Its media strategy and the concerns of activist media outlets have been implicit in this process, both internally, and externally in its proactive interaction with the mainstream media in a bid to influence the wider political agenda.

There are six 'republicanisms', core tenets of belief that are an ideological foundation or starting point: nationalism, militarism, cultural romanticism, socialism, anti-imperialism and anti-colonialism.[51] These have become modified. They can be further simplified to the five 'isms' of republicanism: separatism, nationalism, secularism, socialism and non-sectarianism.[52] However, in the years since the Peace Process, specific key words and concepts are now more central to Sinn Féin: equality, community, nation, struggle and identity are among the most important in their post-ceasefire lexicon. Since the Hunger Strikes, Sinn Féin's re-evaluation of republican identity has gradually elevated concepts of equality, emancipation, empowerment and liberation in various forms to the core of its political agenda, while militarism, armed struggle and electoral abstentionism have become footnotes in ideological history. The party has built on the generalized issues of republican philosophy and gradually come to abandon particularities of strategy, the former means by which it was going to unify Ireland. The lexicon of Sinn Féin had to undergo transformation as methods and strategy became reconfigured. As the armed struggle was replaced with electoralism and deeper integration with the state, its activist base utilized 'the softer language of transition and gradualism', which 'replaced the maximalist imperatives of a revolutionary party'.[53] The party had recognized that within the two states in Ireland there were multiple publics, and not all of those shared the same ideological and political roots as Sinn Féin's Northern leaders in the resistance movement. Hedges noted that the party's newspaper, *An Phoblacht*, was designed to speak to multiple publics and the various preoccupations that they held:

> It was primarily aimed at the nationalist and republican community that was under the cosh during the conflict. There was only the *Irish News* daily newspaper and it took an SDLP line; it certainly wasn't sympathetic to the Republican Movement view. *AP/RN* was primarily aimed at nationalists but it was also aimed at Fianna Fáilers down here and Fine Gaelers, people who weren't aligned, trade unionists and progressives of all colours.[54]

As a result, in the Republic of Ireland issues like drugs, crime, housing and employment are central to the party and its paper's message, while in Northern Ireland party literature prioritizes education, jobs, housing and the environment but 'lards' them with established political issues like policing, fair employment and justice and equality, in a way that, Feeney notes, appears like the party invented those issues.[55]

Nationally and locally, the discourses of the Celtic Tiger, the Peace Process and economic boom and bust of the 2010s have framed the development of Sinn Féin and its attendant media activity. The Celtic Tiger created greater fundamental financial and social inequalities in the Irish state, with average wages for those at the bottom of the socio-economic structures falling, in real terms, throughout the period despite the introduction of the minimum wage, while towards the end of the boom there was a rapid rise in higher earnings.[56] The changing patterns of immigration linked to the Tiger also allowed Sinn Féin to frame its fight in the Republic as one for the rights of citizens, workers and the new immigrants left behind by the boom and who suffered most from the post-2008 crash.[57] The economy gave further opportunity for the party, which linked it to unemployment and emigration, the latter of which, *An Phoblacht* decreed, was at 'crisis point'.[58]

Although there was a clear pragmatic and strategic logic in Sinn Féin's emphasis on social and economic equality issues in the South, its focus was more than mere opportunism. It had noted that the left space had grown in the years of the Celtic Tiger collapse, corresponding with 40 per cent of the electorate not voting for either Fianna Fáil or Fine Gael, but had also seen the left become populated with independents and interest groups.[59] Historically, the non-establishment space in the Republic's polity was around 20 per cent, but Sinn Féin was 'more successfully expanding into that space that has opened up, but the potential size of that space is also bigger now than it ever has been in history'.[60] The coalition of left parties in Ireland had seen it become a space of protest politics rather than the dynamic origin point in the push to challenge the political status quo.

The ideologically and geographically disparate independent electoral voices in the South did not offer a collective threat. Sinn Féin's growth in the Republic, from one Teachta Dála (TD) before the 2002 general election to fourteen in 2011 and up to twenty-three at the 2016 poll, had been as a result of collective enthusiastic and hardworking activist teams embedded in their communities.[61] These activists were involved in a wider degree of social and political activism than their counterparts in the North, and were ideologically crucial for both the party's collective self-image and the national project:

> The centre ground is a crowded political place. Sinn Féin does not belong there and should not be in the business of trading fundamental redistribu-tive policies in the hope of short term electoral gain ... Sinn Féin should continue to develop and defend our platform as a radical left-wing party building left-wing unity, building Irish unity and an Ireland of equals.[62]

Left approaches have helped Sinn Féin to make the link between local activism and national politics, developing inclusion of community at a national level and bridging the gap between grounded physical communi-ties of activists and the imagined Irish nation.[63] The party has also con-flated concepts of social and community activism with political struggle which has driven approaches to activism, producing what the Progressive Unionist Party's David Ervine described as 'in-your-face street politics and agitation', and which recognizes the agenda-setting potential of both grassroots political and media activism.[64] The social and economic mani-festo was also to become more important in the Republic for two reasons. With relatively little financial and political autonomy in the North, mobi-lization on specific issues of economic and social reform would be a waste of the party's resources and time. However, while Ó'Broin asserts that the long view can be taken on macroeconomic policy in the North, 'in the south, failure on the economy leads to failure at the polls'.[65]

Sinn Féin's role as arbiter or primary definer of modern republicanism saw it utilize all strata of the activist sphere to communicate its dynamic political restructuring. The roots of these reforms pre-dated the Peace Process, and the party's gradual development as a political organization, rather than as the subordinate political wing of the IRA, necessitated a re-imagination of both the traditional discourses and mediated public aesthetics of Provisionalism. In essence, Sinn Féin's transformation is not simply ideological, but also bureaucratic and organizational. The party's central function has changed and as a result its activist practices and structures have required transformation: 'Republicanism has evolved from an ideology and organisation whose politics are based on mass revolution-ary movement and armed struggle to a conventional political party whose goals are the preservation of a bureaucratic structure and adaptation of the status quo.'[66] New discourses that supported the developing party would eventually contribute to the ideological demilitarization of the movement in pursuit of new publics beyond those of traditional republicanism and began before official talks about peace were instigated in 1993.[67]

This 'normalization' of revolutionary republican politics was also evinced in the demilitarization of expressions of its cultural and political identity and aspirations.[68] Electoralism and full integration into the constitutional process saw its political ambitions shift from being a protest movement to holding political office and seeking re-election more regularly and in more political institutions than any other party in Ireland. The party's gradual embracing of the constitutional agenda was based on acknowledgement of the conflict between tacit and explicit nationalist aspirations for Irish unity but a lack of popular support for the armed struggle. In the twelve years of the post-Hunger Strike period, the party had gone from openly advocating the ballot paper and Armalite strategy to recognizing the need for PIRA ceasefire in the Hume–Adams talks. The party had in a two-month period in 1981 performed a far-reaching *volte face*, stating categorically in September that, 'outside of a 32-county sovereign independent democracy, the IRA will have no involvement in what is loosely called constitutional politics', before Danny Morrison asked the ard fheis, 'will anyone here object if with a ballot paper in this hand, and an Armalite in this hand, we take power in Ireland?'[69] Although constitutional and electoral politics are not necessarily the same, Morrison's famous *ad hoc* speech, improvised in the heat of a highly contested debate on electoralism, did signify the gradual development of electoral policy dating back to Jimmy Drumm's speech, co-written by Morrison and Adams, at the Bodenstown commemoration in 1977.[70] This electoral policy was not without precedent; Sinn Féin had contested elections in previous periods, including the 1960s. The period 1970–1981 was, in this respect, an aberration. That the party went from floating the idea that 'we find that a successful war of liberation cannot be fought exclusively on the backs of the oppressed in the six counties', to being central to peace talks in little over fifteen years, was a remarkable transformation given this strand of republicanism's initially deep traditionalism.[71]

Sinn Féin leadership had long known that PIRA's armed campaign was the central obstacle to political advancement. Danny Morrison noted that it became apparent while canvassing in the mid 1980s when a voter said, 'I like what you have to say, but I don't like those bombs.'[72] The party's vision was not merely based on this specific anecdotal evidence; Sinn Féin's strategy had eventually to make it explicit that it had departed permanently from militarism early in the Peace Process and this would inevitably lead to the decommissioning of IRA arms. Adams's press officer and confidante Richard McAuley said, 'We're not going to realize our full potential as long as the war is going on in the North and as long as Sinn Féin is presented the way it is with regard to armed struggle and violence.'[73] The acknowledgement of the intellectual and moral friction between the armed campaign and how it hampered the party's wider growth was highlighted in 1988 by the party's current lord mayor of Belfast, Máirtín Ó'Muilleoir, ten years prior to the GFA. Ó'Muilleoir, who would eventually become a media entrepreneur, was closely aligned to the party's strategy, and noted the 'contradictions between the armed struggle and our political work'. He called for a pragmatic position that recognized the political suicide of armed struggle.[74] Ó'Muilleoir's concern, as a post-1981 Hunger Strikes, non-PIRA recruit, was in job creation and economic regeneration, both of which were hampered by the armed struggle.[75] His profile as someone who had not played a part in the armed campaign encapsulated another of the key points of conflict between new Sinn Féin and the older republican volunteers. This was a clash between generations and competing political traditions. The new Sinn Féin generation were characterized as 'draft dodgers' and 'the Armani suit brigade' by some of those who had been through the jail system.[76] *Fourthwrite* and the *Blanket* were partly established by a group of former prisoners as a response to the role that 'draft dodgers' were playing in republicanism's new ideological direction, seeing it as an affront to the sacrifice that they had made.[77] While many former prisoners remained faithful to the Sinn Féin reformist cause and would play key senior roles, a significant number of dissidents and dissenters were former prisoners who rejected the notion that their sacrifice had been for the party to enter government in Stormont. [78]

This reconfiguration of the aspirations of republicanism caused conflict with the ideologically diverging strata of dissenting activists who adhered to differing commitment to republican tradition throughout this period. As the party slowly rewrote the armed force catechism to fit the gradualist needs of the Peace Process, it lost supporters and groups who would utilize the activist and social media spaces to voice their own dissent. Those that diverged from Sinn Féin did so as the party framed often significant changes in political direction within the ambiguous linguistic apparatus of the Peace Process and portrayed them as part of the reconfiguration of republican strategy and struggle.

The ideological and narrative flexibility of the reformist project dated back to the early 1990s, and was best illustrated by the TUAS strategy, which was ambiguously allowed to mean either Totally Unarmed Strategy or Tactical Use of Armed Struggle to those interpreting it.[79] It was designed to mollify traditionalists but also signify commitment to joining the Peace

Process.[80] Murray and Tonge posit that, in being forced to tacitly update the internal assumptions of the historic mandate of the 1918 First Dáil, the party had to use duplicity to reassure 'doubters that armed struggle remained a tactical option'.[81] This constructive linguistic ambiguity was also prevalent in pre-Peace Process activist media, with *An Phoblacht* variously describing IRA ceasefires as 'suspensions' or 'pauses' to assuage the fears of traditionalists.[82] The tactical use of armed struggle may have remained moot but, in effect, constitutionalism and electoralism had replaced it as the centrepiece of republican strategy and methodology. This ambiguity was at the heart of the protests of many dissenters who stated the '"constructive fudge" and "creative ambiguity" ... has made the peace process the intellectual farce it is'.[83] However, the actions of PIRA had become a 'political liability' and, despite the powerful cultural and ideological sustenance it provided the movement, Gerry Adams recognized that Sinn Féin had to become the dominant partner in the Provisional movement.[84]

The internal establishment republican battleground was fixed on moving the primary focus of the movement away from the sustaining factor of armed force and resistance as centralized by the waves of republican campaigns in the twentieth century and to reconfiguring them to the political struggles of 'diversity, equality and respect' that would be fought for in the constitutional, not guerrilla war, arena.[85] A second key issue with constitutionalism, as opposed by dissenters, was that by engaging in constitutional politics Sinn Féin accepted what it had not previously: that 'justice and democracy were possible within the British state'.[86] This in itself was a reversal of what PIRA had rejected in peace talks in the 1970s. As a former senior PIRA commander said of the Peace Process, 'we fought on and for what? – What we rejected in 1975?'[87] The internal ideological clash in this instance was between the constitutional direction of Sinn Féin and how it would offer the chance of 'building an Ireland of Equals', while the phalanx of PIRA was, during the early post-1998 years, used, often murderously, to control and silence dissenting voices.[88]

This period of policing dissent, in the way that PIRA had policed 'antisocial behaviour' during the Troubles, formed one facet of the transitional fulcrum between the revolutionary, armed force period and the purely constitutional future. Although there were a number of PIRA-related instances of violence after decommissioning, most notably the murder of Robert McCartney in 2005, they were more frequent in 1998–2004. Dissent was eventually to be policed in a different fashion.[89] The McCartney murder, carried out by alleged PIRA members, caused enormous problems for Sinn Féin, both in terms of publicity and its immediate electoral cost.[90] It also drew into sharp focus the contradiction between a political party with a supposedly on-ceasefire and decommissioning army which was still involved in brutal acts in its own community. It is in this period that we see the first flowerings of new dissident projects, the first attempts at discerning a new way to republicanism's aspirations that did not include either the compromises of Sinn Féin or the violence of the past. It is also possible to make the link between the development of a greater number of dissenting groups after 2005 and the post-McCartney period, where the violent threat of PIRA in republican communities had to be seen to diminish.

If the main battlegrounds for Sinn Féin became constitutional politics and primarily focused on the socio-economic issues that affected republicans, then a new agenda had to be found for the decades old traditional means of republican cultural expression. While new media and traditional activist media provided a space for both Sinn Féin to publicly articulate the ideological development of the new era, older forms of political expression would also become integrated into the hegemonic power battle. Militarism and romanticizing of the past were central to republican ideological sustenance, inherent to the key dates of its annual calendar of commemorative events. The defiant militarist symbols of the past, however, clashed with the realities of the Peace Process, which delivered much less than the central republican catechism of Irish unification and self-determination. The struggle for Sinn Féin, throughout this period, had not only been to find an effective means of framing the compromises inherent in the Peace Process – countering their portrayal as a dilution of the deeply held common ideological principles of resistance and struggle – but also to manage the dissident and dissenting voices within its own community. The difficulty in developing a comprehensive communications strategy that evinced a new direction was centred on expressing a new focus on political issues of class, gender and political equality while simultaneously re-imagining the cultural expression of a movement whose previous primary outward expressions of its own culture were profoundly militarist. Although not universally exclusive, these issues represented the friction between the older guard of traditional Irish republicanism and the emerging confident post-conflict youth vote that Sinn Féin cleverly captured and developed.[91] For the emerging electorate with little memory of the Troubles, Sinn Féin was not a party primarily linked to armed struggle, but was a central architect of the peace.[92] The symbols of republican history, like the Easter Rising, became cultural footnotes rather than the direct ideological sustenance to the armed struggle they had been during the Troubles, and continued to be for dissidents.

Electorally, the break from overt past militarism has played well with the traditional republican hinterland and the new emerging young Catholic nationalist middle class, the risen people, who had largely diverged from the previous generation's support for the SDLP.[93] The party's trajectory electorally had been sharply upwards, gaining six seats at the 2003 election. This was up nearly 7 per cent on the first elections in 1998, where it had been the second-placed nationalist party after the SDLP, which benefited from the role that John Hume had played in the Peace Process and the brokering of the Belfast Agreement. It had taken 23.5 per cent of the vote in 2004, and in 2007 it gained a further two seats and increased its share to more than 26 per cent of the electorate at a time when the SDLP was in decline in all but its core constituencies. However, the party barely increased its vote at the 2011 Assembly elections, recording a less than 1 per cent increase in its share while taking a further seat. Before the Renewable Heat Incentive (RHI) scandal that dogged the DUP in late 2016 and triggered the 2017 Assembly elections, the May 2016 poll saw Sinn Féin experience electoral decline for the first time in the period of devolution. It was a worrying sign for the newly risen people. It lost a seat in that election, to the People Before Profit party in West Belfast, and saw its share of the vote decline by nearly 3 per cent in a poll that evidenced a growing disenchantment with the ineffectiveness of the Assembly, which had been dogged by political scandal, and where five of the six top parties recorded declines in votes won. As chapter seven's epilogue will outline, that would all change in little more than nine months, as Northern Ireland went to the polls again as the Assembly collapsed under the weight of a £500bn financial scandal. The twin effects of the Brexit vote's disconcerting rise of English nationalism and how it triggered debates over the border and Irish reunification, combined with the DUP's foolish deployment of deeply sectarian cant in the campaign, would see Sinn Féin narrowly avoid becoming the single biggest party in the Assembly and increase its vote by nearly 4 per cent.

In the Republic of Ireland its development as an electoral force has been the result of the outplaying of the Celtic Tiger collapse and extreme economic uncertainty felt in the state, austerity measures imposed by the European Central Bank, and the party's savvy grassroots activism. It has benefited from the decline of Fianna Fáil, the traditionally republican party in the South which was hit by a fallout from years of political and economic scandal which were linked in the public's imagination to its role in two severe periods of recession. It also benefited from a steep decline in support for the Labour Party, the formerly traditional left party in the polity. It began to make major inroads in elections to the Dáil in 2011, when it increased its seats from four to fourteen, with a very creditable third-placed finish by Martin McGuinness in the 2011 presidential election. McGuinness's campaign was itself dogged by political scandal, and, with huge relevance to this book, apparently turned when a tweet sent by a fake McGuinness Twitter account was read out during a televised debate and derailed the campaign of the front runner Sean Gallagher on the eve of the poll.[94] The party was also central to the nationwide protests against hugely unpopular water charges that Fianna Fáil and the Green Party coalition conceived and which the Fine Gael-led government then sought to impose on households around the country.[95] Sinn Féin had its name on posters produced for the nationwide protest against the charges which the *New Statesman* noted allowed it to promote the idea that it was a party for the ordinary people while other parties backed the controversial scheme.[96] Sinn Féin converted this campaigning into electoral gains at the Irish general election in February 2016, when it increased its vote by almost 4 per cent, gaining nine seats and jumping to twenty-three. This made it the third party in the Dáil, and installed it as a potential coalition partner at future elections, should it maintain its current recent electoral trajectory. Its performance, despite criticisms of Gerry Adams's leadership, could, on one level, suggest that the party is disproving Tom McGurk's assertion that it does not know how the Republic ticks.

Away from the symbols and rituals of the Peace Process, Sinn Féin also strategically changed the infrastructure and output of its media and communications, dynamically altering its internal and external media strategies on both sides of the border. The expanded focus of the party obviously required larger, more professional media teams in Dáil Éireann and at Stormont. The party's 'always-on' strategy of producing activist materials and responding to mainstream media narratives had produced highly effective media infrastructure that now went well beyond *An Phoblacht*. With the party's absorption into the political mainstream and increasing electoral support, its reassessment of its aspirations saw it redefine the parameters of activist media and challenge the mainstream press.

Notes

1 In Northern Ireland and the Republic of Ireland Sinn Féin's name is colloquially shortened to 'the Shinners' by both the party and opponents.

2 McGregor, Mark, '"Dissidents" – they mostly didn't think so', *Sluggerotoole*, 27 January 2009. Available at: www.sluggerotoole.com/2009/01/27/dissidents/. Accessed 28 September 2009.

3 Young, Connla, 'New "revolutionary" republican party Saoradh launched', *Irish News*, 26 September 2016. Available at: www.irishnews.com/news/politicalnews/2016/09/26/news/new-revolutionary-republican-party-saoradh-launched-708613/. Accessed 26 September 2016.

4 See: 'Saoradh – the NEW face of Republicanism?' *Joycey's Blog*, 17 October 2016. Available at: www.joyceysblog.wordpress.com/2016/10/17/saoradh-the-new-face-of-republicanism/. Accessed 20October 2016.

5 'Terrier', 'Don't misrepresent Saoradh', *Pensive Quill*, 8 December 2016. Available at: www.thepensivequill.am/2016/12/dont-misrepresent-saoradh.html. Accessed 9 December 2016.

6 O'Ruairc, Liam, 'Defining dissidents', *Pensive Quill*, 18 May 2009. Available at: www.thepensivequill.am/2009/05/defining-dissidents.html. Accessed 18 May 2009.

7 O'Ruairc, 'Defining dissidents'. See also: 'Political stalemate – here we go again', *Newsletter*, 1 September 2008. Available at: www.newsletter.co.uk/news/political-stalemate-here-we-go-again-1-1874761. Accessed 1 September 2008.

8 McIntyre, Anthony, 'Supporting peace but not the process', *Blanket*, December 2001. Available at: www.indiamond6.ulib.iupui.edu:81/pens.html. Accessed 7 December 2009.

9 McDonald, Henry, 'IRA rebuff for Adams prison ally', *Observer*, 5 November 2000.

10 White, Robert W., and Fraser, Michael R., 'Personal and collective identities and long-term social movement activism: Republican Sinn Féin', in Stryker, Sheldon, Owens, Timothy J., and White, Robert W. (eds), *Self, Identity, and Social Movements* (Minneapolis, MN: University of Minnesota Press, 2000).

11 Ní Tuama, Carrie, 'Complacent convenience', *Fourthwrite*, No. 1, Spring 2000.

12 'Statement by Gerry Adams calling on the IRA to end the "armed struggle"', 6 April 2005. Available at: www.cain.ulst.ac.uk/issues/politics/docs/sf/ga060405.htm. Accessed 9 August 2013. Also available at: www.sinnFéin.ie/contents/15207. Accessed 9 August 2013.

13 Bean, Kevin, *The New Politics of Sinn Féin* (Liverpool: Liverpool University Press, 2007), pp. 142–145. See also: English, *Armed Struggle*, p. xxiv. While Bean points to republicanism being embodied by the contributions of the socialist Connolly and the cultural separatism of Patrick Pearse, Connolly has been the dominant historical influence in recent years as dissenters have sought to highlight the opportunity for socialism in a time of recession and growing gap in wealth in Irish and British society.

14 Cunningham, Ciarán, interview, 8 January 2012.

15 'Elections and abstentionism'. Internal party document. Available at: www.rsf.ie/election.htm. Accessed 9 August 2009.

16 See 'Provos should disband now', *Saoirse*, April 2002. Republican Sinn Féin described decommissioning as 'the worst sell-out in Irish history'. See also: Toolis, Kevin, 'Decommissioning: Sinn Féin may pay price for peace', *Daily Mirror*, 24 October 2001.

17 McIntyre, 'Supporting peace but not the process'.

18 McIntyre, Anthony, 'Out of the ashes of armed struggle arose the Stormontistas and they fought ... Ardoyne youth', *Blanket*, 5 September 2002. Available at: www.indiamond6.ulib.iupui.edu:81/stormontistas.html. Accessed 7 December 2009.

19 Todd, Jennifer, 'Social transformation, collective categories, and identity change', *Theory and Society* vol. 34, no. 4, 2005, p. 445.

20 Cadwallader, Anne, 'Historic step towards peace', *Christian Science Monitor*, 23 October 2001. See also: O'Neill, Sharon, Doyle, Simon, and McKinney, Seamus, 'A sequence of surrender: ex-prisoners' reaction', *Irish News*, 23 October 2001.

21 McIntyre, Anthony, 'Republicans acknowledging a democratic basis to partition',*Blanket*, 2 February 2002. Available at: www.indiamond6.ulib.iupui.edu:81/partition.htm. Accessed 10 December 2009.

22 Hall, Michael, *Republicanism in Transition 2: Beginning a Debate* (Newtownabbey: Island Publications, 2011), p. 24.

23 Clarke, Liam, and Jones, Michael, 'Trimble offers olive branch to Adams', *Sunday Times*, 28 March 1999.

24 Price, Marian, 'We want recruits because we are sure of the rightness of our cause', Bodenstown address, 13 June 1999. Available at: www.rsf.ie/boden99.htm. Accessed 7 May 2009.

25 Maillot, Agnès, *New Sinn Féin: Irish Republicanism in the Twenty-first Century* (Abingdon: Routledge, 2005), p. 70. See also: Murray, Gerard, and Tonge, Jonathan, *Sinn Féin and the SDLP* (London: Hurst & Company, 2005), pp. 227–239.

26 McGurk, Tom, 'Does Sinn Féin understand the Republic?', *Sunday Business Post*, 26 July 2009.

27 'Cllr Louise Minihan resigns from Sinn Féin', *Indymedia Ireland*, 17 July 2009. Available at: www.indymedia.ie/article/93210&comment_limit=0&condense_comments=false#comment256150. Accessed 18 July 2009.

28 Tonge, Jonathan, '"They haven't gone away, you know": Irish Republican "dissidents" and "armed struggle"', *Terrorism and Political Violence* vol. 16, no. 3, 2004, p. 672.

29 The *Blanket* provided a space for diverse opinion from both within republicanism, especially for those dissenting from the Sinn Féin Peace Process strategy, as well as socialists, trade unionists and a number of loyalists and unionists.

30 McIntyre, interview.

31 Maillot, *New Sinn Féin*, p. 3. Bean, *New Politics of Sinn Féin*, p. 177.

32 Maillot, *New Sinn Féin*, p. 1.

33 McIntyre, Anthony, 'Republicanism ... alive or dying?', *Fourthwrite*, No. 28, Winter 2007. Available at: www.indiamond6.ulib.iupui.edu:81/AM130108.html. Accessed 11 December 2010.

34 Maillot, *New Sinn Féin*, p. 129.

35 O'Ruairc, Liam, 'From Havana to Pyongyang', *Blanket*, February 2002. Available at: www.indiamond6.ulib.iupui.edu:81/pyongyang.html.This is the first in a series of important articles by O'Ruairc that addressed the historic international dimension to Sinn Féin policy. Accessed 10 December 2010.

36 'International solidarity,' eirigi.org. Available at: www.eirigi.org/campaigns/international/index.htm. Accessed 3 May 2009.

37 See: 'Vote No on 2 October', *An Phoblacht*, 24 September 2009. 'Vote No to Lisbon 2', *Saoirse*, September 2009. 'Getting the message out – vote No to Lisbon 2', eirigi.org, 10 September 2009. Available at: www.eirigi.org/latest/latest100909.html. Accessed 11 September 2009.

38 McIntyre, Anthony, 'Toome debate', *Blanket*, 21 December 2006. Available at: www.indiamond6.ulib.iupui.edu:81/AM1020107.html. Accessed 22 December 2006.
39 Maillot, *New Sinn Féin*, p. 3.
40 O'Kane, Eamonn, 'Anglo-Irish relations and the Northern Ireland peace process: from exclusion to inclusion', *Contemporary British History* vol. 18, no. 1, 2004, p. 95.
41 Adams, Gerry, 'To cherish a just and lasting peace', *Fordham International Law Journal*, vol. 22, 1998, p. 1187.
42 McKearney, *The Provisional IRA*, pp. 212–213.
43 McIntyre, Anthony, 'Irish Republican Writers Group and the battle for new ideas', *Socialist Democracy*, 2001. Available at: www.socialistdemocracy.org/ ProblemsOfPeace/POPTheIRWGAndTheBattleForNewIdeas.html. Accessed 11 September 2012.
44 Craig, Joe, 'What's so radical about Sinn Féin?', *Green Left Weekly*, 12 June 2002. Available at: www.greenleft.org.au/content/ireland-whats-so-radical- about-sinn-fein. Accessed 11 December 2012. Also available at: http:// www.socialistdemocracy.org/News&AnalysisIreland/News&AnalysisIreWhatsSo RadicalAboutSinnFéin.htm. Accessed 11 December 2012.
45 Splintered Sunrise, 'Dissidence in the new dispensation', *Splinteredsunrise*, 20 April 2009. Available at: www.splinteredsunrise.wordpress.com/2009/04/20/ dissidence-in-the-new-dispensation/. Accessed 21 April 2009.
46 Ó'Caoláin, Caoimhghín, 'Ireland, republicanism and Sinn Féin', *An Phoblacht*, 10 April 2003.
47 Adams, Gerry, 'A further shore is reachable from here', McCool/Coyle/Carlin Memorial Lecture, Derry, 16 August 2000. Sinn Féin press release. Available at www.sinnFéin.org/releases/00/pr081600.html. Accessed 11 May 2012.
48 See also: G. Adams, 'Presidential address to the Ard Fheis 1997'. Available at: www.sinnFéin.ie/contents/15174. Accessed 11 May 2012. The phrase 'voice of an idea' comes from a speech about Robert Emmet delivered by Patrick Pearse in New York in 1914. See: 'How does she stand?', *Collected Works of Pádraic H. Pearse* (Dublin: Phoenix Publishing Co., 1924), p. 76.
49 For an overview of the influence of the new Catholic middle class on establish- ment republican politics, see: Bean, *New Politics of Sinn Féin*, pp. 40–44.
50 Maillot, *New Sinn Féin*, p. 73. The political analyst Pat Montague says that what separates Sinn Féin from other parties is its confidence in both its message and direction.
51 Tonge, Jonathan, 'The political agenda of Sinn Fein: change without change?', in Stanyer, J., and Stoker, G. (eds), *Political Studies Association Annual Conference* (Jordanstown, Belfast: Political Studies Association, 1997), pp. 750–760.
52 McIntyre, Anthony, 'Be honest Mr Adams: you no longer have a strat- egy for a United Ireland', *Pensive Quill*, 3 April 2009. Available at: www.thepensivequill.am/2009/04/be-honest-mr-adams-you-no-longer- have.html. McIntyre made the comment about the five isms in reply to a comment on his blog. The original piece appeared in *Parliamentary Brief*. Accessed 4 April 2009.

53 Bean, *New Politics of Sinn Féin*, p. 141.

54 Hedges, John, interview, 26 November 2016.

55 Feeney, Brian, *Sinn Féin: A Hundred Turbulent Years* (Dublin: O'Brien Press, 2002), p. 436.

56 Voitchovsky, Sarah, Maître, Bertrand, and Nolen, Brian, 'Wage inequality in Ireland's "Celtic Tiger" boom', *Economic and Social Review* vol. 43, no. 1, 2012, pp. 99–133.

57 'Putting equality at the heart of the economy', *An Phoblacht*, 18 January 2006.

58 'Ógra joins emigration protests at airports and seaports', *An Phoblacht*, 27 August 2010.

59 Ó'Broin, Eoin, interview, 2 June 2012.

60 Ó'Broin interview.

61 Maillot, *New Sinn Féin*, p. 98.

62 Ó'Broin, Eoin, 'Sinn Féin election growth to be found as republican, left alternative', *An Phoblacht*, 7 June 2007.

63 Shirlow, Peter, and McGovern, Mark, 'Language, discourse and dialogue: Sinn Féin and the Irish peace process', *Political Geography* vol. 17, no. 2, 1998, p. 179.

64 Quoted in Maillot, *New Sinn Féin*, p. 64.

65 Ó'Broin, Eoin, *Sinn Féin and the Politics of Left Republicanism* (London: Pluto, 2009), p. 282.

66 Bean, Kevin, 'Every picture tells a story', *Fourthwrite*, No. 1, 2000.

67 Moloney, Ed, *A Secret History of the IRA* (London: Penguin, 2002), pp. 350–352. Moloney notes the de-escalation of Provisional armed activity in Derry after local public outrage at the Coshquin bombing in October 1990 which involved a local man being made to drive a 1,000lb bomb to an army border check point because he had worked for the security forces.

68 McDowell, Sara, 'Armalite, the ballot box and memorialization: Sinn Féin and the state in post-conflict Northern Ireland', *The Round Table: The Commonwealth Journal of International Affairs* vol. 96, no. 393, 2007, pp. 725–738.

69 'IRA attitude on elections', *An Phoblacht/Republican News*, 5 September 1981. Morrison, Danny, 'By ballot and bullet', *An Phoblacht/Republican News*, 5 November 1981. See also: O'Ruairc, Liam, 'Going respectable', *Weekly Worker*, No. 573, 21 April 2005.

70 Morrison, Danny, interview, 5 November 2011.

71 Drumm, Jimmy, 'Annual Wolfe Tone commemoration speech', *Republican News*, 25 June 1977.

72 Morrison interview.

73 Wilson, Robin, 'Time for magnanimity', *Fortnight*, September 1992.

74 Moloney, *A Secret History of the IRA*, p. 299.

75 Moloney, *A Secret History of the IRA*, p. 299.

76 See: Hill, Geoff, 'Devolution countdown: Seamus returns to the fast lane', *Newsletter*, 30 November 1999. This is the earliest reference to the phrase in the mainstream media: 'Cedric Wilson launched into a detailed history of the Troubles during which he once, quaintly, accused Mitchel McLaughlin of being a draft dodger because of his lack of active involvement in the IRA. Shame on you, Mitchel.'

77 Stanage, Niall, 'Hughes no longer toes the provo line', *Sunday Tribune*, 17 December 2000. Available at: www.indiamond6.ulib.iupui.edu:81/BH110208.html. Accessed 10 September 2009.

78 Former PIRA prisoners that hold seats for Sinn Féin include Gerry Kelly MLA, Carál Ní Chuilín MLA, Pat Sheehan MLA, Fra McCann MLA and Conor Murphy MP. For an evocation of the dissenting position, see: Breen, Suzanne, 'A life dedicated to the IRA and a broken heart', *Sunday Tribune*, 24 February 2008. See also: Hughes, Brendan, 'They think it's all over', *Blanket*, 4 February 2002. Available at: www.indiamond6.ulib.iupui.edu:81/allover.html. Accessed 9 September 2009.

79 'The TUAS document'. Available at: www.cain.ulst.ac.uk/othelem/organ/ira/tuas94.htm. Accessed 11 May 2012.

80 Moloney, *A Secret History of the IRA*, p. 432. TUAS document, pp. 498–501. On the ambiguity of the TUAS document, see also: Bean, *The New Politics of Sinn Féin*, p. 188. Dissident armed group the Real IRA would use the term in its 2009 Easter message after the murders of security force members early that year. 'Actions by volunteers of Óglaigh na hÉireann in the last year have proved that the tactical use of armed struggle can, and does, bring results.' 'Real Irish Republican Army (RIRA) Easter Statement, 13 April 2009'. Available at: www.cain.ulst.ac.uk/othelem/organ/ira/rira130409.htm. Accessed 10 September 2010.

81 Murray and Tonge, *Sinn Féin and the SDLP*, p. 265.

82 Moloney, *A Secret History of the IRA*, p. 429.

83 A. McIntyre, 'An ambiguity that corrupts', *Observer*, 2 September 2001.

84 Feeney, *Sinn Féin*, p. 428. Feeney notes Adams pledged to make 'electoralism a central part of Sinn Féin's strategy'.

85 Bean, *New Politics of Sinn Féin*, p. 210. The quote is from Sinn Féin's 2007 Assembly election manifesto.

86 Smyth, Jim, 'On the road to god knows where: understanding Irish republicanism', *Capital and Class* vol. 86, no. 1, 2005, p. 155.

87 A. McIntyre, 'A dark view of the Process', *Fourthwrite*, Spring 2000.

88 'Building an Ireland of Equals' became a central trope of the communications policy of Sinn Féin. Its flexibility allowed women's rights and those of the sexually marginalized to become incorporated into party literature. For an example of its flexibility see: 'An Ireland of equals in a Europe of equals', *An Phoblacht*, 2 June 2004.

89 Chrisafis, Angelique, 'How pub brawl turned into republican crisis', *Guardian*, 28 February 2005. See also: Breen, Suzanne, 'Provos move to smash dissent', *Sunday Tribune*, 3 December 2006.

90 'Murder lost seat for Sinn Féin', *BBC News Online*, 10 May 2005. Available at: www.news.bbc.co.uk/1/hi/northern_ireland/4532073.stm. Accessed 11 May 2005.

91 Maillot, *New Sinn Féin*, pp. 96–97. It must also be noted that the foundation of the Provisionals in Belfast in the early 1970s was based in a large recruitment of young people and that the party has traditionally had a vibrant youth culture. See also: Bean, *New Politics of Sinn Féin*, pp. 58–59.

92 Bean, *New Politics of Sinn Féin*, pp. 58–59.
93 Bean, *New Politics of Sinn Féin*, p. 40.
94 Ryan, Philip, and Swords, Warren, 'The tweet that changed the course of Irish presidential election was "just a bit of fun"', *Irish Daily Mail*, 30 October 2011. Available at: www.dailymail.co.uk/news/article-2055197/Irish-presidential-election-2011-Tweet-changed-course-just-bit-fun.html. Accessed 1 November 2011.
95 See: 'Water charges – a tax too far: a Sinn Féin policy position paper', November 2015. Available at: www.sinnfein.ie/files/2015/WaterChargesDoc_Nov2015.pdf. Accessed 2 December 2015.
96 Dunne, Ciara, 'How did Sinn Féin become contenders in the Irish election?', *New Statesman*, 30 March 2015. Available at: www.newstatesman.com/politics/2015/03/how-did-sinn-f-become-contenders-irish-election. Accessed2 April 2015.

3

Contemporary Irish republicanism since 1998: dissos and dissenters[1]

If it is easy to identify those that the media refers to as 'dissident republicans', it is far more difficult to identify and define what they mean by 'dissident republicanism'.[2]

The second bloc: traditional dissent

The compromises of the Peace Process and electoralism remained an issue for some traditionalists who were constants through the modern era of republicanism prior to 1998. These groups would become more marginalized through the period under analysis. Politically dissenting organizations like the Irish Republican Socialist Party, Republican Sinn Féin and 32 County Sovereignty Movement were active, to a greater or lesser extent, prior to 1998, but – if one sees electoral success and media attention as two measures of political activity – the influence of both their political strategies and activist media are naturally more diminished than that of Sinn Féin. Their visibility and the effectiveness of their communication would become lessened both in the face of Sinn Féin's growing electoral and social power and with the emergence of dissenting groups that would later share the anti-Good Friday Agreement space.

The dissident and dissenting groups that pre-date the Peace Process were not a wholly unified ideological bloc and reflect the diversity of republican thinking. They primarily reflect the divergent approaches to elections and recognition of the political institutions of the three states in which republicanism found itself active: the parliament at Westminster, the Dáil in the Republic of Ireland and the Northern Ireland Assembly. They also represent confusion and eternally quixotic interpretation of the political realities of the changed Irish electoral landscape encapsulated in Sinn Féin's growth. In a series of pamphlets produced to explain the various dissident and dissenting positions, one respondent noted solipsistically, 'I believe Sinn Féin is out of kilter'; another quixotically, 'We can't blame the population for voting Sinn Féin.'[3]

The IRSP competed in elections from 1977, three years after its formation following a split from the Official Republican movement, and, in the midst of the political turmoil surrounding the Anti-H Block and Hunger Strikes campaigns, won two Belfast City Council seats in 1981, on a joint ticket with People's Democracy.[4] However, in the period after the tumult of the Hunger Strikes, it failed to capitalize on developing support for militant republicanism, and the already dominant Provisionals in Sinn Féin would ultimately control the socialist republican space. The IRSP's commitment to a revolutionary Marxist Leninist socialism failed to become updated to recognize wider transformations in the global left that came with the collapse of the Soviet bloc. Its failure to tailor its idealism to the changing political dispensation meant it had a diminished profile.[5] However, fighting elections, and the *de facto* recognition of parliaments in Northern Ireland, the Republic and at Westminster that this entailed, remained the central objection of the less doctrinaire socialism of RSF and 32CSM. Both of these organizations were not products of the socialist class struggle, but of the two most recent splits from Sinn Féin along divergent approaches to the republican catechism and abstentionism, in 1986 and 1997 respectively. Both organizations were made up of hard line traditionalists, and had their main constituencies in the Republic of Ireland and in the borderlands especially. They were also committed to upholding the ideals of the War of Independence (1919–1921). For RSF, which split from Sinn Féin on the issue of abandoning abstentionism in 1986, the only parliament that could be ideologically recognized was 'the Second Dáil, the last one [that] voted in an all-Ireland election, remained the lawful government of Ireland'.[6] Reflecting the original declaration of RSF on its split from Sinn Féin, 32CSM saw the only blueprint for the aims of republicanism as 'the Declaration of Independence, in word, deed and spirit, as established in 1918 and ratified by Dáil Éireann on January 21st 1919'.[7]

Former Provisional leader Ruairí Ó Brádaigh, who split from Sinn Féin in 1986 because of the decision to abandon abstentionism and allow the party's TDs to sit in the Dáil, led Republican Sinn Féin originally and is still a huge ideological influence over the party. That split was perhaps the most important in the modern republican movement and set the parameters for the reconstruction of the republican sphere throughout the period under analysis. RSF was also linked to the armed organization Continuity IRA, which was also established as a result of the split from the Provisional IRA.[8] On occasions, RSF has consistently denied the link between the organizations, refusing to act as a conduit to CIRA in the aftermath of the Omagh bomb.[9] Reflecting older ideological purity, it has retained a traditionalist refusal to recognize the political apparatus of either state and therefore will not stand in parliamentary elections. Despite the fact that this has been a significant reason for a failure to grow beyond its natural constituency, is has reiterated:

> Republican Sinn Féin is abstentionist. We do not recognise the legitimacy of the Six or 26-County States in Ireland, both of which were created by acts of the British parliament in Westminster as a denial of the wishes of the Irish people. Therefore, we do not give voluntary recognition to either jurisdiction.[10]

This intransigent traditionalist stance allowed RSF to be seen as a relic of the early twentieth century, with little to offer the transformed political landscape beyond its relatively small activist base. In the 2007 Assembly elections none of its six candidates managed to poll more than 500 votes – gaining less than 0.4 per cent of the total votes cast.[11] The Northern Ireland Civil Rights Association founder and former Official Republican Des O'Hagan captured the central criticism of RSF: 'Republican Sinn Féin still think this is the 1950s ... or even the 1920s.'[12] RSF was, naturally, also opposed to the Peace Process on the basis that it deepened partition and maintained British rule in Ireland, insisting, 'there will be no full and final closure to the conflict between Irish republicans and English imperialism until the British government signals to the world its intention of leaving Ireland forever.'[13]

RSF's key strategy for the future of Ireland remained Éire Nua, a blueprint for a united Ireland governed on a federal system based in the four provinces originally drawn up in a fifty-six page pamphlet in 1971.[14] Associated with the party's then primarily republic-based leadership, it was Sinn Féin's policy until 1983, when it was abandoned for support for a unitary republic. This was also a central issue in the ending of Ó'Brádaigh's time as the president of the party, with Gerry Adams assuming leadership at the ard fheis of that year. The policy had been discredited for a number of years by the Adams camp within Sinn Féin as a means of undermining Ó'Brádaigh.[15] In carving the country up into four provinces and recognizing the legitimacy of the unionist identity in Ulster, it did not provide a realistic basis upon which to campaign for elections, especially not in the modern era.[16] The acknowledgement of the unionist majority in the North was conceived so as to provide proof that republicans did not 'believe in a steamrollering unitary state', but the federal structure was designed to temper abuses and discrimination of the Northern state from 1920–1972.[17] Belfast Provisionals had rejected the original document as a 'sop to unionists'.[18] Jim Gibney noted it was unpopular because it could be read as giving more power to abuse republicans further.[19] The policy is perhaps more important for the role it played in the power struggle in Sinn Féin in the early 1980s than for any long-term credibility. Certainly it did not provide a basis for a long-term interrogation of policy with RSF. When the updated Éire Nua document was released by RSF in 2001 it was a modestly rebranded version of the original with added emphasis on a social and economic programme.[20] With little detailed reference to how it would be implemented or agreed, RSF did not develop its defining policy 'beyond a broad set of federal principles'.[21]

Éire Nua, at the very least, represented the long-term policy stasis of RSF, which had moved little in forty years and not responded to the dynamic recalibrations of the social and economic landscape of Ireland. With the political landscape altered by both the effects of the changed institutions of the Good Friday Agreement and the influence of global capitalism, North and South, it remained a poor foundation upon which to build consistent support. Regardless, RSF stayed loyal and true to the principles of republicanism upon which it was founded. The age of its activist base had grown older without being significantly replenished by new membership.[22] It was accused of having a *Dad's Army* reputation for dressing up in uniforms at commemorations and having neither the credibility nor the dynamism to offer a credible platform to articulate the concerns of republicans diverging from either Sinn Féin or IRSP.[23] These have latterly tended to be involved in éirígí or RNU, or both, or simply have avoided alignment at all. The overwhelming popular support for the Peace Process also meant that RSF struggled to build its public profile significantly. Activists struggled with being isolated: Geraldine Taylor, a republican veteran in Belfast noted, 'I was practically on my own in Belfast.'[24] However, she noted sales of *Saoirse* had increased as the process developed and youth membership also grew, particularly in places where dissidence was most visible: Ardoyne in North Belfast, Newry, Armagh and Lurgan.[25] Limited street-level activism which failed to extend beyond commemoration and small demonstrations saw the party effectively locked into a praxis that had markedly failed to capture much attention beyond a narrow sector of the dissident republican sphere. In the area of traditional street protest, it made its presence felt in areas like North Armagh and North Belfast, and it was prominent in protests against the controversial Ulster loyalist Love Ulster rally in Dublin in 2006 and against Queen Elizabeth II's visit to Dublin in 2010.[26] The party has also been at the forefront of maintaining traditions of commemoration, with uniformed colour parties that hark back to the PIRA and INLA funerals of the 1970s and 1980s. This militarist underpinning was enough to attract the producers of *Vice* magazine's online documentary series, who filmed young RSF volunteers on parade and getting military training for the short film 'The Republic's dissident youth: Ireland's young warriors' in July 2015.[27]

With a traditionalist stance and an older activist base, this media activism also fell within conventional forms. Unlike IRSP or the 32CSM, RSF maintained disciplined and regular monthly publication of *Saoirse*, which, in a period of technologically advanced online media strategies and the cutting edge graphic design of *An Phoblacht* and *Look Left*, remained a traditional echo of *An Phoblacht* from the revolutionary period of the 1970s/ 1980s; its editorial diet mostly a mixture of commemoration, news from cumanns and campaigns, pages of overseas news from radical groups and ideologically congruent struggles.[28] However, it is to be commended for its commitment to producing *Saoirse* while other organizations' papers or media outlets have fallen by the wayside, and in recent years to have re-invigorated it with a redesign which has made it more modern. The organization's argument for maintaining *Saoirse* has always been that not only does it provide an external face, but it also provides coherence and focus internally.[29] Although RSF did not initially become deeply embedded in online or social media, reflecting, President Des Dalton said, that its activist base was not interested or deeply integrated in these platforms, it did maintain publication of its weekly online *Irish Republican Information Service* until 2014.[30] Within the context of the online sphere, in which there can be discerned a restructuring of the republican public sphere, like most other political groups in Ireland RSF had active communities centred on Facebook. However, this is indicative of the popularity of Facebook, which was the most overwhelmingly popular social media site in Ireland, rather than any innovation on RSF's part.[31] The party did not have any centralized strategy for social media until the early 2010s; it only joined Twitter in 2011 but has often had periods of inactivity on such platforms. Rather, the party hierarchy ceded this type of activity to members of individual cumanns.[32]

Within the specific context of the thematic or ideological concerns common to the articulation of the issues of republicanism in this period, RSF continued to show interest in similar European radical hinterlands as Sinn Féin, demonstrating kinship with sub-state separatist independence movements. Ó'Brádaigh, while president of Sinn Féin had been keen to develop a pan-Celtic alliance in Europe; the blogger Splintered Sunrise noted in a reply to a post on Éire Nua on *Cedar Lounge Revolution* that, 'Ruairi did and does have a strong streak of romantic pan-Celticism, but he was also the guy who was keen to forge links with the likes of the Basques and Catalans and Corsicans.'[33] The party continues to hold a large archive of materials from activist groups in Europe in its Dublin headquarters, but it has limited co-operation with the high-profile Basques and Catalans. The close links between Sinn Féin and the Basque separatists Herri Batsuna has seen previous links with Republican Sinn Féin severed.[34]

The party has built a closer alliance with the Breton separatists Emgann, and RSF president Des Dalton has regularly spoken in Brittany.[35] It took a similar position on the Basque peace process and the ceasefire of ETA as it did with the Northern Irish Peace Process, noting,

> the struggle over so many decades of Basque people for national liberation is at a permanent end. The involvement of the same forces that have been at work in Ireland, and especially of Provisional leadership, in bringing about this outcome for a friendly people is to be deplored.[36]

32CSM, which has maintained a direct and overt link to the Real IRA/ New IRA, and informal links with Republicans Action Against Drugs, was very active in the years 1998–2005, in terms of its integration into the wider political sphere. However, it has retreated since then, rebuilding and concentrating in areas where it had developed support, especially Derry and Dublin. This has had little to do with building any great grassroots political support, despite having member Gary Donnelly elected to Derry and Strabane Council on an independent platform in 2014.[37] Its success has largely been due to its hostile attitude towards drug dealing and anti-social behaviour in its working-class hinterlands. This was the subject of a *Vice News* documentary shot in Derry in 2014 which outlined the punishment beatings, intimidation and killings of which its affiliate organizations are accused.[38] Its affiliation with armed action against drugs in Dublin also saw it involved in the political, social and public relations fallout of the murder of RIRA member Alan Ryan, who was murdered by an underworld gang and who received a paramilitary funeral which caused controversy in 2012.[39]

The party also held a hard line, traditionalist stance on the Peace Process, having split from Sinn Féin in 1997 in opposition to the Mitchell Principles and the eventual enshrinement of a unionist veto in the negotiations and the acceptance of the continuation of partition.[40] The enduring affiliation with RIRA would seem to be a central problem with building a bigger platform in Northern Ireland, where there is overwhelming support for peace and against any return to an armed campaign. As an organization with an overt link to an armed group that was highly active, it was the initial home for those for whom an armed campaign was the central defining characteristic of republican ideology. As far back as 2002, a 32CSM member told one republican writer, 'In other areas such as Derry, there is growing support for people who want to carry on with the armed struggle.' McIntyre had concluded of Real IRA that, 'the organisation is an albatross around the neck of a radical republican alternative'.[41]

However, as this time period progressed, there was little progressive or radical about 32CSM. Its regressive approach allowed Sinn Féin to denounce it, insisting that, 'there is no other logic or political purpose to their campaign. Their actions amount to sabotage against Irish republicanism.'[42] The shooting of two British soldiers by RIRA in Antrim in 2009 caused widespread revulsion at a period of other fatal attacks in security force personnel.

In terms of its media activism, between 1998 and 2005, 32CSM appeared to be committed to developing a national platform and a conventional media strategy, including a well-maintained website, regular publication of its newspaper *Sovereign Nation*, and a series of pamphlets outlining its position and aimed at trying to build popular support. *Sovereign Nation* was smaller than RSF's *Saoirse*, with an average edition having twelve pages, and it also lacked the professional layout and content of its competitor.[43] The smaller number of cumanns that made up the organization might explain the greater difficulty in finding content and sustaining production and distribution. However, it served as an adequate ideological vehicle for the party when it did come out, encapsulating 32CSM's approach to the Peace Process and British rule in Ireland. At the centre of its opposition to the Peace Process was the confirmation of the continued partition of Ireland, the organization arguing that: 'the colonial nature of partition is demonstrated by over 80 years of empirical political proof which has witnessed conflict and sectarian division on an unprecedented scale. It must end completely.'[44] 32CSM's inability to build and sustain any sense of momentum on the ground was naturally mirrored in the pattern of production of its media and communications. The party newspaper, *Sovereign Nation*, like *Starry Plough* for IRSP, was published at infrequent intervals, stopping in 2002, reappearing infrequently in 2004–2005 and then relatively rarely since 2006. The central party website also disappeared in 2010, with individual cumnns using free blogging platforms to publicize their work.[45] This lack of central organization may indicate a crisis in financial and human resources as well as an attempt at maintaining a lower profile for security purposes. Either way, Facebook appears to be the central organizing point for cumanns, while some individuals have used Twitter in recent years, but only in personal capacities.

The second original bloc of still active and longer established political dissenters that emerged from splits in the militant republican movement during the revolutionary post-1969 period includes the Irish Republican Socialist Party – the left-wing Marxist party which split from the Official IRA in 1974 – and the Workers' Party, which was Official Sinn Féin after the 1970 split and retained the shared party name until 1982. Both maintained left-wing approaches to the republican cause but differed in their stances towards the Good Friday Agreement. IRSP maintained the

Marxist standpoint that it had been committed to since 1974. The party rejected the Peace Process, stating it

> comprehensively rejects the Good Friday Agreement as an imperialist-backed undemocratic sabotage of true peace and freedom in Ireland. The party is guided by the analysis of James Connolly: that the class struggle and national liberation struggle cannot be separated, and is the only movement that upholds that analysis.[46]

The Workers' Party, although sharing Marxist Leninist roots with IRSP, had since its renaming in 1982 and subsequent further split with the Democratic Left in 1992 and republican left later again, developed a less doctrinaire socialist perspective.[47] It saw the Peace Process as a vital element in a journey towards building a secular socialist state and supported the Good Friday Agreement, seeing it as the primary means of combating sectarianism:

> It was in this spirit, and with reservations, that we supported the Good Friday Agreement. We viewed it not as a final settlement but as a first step towards our goals of integration and citizenship. On this basis, we believe our vision of secular, democratic, socialist politics can best take root.[48]

These two parties have been involved in markedly different forms of media activism through the period under consideration. The IRSP could claim to be the largest and most active left-wing party in the socialist republican bloc at the beginning of this period. However, at the end of the period it had been superseded by both éirígí and RNU in terms of profile and media activity.[49] The decline in profile and the resignation of key activists like Gerry Ruddy and Liam O'Ruairc, who had been central to the media operation, were reflected in its failure to sustain publication of the party paper, *Starry Plough*.[50] Former senior party members were involved in the *Red Plough*, an independent socialist republican blog established after they left the party.[51] A large number of rank and file members would also initially find a new home in RNU.[52] As the INLA's last ceasefire was announced in 2009, the ideological atrophy was revealed with the assertion that, 'the IRSP will soldier on without much in the way of political support, just as all militant republican parties did prior to the green tide of Sinn Féin's electoral breakthrough after the 1981 hunger strikes.'[53]

The Workers' Party elevated its profile in media activist terms when it launched the bi-monthly general political interest magazine *Look Left* in 2010, reflecting a highly active media strategy which aimed to create a traditional political journal while recognizing the Internet as a new site of electoral and social engagement.[54] The party, which had been riven by splits and defections throughout the 1980s and 1990s, had failed to sustain the publication of a party newspaper or magazine for long periods. The

United Irishman remained the voice of the Officials until 1980, and other publications like the *Irish People, Northern People, Women's View* and *Workers Weekly* also played a part in activist media campaigns during this time.[55] While the party spent much of the 1990s recovering from defections that continued to affect it and rebuilding, new members became highly active figures in the vibrant Irish blogosphere, most notably activists and writers like World by Storm and Garibaldy writing for *Cedar Lounge Revolution*, an award-winning political blog.[56] The latter was also a frequent writer and commenter on *Sluggerotoole.com*, the most prominent political blog in Northern Ireland. These writers were a bridging point between the old political traditions of activist media which complemented party work and the newer forms of blogging and new political writing situated online. *Look Left* began life as a traditional party publication, but its focus soon became broadened to include a more diverse range of subjects, including popular culture and sport, and a range of contributors from outside of the party. This broader concern saw it adopt the style and tone of more international publications like *New Internationalist* and reflected a broadening of interests of many on the left in Ireland. It also incorporated elements of popular culture which reflected the experience of some of the writers in the football and music fanzine movements.[57] Football, in particular, has been a recurring subject of the magazine. Although it had small print runs of 5,000 or fewer, its distribution in the large high street newsagent Eason's in Ireland and political bookshops in Britain developed its profile and standing.[58] Although the party failed to add to its two councillors in the Republic of Ireland, it did claim growing numbers and new local branches forming after the publication of *Look Left*.[59]

The Internet: blogosphere, the *Blanket* and *Fourthwrite*

The third bloc of republican dissent encompassed the activist writings of republicans from across the ideological spectrum using the Internet as their home. At the start of the twenty-first century, the development of blogging technologies and affordable online media made possible a growth in political engagement and saw new communities of politically engaged people coalescing online. In Northern Ireland, they came together from a range of political perspectives, like those on *Sluggerotoole.com* and *Debatecentral.com*, while the blogosphere hosted diverse voices like pro-agreement Chris Gaskin and anti-agreement, traditionalist republicans like Republican Sinn Féin-allied writers responsible for *1169 and Counting*.[60] However, as was the case for much of the blogosphere, republican writers' presences were not sustained over a significant period of time and their influence or reach did not extend beyond the small coterie of interested readers, many of whom also congregated on 'secular' sites like *Sluggerotoole.com* and *Politics.ie*. The Irish left-wing blogosphere showed a passing interest in republicanism specifically and Northern Ireland generally. Belfast writer Splintered Sunrise, whose blog carries the same name, was among the most active, and was nominated for several Irish blog awards while regularly being voted in the top 100 left-wing blogs in Britain.[61] He was also found by academic researchers to be one of the central figures in the new ecology of the Irish political blogosphere.[62]

Cedar Lounge Revolution was also part of a cluster of Dublin-based left-wing sites that made a significant impact on the political environment, although republicanism was a secondary concern to the impact of corruption and economic collapse on the Irish state. Their primary impetus was not to make a significant contribution to the political blogosphere, but simply to break away from the often combative *Politics.ie*'' forum.[63] In deliberative terms, the blogger Garibaldy asserts, this was a space where a kind of organic intellectualism was having an effect on general opinion, but away from republican politics.[64] Crucially, these were writers in the Republic of Ireland, where the blogosphere had been more fully utilized as a 'citizen journalism' space and where the Republic of Ireland's blogging community was an active and fertile space of comment, but few turned their attention in a sustained way on Northern Ireland.[65] World by Storm noted that the Irish political blogosphere was unlikely to make a major impact because it was 'a minority pursuit and a very middle class pursuit, although not exclusively'.[66] Perhaps the only really telling contribution from the blogosphere on the republican political environment came as a result of the structural and ideological changes within Sinn Féin. The *Sinn Féin Keep Left* blog, which started in 2009, was aimed at promoting left-wing discussion in the party, particularly after the high-profile defection of the Dublin Sinn Féin councillor Killian Forde to the Labour Party in 2009.[67] It documented the ongoing internal battles between socialists and reformists in the party in Dublin, but admitted it had achieved little in its eighteen months of publishing, acknowledging that 'the aim of this site was to encourage left-wing debate amongst party members and supporters. Unfortunately, we have not succeeded in this aim.'[68]

Other than some specific examples where the offline world was being discussed in the online, the blogosphere and Internet discussion forums, unconnected to the parties and activists, made little deliberative difference to the structure and discussions of republicanism. *Sluggerotoole.com* was, throughout the period, the most active of the Northern Irish blog sites and made a significant contribution to the political life of the North. Its influence went beyond that of most blogging sites, with 96 per cent of the MLAs at Stormont regular readers.[69] It has also been the home of republican writers who contributed important commentary, including both Mark McGregor, who was critical of Sinn Féin, and former party loyalist, Chris Donnelly. Its editor, Mick Fealty was also a contributor to the *Blanket* and an associate of its editors. Fealty also contributed widely to the main-stream media as a commentator on both Northern Ireland politics and the potentials of the online environment. Slugger was only occasionally host to important revelations or discussions on republicanism, the disputed claims over the supposed deal offered by the British government during the 1981 Hunger Strikes, opened by Richard O'Rawe's book *Blanketmen*, being one. In this case, a Slugger blogger, 'Rusty Nail', who was Carrie McIntyre from the *Blanket*, was the instigator across multiple posts.[70] On one occasion, McIntyre and Danny Morrison, under Internet usernames, engaged in an angry debate about the events of a meeting between Sinn Féin and the families of the dead men, and revealed their identities behind their online pseudonyms.[71] This brought offline events into the online world, but there were few examples of the online world setting the political agenda. Fealty nonetheless noted, 'boundaries are being broken down every day in cyberspace, as nationalists and unionists alike debate the latest news in online forums', and that the Internet was being used by politicians 'for flying kites, or taking soundings of how people outside their own constituency are likely to read their policy detail'.[72] With the benefit of some years' experience, Sinn Féin's Eoin Ó'Broin countered, 'a lot of that stuff is over stated and over theorised'.[73]

There was also engagement in activity on republican-specific message boards and forums. Among these, although not exclusively, were *Irish Republicans.net, Irish Republican Bulletin Board, Up the Ra! Forum, Irish Republican Socialist Forum* and *Éire Shaor*. These sites did not gain main-stream visibility, and there are four reasons why they did not. In some instances they were policed by Sinn Féin and shut down if there appeared to be any potential of the party being damaged, as in the case of *Irish Republican Bulletin Board*.[74] Secondly, the membership of these sites appeared to be highly transitory, moving often between sites and not building deep engagements or relationships to deliver any impact on the republican sphere. Thirdly, some forums, like *IRBB* and *Up the Ra!* were closed to public membership and did not build sufficient numbers to effect a significant contribution to the republican sphere. Fourthly, the majority of the posts on bulletin boards and forums should not be considered as serious interventions in the republican sphere. Most of these sites were the home of republican militants offering little other than inflammatory and sectarian opinions. They were not spaces of political activism, even as defined in the vague terms of Internet activism. Like message boards and forums for football supporters, they were a place for partisan opinions which had little effect in the offline or political lifeworld. For all intents, these spaces were populated by Internet users with no active interest in political activism.

The most prominent and productive activist journalism outlets brought together the work of a number of former PIRA prisoners, as well as left-wing activists, who would signpost their dissatisfaction with both the development of Sinn Féin and the Peace Process in *Fourthwrite* and the *Blanket*. These publications continued the tradition of republican pamphleteering, with *Fourthwrite* a traditional hard-copy political publication, and the *Blanket* an Internet magazine. They were highly significant in the analysis of this tertiary bloc largely for two reasons. First, they were a catalyst to the development of the fourth bloc of newer republican activist groups that developed after 2006 because they offered the first sustained critiques of the changed cultural and political direction of establishment republicanism not linked to RSF and 32CSM. Secondly, they were important within the parameters of this book as they provided a sustained period of engagement in activist writing and developing spaces of dissent online that are comparable with any in the contemporary British or Irish political sphere. Their effects, although not sustained until the present, should not be underestimated. *Fourthwrite* was one of the best selling local interest political magazines in Belfast when it was published, and the *Blanket* would inform briefings for governments.[75] They were the first longer-term attempts at seeking to discern another way forward for republicans for whom the process of peace represented a capitulation of Provisionalism's values.

The writers of both magazines began with the Irish Republican Writers Group (IRWG), but would develop this platform working first on *Fourthwrite*, before, ironically, a split would see the establishment of the *Blanket*, which would be published concurrently with a significant degree of overlap. Tommy McKearney (*Fourthwrite*) and Anthony McIntyre (the *Blanket*) would continue to publish in each publication as well as contributing to a range of publications across the left spectrum and the national and international media. Articles from *Fourthwrite* would also be republished on the *Blanket*, highlighting the shared personal commitment of those contributing to articulating reasoned and non-militarist, non-traditional dissident critiques of establishment republicanism and the Peace Process.

The overwhelming tone of the key writers on the *Blanket* and *Fourthwrite* was of their disappointment in the course of the Provisional movement, of what was, for them, a sellout of the values for which some had served long jail sentences. Although beginning as a loose coalition of former prisoners, friends and politically aligned allies, their commitment to a sustained engagement with critiques of Provisionalism and the Peace

Process forged an important sounding board space which would be utilized and built on by many of those that would form éirígí and RNU.[76]
These writers were often present at éirígí and RNU commemorations;
McKearney spoke at éirígí commemorations and McIntyre gave the Easter
oration for RNU in 2008.[77] However, this does not signify a universal
fealty: McIntyre noted that many of those who would go on to form éirígí
in Belfast were initially dismissive of *Fourthwrite* and the *Blanket* when
they were still members of Sinn Féin.[78] They sought to situate their dissatisfaction with the Peace Process both within critiques of Provisional
authoritarianism and within a global left-wing class analysis that highlighted the deep problems that neo-liberalism would bring to Ireland and
which would be borne out by the post-Celtic Tiger crash. For them, the
drift to the middle ground by Sinn Féin stripped republicanism of its
radicalism and its potential. For them what should not be forgotten was
that, 'Irish republicanism at its best has been radical, democratic and revolutionary.'[79] They were also inclusive, not aimed at a narrow party agenda,
but open to a variety of viewpoints from contributors across the republican
and radical spectrum:

> Both the *Blanket* and *Fourthwrite* are magazines that give voice to the
> unheard, to the left and the disaffected. They provide an intellectual chal-
> lenge to the status quo. They give voice to the growing unrest with the
> direction taken by the provisionals. Unfortunately, as of yet, the status quo
> (and that includes the provisionals), feels it can ignore the challenge and
> treat the criticisms with disdain.[80]

The Peace Process, which was, to some extent, predicated upon 'normal-
izing' Northern Ireland within the parameters of the neo-liberal agenda
and economic regeneration, would be a foundation stone for critiques of
the fourth bloc of politically active groups emerging in the timeframe
under scrutiny.[81] This bloc would initially coalesce or find a space on the
Blanket as means to articulate critiques of the Peace Process and find a
credible republican 'third way', predicated on emphasizing that republicanism was not the sole property of Sinn Féin, nor was militarism an
option.[82] Although *Fourthwrite* would be greeted with enthusiasm by the
spectrum of dissenting republicanism, and reviewed favourably by at least
one loyalist publication, which described its content as 'thoughtful stuff',
it was the *Blanket* that had a more profound effect throughout its time of
publication (2001–2008).[83] It was important not simply because it was a
space for former senior activists dissenting from the Provisional line, but
because of the wide spread of contributors, including loyalists.[84] McKearney and McIntyre were also involved with *Other View*, a magazine written
and produced by former loyalist and republican prisoners which has

become a neglected footnote of the activist journalism sphere at this time. It is notable because of the contributions of Billy Mitchell, a former loyalist commander who contributed regularly and tellingly to both *Fourthwrite* and the *Blanket*.

Ultimately, it was on the pages of the *Blanket* and *Fourthwrite* that a period of cultural dissent flowered and the third period under analysis (2006–) was born. The magazines, in offering a space to republicans, loyalists and many more besides, were an attempt at rediscovering the radicalism that McKearney avowed. Whether directly or indirectly, they provided the inspiration or climate for action that the fourth bloc of republican dissenters would initially seek to develop, if later abandon. The magazines became a credible communication space for Anti-Good Friday Agreement republicans and are liminal documents of a political activist space in transformation and transition.[85] This activist journalism space could also be seen as a liminal space in another way, in that it publicly displayed the twilight of some forms of republicanism. With the writers of the *New Republican Forum* and its magazine, *Forum*, what is evinced is a space in which the discontented and ideologically crisis-hit prisoners of the Real IRA signposted their withdrawal from the political sphere as a meaningful presence.

In the later years of the timeframe under investigation, the Real IRA and Continuity IRA became prominent again as a result of the escalation in dissident violence from 2009 onwards and the establishment of the New IRA. The threat that dissident violence posed to the Peace Process became a significant mainstream media narrative.[86] The murders of security forces personnel in 2009–2011 and several bomb attacks saw media attention re-focus on the dissident threat, with the head of MI5 noting, 'while we do not face the scale of problems caused by the Provisional IRA at the height of the Troubles, there is a real and increasing security challenge in Northern Ireland'.[87] The Real IRA, and its prisoners in jails in the Republic, had also, for a period, been involved in attempts at recalibrating their own ideological and strategic viewpoint to the post-GFA world through the *New Republican Forum* and *Forum Magazine*. The *Sunday Times* stated, 'dissident republicans are trying to rescue their organisation from oblivion by launching a smart new magazine and website to propagate their anti-Good Friday agreement message.'[88] Running from 2002–2006, this was a credible attempt at broadening the horizons of an organization that had been predicated upon physical force and the maintenance of the traditionalist militancy.[89] *Forum Magazine.* gave public face to the internal debates and fractures that were emerging in this strand of dissident thinking, perhaps signposting its lack of sustainability as a long-term political project, and the transition towards conventional criminality of which it was accused by sections of the media in the Republic. An interview with Declan Carroll, the spokesperson for republican prisoners in Portlaoise prison, captured the internal frictions in the Real IRA:

> We are totally convinced that the Belfast Agreement cannot and will not deliver Irish Freedom. But we are equally as adamant that the current strategy of the main dissident groups is futile and is preventing the emergence of a genuine democratic republican alternative to the provisional movement.[90]

However, whether it was financially difficult to sustain or there was an insufficient number of activists willing to keep the project going, the magazine ceased publication in 2006. Linked to former senior PIRA member Michael McKevitt, it emerged from the split in the Real IRA, where political prisoners from the organization accused its army council of colluding in smuggling and criminality. However, there were only thirty-five prisoners supporting the split, fewer contributing regularly to the project and there were a limited number of other writers and contributors, some of which included those who were writing for the *Blanket* and *Fourthwrite*, including McKearney, McIntyre and Liam O'Ruairc. There was cross-platform publication of several *Forum* articles on the *Blanket*, including an interview with McKevitt from jail.[91]

The failure of *Forum* to sustain publication beyond 2006, while both *Fourthwrite* and the *Blanket* survived and remained valued, is perhaps illustrative of the twilight of traditionalist militant republicanism as an intellectual force in this realm of political activist media. One of the effects of the Peace Process was to reconfirm that traditional physical force republicanism could never claim a legitimate mandate from republicans, nor did it have a credible deep intellectual commitment beyond militarism. It certainly did not develop a credible alternative to the Sinn Féin constitutional project, or rather, did not have the cultural capital to combat the momentum behind both Sinn Féin and the 'propaganda of peace'. A facet of this failure to move beyond critiques of Sinn Féin could quite legitimately be seen in a basic content analysis of *Forum*. The *Blanket* was accused of an 'obsession' with Gerry Adams and frequent *ad hominem* attacks on Sinn Féin and its leaders.[92] However, a great degree of the content of *Forum* was simply predicated on rejectionist critiques of establishment republicanism without ever articulating a credible alternative to the Peace Process.[93]

At a much later stage, another magazine, the *Hibernian*, launched with an almost diametrically opposed social and political position to both *Fourthwrite* and the *Blanket*, yet remaining steadfast in critiques of Sinn Féin. It ran between May 2006 and September 2008 and was based on a conservative, ultramontane Catholicism, and sought to reclaim a Catholic republican space that was on the wane in a country which was becoming more secular. Launched by the former PIRA member Gerry McGeough, it had a strong anti-Sinn Féin, traditionalist agenda. McGeough, who was also a former prisoner, was a Sinn Féin ard comhairle member until 2001, including leading the anti-Nice Treaty campaign as national director.[94] The *Hibernian* primarily covered Catholic religious issues, urging for a return to traditional mass and family rosary, while it complained about the perils of homosexuality, divorce and abortion in Ireland. Henry McDonald described its oeuvre as 'evoking an old-style nationalism derived from the Gaelic/Catholic fantasies of Patrick Pearse'.[95] McGeough later became a *cause celebre* for republican dissidents when he was arrested by police and convicted of the attempted murder of an off-duty member of the security forces in 1981.[96]

The *Hibernian* was a Catholic magazine which had republican interests. Its design, production values, size, paper and binding were influenced by *Ireland's Own*, a nostalgic magazine much beloved by the rural Catholic classes, while its religious content was heavily influenced by older Catholic religious publications, particularly rosary and lives of the saints pamphlets. Support for the return of the Latin mass and nostalgic tales of saints and Catholic uprisings featured alongside regular articles on the European Union and the new world order. The Pearsean ideals reported by the *Observer* revealed themselves in the first edition of the magazine, which asked, '1916: a Catholic rebellion?' The edition also featured an interview with an exorcist.[97] Given McGeough's background in anti-EU campaigns, and the prominent place that Ireland's position within the EU had in public life, the magazine featured a run of two cover stories: 'God Save Ireland' and an interview with the 'Millionaire Patriot', Declan Ganley, the right-wing millionaire who became the face of the 2008 Lisbon Treaty No vote.[98] The traditional, right-wing Catholic ethos was strident: the cover of issue 18 urged Irish women to 'Have more babies!' and issue 19 posed the question, 'Ghosts: are they souls in purgatory?' In the final edition, editor McGeough averred:

> The tyranny of Political Correctness prevents people from speaking out against the evils of feminism, the promotion of homosexuality, abortion, contraception and divorce lest they be attacked by the liberal/masonic media, et al. At the *Hibernian* we have only shown contempt for political correctness and have never shied away from the promotion of Catholic Order in society.[99]

The article was illustrated with a picture of Patrick Pearse, but with no explanation why in the text, other than that the magazine hoped to have 'kindled a spark of Catholic Nationalism and sense of Irish pride among true gaels'.[100] Of the republican-specific content, Irish American lawyer and former publicity director for NORAID, Martin Galvin, contributed several articles, as he did to both *Fourthwrite* and the *Blanket*. These included a twenty-fifth anniversary of the Hunger Strikers piece, as well as a call to reject policing and justice reforms and another outlining the treatment of McGeough by the legal system.[101] One contributor railed against Sinn Féin's obsession with socialism, saying, 'The words Sinn Féin were once synonymous with the battle to protect Irish national and cultural integrity. But in their current guise, they've done more to undermine the cause than to protect it.'[102] *Fourthwrite* contributor, Mags Glennon said:

> McGeough's magazine speaks of a 'crusade' and ignores any historical figures not white, straight and Catholic. It also has extremist anti-contraception and anti-women articles. The Catholic right constituency it is aiming for is rapidly diminishing in Ireland, but he is attempting to marry strict Catholicism with nationalism and anti-immigration views.[103]

The fourth bloc 1: éirígí and Republican Network for Unity

After the demise of *Fourthwrite* and the *Blanket*, the radical republican ground would be occupied by those that would forge the fourth bloc and that was primarily encapsulated by the political party éirígí and the pressure group Republican Network for Unity. They became important because they identified and articulated an anti-establishment republican position which was allied to a commitment to grassroots political activism that evinced a new media activism, which, in turn, built their public profile significantly. While *Fourthwrite* and the *Blanket* were satisfied with a sustained period of cultural intervention, éirígí and RNU's political intervention was to engage Sinn Féin politically in its own communities and ideological hinterland. Although éirígí and RNU were similar in their political opposition to the Peace Process, their specific ideological contexts and wider political interests saw them diverge.

éirígí was established in 2006, at the ninetieth anniversary of the 1916 Rising, by a group of former Sinn Féin activists in Dublin who had become disenchanted with the party leadership's 'desire for embourgeoisement and an obsession with image'.[104] The party name, meaning 'Arise' in Irish, was taken from the Desmoulins quote, 'the great appear great because we are on our knees, let us arise', which was beloved of Connolly and the republican socialist radical and union organizer, James Larkin.[105] For éirígí, its emergence was as a result of being centrifugally pushed away from Sinn Féin, which was administering British rule in Northern Ireland, including the administration of neo-liberal policies such as Private Finance Initiatives. Sinn Féin, it noted, 'is blinkered and fundamentally compromised by their ultimate acceptance of the confines and limits of the capitalist system'.[106] The party noted that Sinn Féin, as an active member of the political system on both sides of the border, was implicated in private corporations 'incrementally taking control of all aspects of the national infrastructure'.[107] These included schools, hospitals, motorways, railways and energy networks being controlled by Public Private Finance initiatives and private finance.[108] There were, however, questions asked about how new or radical éirígí was. Republican critic, Jim Cusack, said:

> the éirígí mob is, generally speaking, university educated and articulate. The term 'republican socialist' has more of a buzz to it than going to Socialist Workers Party meetings and listening to interminable middle-class lefties going on and on about rights for the working class. It is also more hip than the Ruairi Ó'Brádaighs sitting there in their ould kitchens spouting about the First Dail.[109]

World by Storm, soon after the party's establishment and publication of its first policy document, against imperialism, headlined a post, 'éirígí – new dawn fades? Or non-Sinn Féin republicanism boldly going where many have gone before ...', and effectively asked if there was anything radical about the party at all. On the basis of their anti-imperialism document, he noted a lack of a new or coherent analysis beyond traditional republican confines, concluding it was very conservative. He did, however, welcome that the party had at least begun the process of thinking about a 'post-SF future on the left ...'.[110]

éirígí's core message and activist repertoire were initially predicated upon recapturing a traditional, socialist, working-class activism that emphasized and reclaimed traditional Connollyite values from those in establishment republicanism that had reduced them to an 'historical curiosity'.[111] There was an internal crisis in Sinn Féin, particularly in Dublin, where the party was involved in an accelerated transformation from the kind of street-level pressure group it had been in the North until the Peace Process, to being a fully functioning constitutional party in the polity of the South. In this, there were again accusations of the party moving to the centre ground, abandoning its core constituency and seeking to appeal to the middle classes. The emergence and development of éirígí were symptomatic of the shift in Sinn Féin's activism and the social profile of its candidates. Several members, including the Dublin, Leinster, Munster and twenty-six county organizers defected to éirígí because of a perception that policies with a socialist edge were 'being watered down'.[112] One policy on health service reform, which had been written in consultation with unions and hospital consultants and passed by the ard chomhairle, was completely revised when it was brought to ard fheis. MacCionnaith noted that, 'they were two different documents and certainly didn't have any bearing on what we were advocating'.[113] The inference was that the radical, Connollyite socialism to which Sinn Féin paid lip service in activist literature and events was off-limits in the policy arena in a bid not to scare off voters in the Republic of Ireland. MacCionnaith, and other defectors, had been uncomfortable with the direction of Sinn Féin from as far back as 1998, but they remained active through 'misplaced loyalty to the organization that we were still members of'.[114] Their dissatisfaction lay in their belief that the left-wing element of Sinn Féin's socialist republicanism had been on the wane for more than two decades before éirígí was formed: 'we had been advocating for more leftwing education in the internal education policy and introducing new members to left wing politics; however that was frowned on since the mid 1980s.'[115]

Close to the party's first year anniversary, Leeson stated: 'like many, before and since, each of us had recognised that the gap between our personal political analysis and that of the collective Sinn Féin leadership's had become untenable'.[116] Ultimately, for éirígí, Sinn Féin's acceptance of the GFA had proven not to be fit for purpose in the push for unity. MacCionnaith, interviewed for *Fourthwrite* while he was still a Sinn Féin member, perhaps signposted his unease and noted the transitional nature of the agreement: 'when is the period of transition due to start and when will it end? We have yet to see it.'[117] For éirígí, Sinn Féin's Northern leadership struggled with the specific political contextual realities of its electorates on either side of the border, and offered little hope of providing a credible socialist alternative. It was also guilty of lacking democracy in practice. This standpoint was partly echoed by one political commentator, who observed that the party struggled 'to come to terms with the modern Ireland beyond their own British subsidised stronghold in Northern Ireland', and in particular the intricacies of the economics of the Republic and the state's shifting demographic profile.[118] Sinn Féin's drift towards the middle class, and in particular in the choosing of middle-class candidates to stand in the South, is more contestable. McKearney points to one instance when the promotion of the middle-class and 'photogenic' Mary Lou McDonald above former republican prisoner Nicky Keogh for the 2002 general election had contributed to the unease that led to the establishment of éirígí.[119] However, the purely class-based analysis is difficult to sustain; it was more rooted in ideological changes in doctrine, which was particularly evidenced by McDonald's sister, Joanne, going on to become one of the founder members of éirígí.[120] Mary Lou McDonald, whose candidacy for Sinn Féin bore fruit when she won a 2004 European election seat and a Dáil seat in 2011, has however gone on to become one of the key symbols of the party's commitment to women and

equality. Within the context of éirígí and the other groups on the republican dissenting spectrum, few have been able to replicate the high commitment to women's issues that Sinn Féin has, and their ranks have been
male dominated.

éirígí's project was about reclaiming republicanism's left radicalism and
the values that it felt has been lost in Sinn Féin's political development
towards the centre ground. These included the initial campaign to 'Reclaim
the Republic' as imagined by the 1916 Proclamation, and where the party
distributed thousands of copies of the proclamation in working-class areas
of Dublin, Belfast, Derry and North Belfast.[121] However, this was also self-
consciously set within the context of global left-wing perspectives and
taking ideological sustenance from successful liberation movements like
that of Venezuela as well as those of the growing anti-globalization and
anti-corporate movements.[122] The party's anti-colonial stance clearly fed
into the narrative of anti-globalization, and its strategies of street theatre,
occupations and attention grabbing agitprop aesthetic stunts on posters
and campaign materials saw it develop the republican space beyond activist journalism to activism in its political and performative senses. éirígí
sought to develop its profile in local communities through traditional
forms of street activism learned from its activists' time in the Provisionals, but also by implicating its struggle in the global left as represented
in Ireland. Mac an Mháistir said: 'I am an Irish Socialist Republican by
accident of geography only. I am a socialist republican because I am, and
always have been, against injustice. I see the people of Belfast, Brixton,
and Birmingham not as my enemy but as my brothers and sisters.'[123] The
Celtic Tiger collapse, the deepening recession in the Republic and the
effects of global corporations abandoning the Republic were the primary
catalysts for the party: 'poverty, exclusion and conflict in both Ireland and
internationally, are caused primarily by the joint system of capitalism and
imperialism'.[124] The referenda on the Lisbon Treaty in the Republic saw
the party garner headlines, even from traditionally anti-republican news
outlets like the *Irish Independent*, for its innovative and active campaigning for a No vote.[125]

In terms of winning political representation, the party acknowledged a
'wait and see policy', and spent its first five years orienting itself and building a platform upon which it could fight elections when it felt it was ready
to do so meaningfully. It felt that contesting elections too early could be
a rock upon which it might flounder and that it opposed the institutions
in which it would be expected to stand. MacCionnaith noted, 'any éirígí
engagement must and can only be premised on a clear understanding that
the existing elected institutions must ultimately fall before a new, genuinely democratic system can emerge.'[126] In this sense, this was an updating of the abstentionist stance of traditionalists but rationalized within

the confines of the Good Friday Agreement era. Daithí Mac an Mháistir noted that éirígí was situated in the global 'one per cent network', but did not intend on running candidates in elections until it had developed an ideological and structural platform which would allow it to have meaningful influence. This would include a media activist operation which would allow it to challenge 'an agenda that was being set by the mainstream media and the political establishment'.[127]

While some disaffected Sinn Féin councillors, like Louise Minihan in Dublin, joined the party formally, others supported it while maintaining the dissenting republican tradition of sitting as independents, including Barry Monteith (Dungannon) and Bernice Swift (Fermanagh).[128] It has yet to develop the wider structures of an electioneering organization despite registering as a political party in late 2009. Whether this was due to the financial implications of fighting elections, or not having the numbers of volunteers required to strategically plan and fight an election, the party only stood in two seats in Belfast in the 2011 and 2014 council elections. It also stood candidates in Dublin, Wicklow and Wexford in local council elections in the Republic of Ireland in 2014, not winning a seat and Louise Minihan losing hers. The party also acknowledged the legacy of the past and difficulty of growing in the financially unstable space that was the post-Celtic Tiger Republic of Ireland. Chairman Brian Leeson noted, 'we understand the difficulties of shedding old ideas and loyalties and understand the difficulties of mounting a revolutionary initiative in the current climate.'[129] However, the party did punch above its weight in terms of publicity, and cut a quick niche in the Irish activist media milieu in Ireland.[130] It developed a highly functioning and visible activist repertoire which gained it headlines and a higher profile than perhaps its membership base deserved, but it never entirely escaped the confines of traditional republican issues for purely socialist equivalents. In the comments on Belfast Gonzo's blog post, Garibaldy noted éirígí's 'cartoonish' depiction of unionist marches, and focus on troops out and policing and justice issues saw the party occupy a conventional republican space: 'They are nationalists. Left nationalists, yes, but still primarily nationalists as they prove every day.'[131]

The fourth bloc 2: Republican Network for Unity and the four Ps

The final organization to establish and mobilize in a meaningful fashion politically and within the activist media milieu was Republican Network for Unity. Originating from the organic coalescence of Belfast and Derry AGFARs who diverged from Sinn Féin in the period prior to the St Andrews Agreement which delivered reforms in policing and justice, it was also concerned with countering Sinn Féin domination in republican communities. If éirígí were about appropriating the heart of left republicanism, Republican Network for Unity emerged as a reaction to specific political and social reforms associated with the terms of the Good Friday and Belfast Agreements. The primary catalyst for the coalescence of RNU was the final acceptance by Sinn Féin of policing and justice reforms under the auspices of the St Andrews Agreement. The Network and its activist media are the best example of the uncertain and liminal nature of the Irish republican dissident sphere in the period after PIRA decommissioning and the signing of the St Andrews Agreement.

RNU's initial mobilization lacked the definitive commitment to either democratic involvement in the manner of éirígí, or the rejectionist stance of traditionalists in RSF or 32CSM, but its community activism would be centred on the four Ps: Peace Process, policing, parades and prisoners. Everything that RNU would be active in and produce media materials for would come as a direct response to these four issues.

The organization began in opposition to Sinn Féin's acceptance of policing and justice plans, linking them to a betrayal of the republican struggle. RNU represented the blurred lines between organizations and ideologically congruent groups and the liminal, changing nature of the republican dissident sphere, often chaotic, where people jumped from organization to organization seeking a solution or safe home. RNU developed as a loose confederation of activists holding congruent, if not universal positions against the Peace Process and with previous links to the Provisionals, and who were still attached to 32CSM, INLA and IRSP. As the *Blanket* and *Fourthwrite* acted as the first spaces for voicing AGFAR opinion and articulating an alternative to the Peace Process, RNU would become an organization and space where a diverse range of people from across the republican spectrum would coalesce.

Starting out as Ex-POWs Against the RUC/PSNI & MI5 before changing its name to Republican Forum for Unity prior to the Wolfe Tone Bodenstown commemoration in June 2007, its initial concerns were to highlight the influence of the security forces in establishment republican policy and the betrayal felt by former volunteers, for Sinn Féin's endorsement of policing reforms in Northern Ireland in particular. Specifically, calls for republicans to co-operate with the PSNI and with any historical inquiries into the events of the Troubles were most difficult to accept.[132]

> We fear that this 'tactic' [engagement with the PSNI) will cement and advance pro British interests as well as further demoralise and disempower an already vulnerable grassroots republican base. As such we cannot contemplate actively supporting such a force or its cosmetic civilian bodies in the form of policing boards or DPPs [district policing partnerships]. To do so would contribute to the upholding of the status quo in occupied Ireland.[133]

The police force, which had 'criminalised' republican volunteers, which had not been disbanded or reformed, was being supported by Sinn Féin. In turn, and in keeping with wider dissenting republican opinion, this acceptance of policing was a *de facto* acceptance of the legitimacy of the Northern Irish state, the antithesis of the struggle in which many of these volunteers had been active. 'The Provisional IRA has for the most part been disarmed because its weapons were judged to be illegal but the PSNI has been allowed to maintain its armoury.' Another writer captured the sentiment that informed RNU: 'the Provisional movement had to accept the state's monopoly of legitimate violence.'[134] Urging republicans to collaborate with the police was a final betrayal of the ideological foundations of the armed struggle:

> Sinn Féin's endorsement of the RUC/PSNI is of course also an acceptance of the British occupation of Ireland, given that nationalists and republicans are being encouraged to work in a proactive way with a police force unwilling to even negotiate its accountability regarding 'security issues' nor the tactics it uses to maintain the security of the British state here, a police force it is important to add, which celebrates the framing and wrongful imprisonment of republicans as well as openly advocating a policy of targeting vulnerable young people for use as informants.[135]

The same force was also failing to police republican areas, and drug dealing and anti-social behaviour had risen as the Provisionals retreated from its former role in this respect.[136] RNU was thus an organic grassroots political reaction to the inherent ideological, structural and social transformations in the republican sphere and republican communities.[137] It represented a resting place for former Provisionals for whom there was nowhere else to go. One activist said it was initially a space to discuss 'how things had got so bad on the ground and whether we should just go home or hang around and do something'.[138] With two years to reflect on the development of RNU, a senior New York republican noted:

> Those who spearheaded the formation of the Republican Network for Unity and the Ex-prisoners against the RUC from which the RNU emerged, were veteran Republicans who fought, suffered imprisonment, risked their lives and dedicated their lives to the struggle no less than those who now back Stormont. They found it heartbreaking to disagree and walk away from the leadership and organization to which they had given so much over so many years. They walked away as republicans who felt that loyalty to the struggle trumped loyalty to the party or party policy.[139]

The primary underlying impetus for the formation of the organization was the growing revelations of the infiltration of the upper echelons of Sinn Féin and PIRA by British security services. Freddie Scappaticci and

Denis Donaldson, both close to the Adams leadership, were revealed to be British informers in 2003 and 2005 respectively. One of the main points of disillusionment for the dissenters was that the leadership that had done much to silence dissenting opinion in the early years of the Peace Process had informers close to its inner circle. Scappaticci was the senior officer in PIRA's internal policing unit, 'the nutting squad', and Donaldson was Sinn Féin's administrator at Stormont.[140] The oration at RNU's first Bodenstown commemoration noted that the 'republican movement had been split and fragmented beyond all recognition' and that many were 'disgusted by former comrades who betrayed all we had fought for'.[141] The aim for republicans was 'rebuilding the movement' and 'to win back the ordinary republican people'.[142]

The group was initially at pains to emphasize that it was neither anti-policing nor linked to any kind of armed group, but opposed Sinn Féin's endorsement of 'British Crown forces in Ireland'. This rendered the initial phase of protest futile and the name change was required for the group to remain relevant.[143] Throughout its existence, it consistently denied security force-derived media intimations that it was linked to the armed dissident group Óglaigh na hÉireann (ONH), and that key senior activists were involved in both organizations.[144] It did have an ambiguous relationship with ONH, which was itself a faction of the Real IRA.[145] Members of RNU, in their capacity as members of Concerned Families Against Drugs (CFAD), worked together on occasions in community policing and confiscating and destroying drug dealers' stock.[146] Like other groups emerging from the dissident sphere, it also held the ambiguous position of not supporting an armed campaign but not condemning those that did. Sharing the same historical worldview as RSF, it noted in an early public letter to the media, 'While we do not advocate armed resistance, we take a long-term historical view of British involvement in Ireland. No matter who attempts to rewrite our history the fact remains that there will always be resistance to this occupation.'[147]

The organization was aware of the relative resurgence of dissident opinion, but countered that public support for it remained low, a spokesman noting: 'there is no appetite whatsoever on the ground for military engagement with the British security forces, but these groups are growing.'[148] But it also confused its public position on such a campaign by sending 'comradely greetings' to ONH at its ard fheis in 2011.[149] The relationship with armed struggle was further complicated when Tony Taylor, chair of the organization's Derry cumann, was arrested in possession of a rifle in August 2011.[150] Media commentators and those from the academy have thus far portrayed RNU as attempting to fulfil an umbrella role, which offered 'a wide variety of republicans disaffected by the compromises yielded in the peace and political processes' shelter and space to develop at a time of uncertainty.[151] Its overall intention as an umbrella organization was to unite 'dissidents in the broad ideological goal of agitating for a united Ireland, but little else'.[152] However, RNU rejected the notion of simply being a vehicle to resurrect the concept of a republican umbrella project. It began initially with a phase that investigated the possibility of unity among AGFARS, but it became a very clearly defined individual entity from 2008 onwards.[153] Cunningham argued, 'there was an inaccurate belief that we were an umbrella group for dissident republicans, which we weren't, but that was manna for some journalists.'[154]

Having started via an initiative by Derry republican Danny McBrearty, the group soon morphed into the Forum for Unity by late 2007. This was in effect something resembling a consultative process in which a number of well-attended public meetings were held to establish whether there were grounds for collective action, especially in building a strategic and meaningfully engaged new group to challenge Sinn Féin. Although the meetings were deemed a success, it became clear for those that would go on to form RNU that neither IRSP nor 32CSM were interested in doing something 'concrete or permanent'.[155] Although they shared many of the same disenchantments with the Peace Process and Sinn Féin, they were not interested in building a new political entity. Throughout 2008, the drift between IRSP, 32CSM and RNU would become more pronounced, but it was not permanent until early 2009.[156] At this point, RNU became a means of investigating the way forward for republicans who could not accept the Peace Process or policing reforms, but who remained unwilling to stand for election within the institutions of the devolved Assembly.

Five years after striking out as an individual organization it came to acknowledge that the optimum space for it to operate as an activist organization with its attendant activist media strategies was 'outside of the Peace Process'.[157] It had learned the lessons of the schisms of the 1970s, and had sought to investigate the possibility of uniting various blocs and factions of those unattached or defecting from other groups:

> The message is simple: we acknowledge your contribution and we thank you, but we need your help again to ensure that the flame is kept alive and that all Republicans have ownership of it and it can never again fall into the hands of a fascist leadership.[158]

Among the 300 plus people that signed an initial pledge published on the *Blanket* many would not remain as RNU members after late 2008 and the gradual erosion of the Forum for Unity. However, in the beginning it was an important space where many former PIRA and INLA prisoners and disaffected members of the Provisionals and IRSP came to mobilize with the 32CSM on an equal basis outside of the Peace Process. The decision to meet and establish a dialogue echoed a similar endeavour by many of these signatories in 2004, which concluded, 'republicans should stand with each other in repossessing the ownership of their struggle. It does not belong to a clique, it is owned by all the people who believe and participate in it.'[159] They were joined by a broad range of republicans who shared preoccupations with the role of British/security forces and the PSNI. These figures included high-profile former republican volunteers like former Sinn Féin director of elections in Belfast, Tony Catney, who had allegedly been denied membership of éirígí; former high-profile INLA volunteer Christopher 'Crip' McWilliams; Marian Price, the 32 County Sovereignty Movement spokesperson; her sister Dolours, and Gerry McGeough.[160] Dolours wrote regularly for the *Blanket* and later denounced what she described as 'the mugging we got in the dark alley the Provisional leadership led us up.'[161]

As many of the independents and 32CSM signatories left the forum and RNU proper developed, those that remained came to realize that there were common reasons why they had drifted away from their original groups, whether they were former Provisionals, 32CSM or IRSP. Many within the ex-prisoner community had put in too much work to walk away after the collapse of the forum. Among the most prominent and recurring motifs that tied them together was a collectively held frustration at the hierarchical and undemocratic nature of the republican organizations to which they had belonged, and, for those coming from 32CSM, a frustration at the persistence of the militarist agenda.[162] If the Internet could be read as a liminal space in which transformations in culture and politics were developing, then RNU was a liminal project in which its early years were spent interrogating the future which reflected these concerns, but attempted to do so beyond the continued nihilistic rejectionism or militarist, sovereignty-based analysis of the dissidents. RNU's analysis was a realistic appraisal of the dissident sphere, while rejecting the analysis, yet it also asked the question of the Peace Process: 'Some dissidents continue to believe that armed resistance with its political, military and publicity dimensions is central to challenging British rule. Those who pretend these Republicans are unimportant, dismiss them as criminals, ignore them or expect Sinn Féin to control them, have badly miscalculated.'[163]

Crucially, while acknowledging the presence of the dissidents, RNU was in the process of redefining the term 'militant' or 'dissident' in its own eyes, preferring to define its own ideology as 'revolutionary republicanism'. Revolutionary republicanism deliberately took RNU away from the dissident milieu while remaining rooted in core republican values of 'national liberation, socialism, and international solidarity in line with the principles of the 1916 proclamation yet manifest in its most precise, progressive and visionary form'.[164] This attempt at distancing itself from the dissidents who had emerged as the key opponents of the Peace Process and emblems of anti-progressive republicanism would be what RNU spent its early years formulating. RNU had 'spent four years exploring what we were, what we were about', and coming to the conclusion that a Northern militarist analysis was leading republicans to misunderstand the deep effects of the GFA on republicanism as an ideological construct:

> With militarism there was a lack of class analysis. Too much of an emphasis on nationalist militarism was leading us to miss the point of what the GFA was about for republicans. Militarism is not enough to tackle GFA because it leaves too many questions unanswered. A traditional, nationalist militarist framework also leaves questions of multi-national and IMF involvement in the south unanswered.[165]

RNU's development was about growing away from the analysis that always began with the problem of sovereignty. An activist noted that dissident groups approaching issues from the point of view of sovereignty was like 'driving a car with the brakes on, the majority of the 32CSM would be left leaning but their constitution does not allow them to express that, sovereignty has to be injected into every article they do'.[166]

RNU in its early years would focus not on producing mainstream media materials or building a traditional support base that could be transferred into votes if, and when, the time came to fight elections. Unlike éirígí, that had a highly functioning activist media strategy from the outset and a clear plan to be constituted as a political party, RNU's focus was on recapturing the revolutionary republican activist space and milieu through grassroots activism. Focusing on core issues and causes no longer part of the Sinn Féin portfolio, it used established dissident and alternative media outlets for statements and reports.[167] Around 2012–2013 it began to build a relationship with mainstream media outlets, in particular the *Andersonstown News* – despite the paper being owned by Sinn Féin's Ó'Muilleoir – which it believes to be less dismissive of RNU policy than it was when the group first formed.[168] Its focus in this period was primarily on issues against drugs and landlordism which it perceived to be the most pressing in republican communities.[169]

> For the first time during the history of dissidents, as Sinn Féin would call us, we were going in, and helping, communities. Communities had been fed a diatribe by Sinn Féin about dissidents being criminals, malcontents and touts, or, at best, militarists. The community had no evidence to the contrary because no-one had put a toe in the water of community politics.[170]

The growth of RNU in later years in republican communities was also linked to the standing of individual members in their own areas, with

Martin Óg Meehan having a high profile in Ardoyne, and Danny McBrearty and Tony Taylor in Derry. Meehan's profile was high in Ardoyne, as a former Provisional prisoner and son of a senior Provisional. He was active in RNU as well as in CFAD and the Greater Ardoyne Residents' Committee, and the work of these groups was documented on his Ardoyne Republican blog.[171] CFAD targeted drug dealers in West and North Belfast and gained some publicity for recovering Class A drugs from houses in Ardoyne and Ballymurphy in Belfast and Derry.[172] Community policing of this kind had a twofold effect for RNU: it established its credentials in communities that were experiencing problems and for whom Sinn Féin could no longer offer community policing as once it could. Secondly, it provided 'evidence' that policing reform had no real effect for republican communities. Cunningham notes that communities had seen drug dealers arrested repeatedly yet return to their areas and resume. RNU argued that Sinn Féin's support for the police and high profile within Stormont meant that it could no longer deliver community welfare in both the fight against drugs and policing loyalist marches.[173]

Where it was once the leading protest group at flashpoint areas like Ardoyne, now senior Sinn Féin representatives accused dissenting groups like RNU of causing riots that threatened the Peace Process.[174] Meehan noted that the riots were indicative of the disillusionment among working-class republicans, claiming, 'there's been no peace dividend for these areas and Sinn Féin can't explain why.'[175] Sinn Féin MLA Gerry Kelly defended police actions during riots in 2009 caused when Orange Parades were routed past Ardoyne. This, said RNU, signalled another betrayal of republican communities. During the disturbances, police fired at least fourteen plastic bullets. Meehan said.[176]

> The aggressive presence of PSNI riot squads intent on facilitating sectarian parades inevitably caused a violent reaction ... Whilst I respect Gerry Kelly's electoral mandate, he needs to acknowledge that the majority of people in Ardoyne are angry that he or his party have not condemned the injuring of 10 people by plastic bullets, the hostile use of water cannons and antagonistic actions by the PSNI.[177]

Thus two of the four Ps – policing and parading – were umbilically linked in the struggle for power in republican areas. With the signing of the Hillsborough Castle Agreement in 2010, policing and justice was devolved to the Northern Ireland Assembly to satisfy Sinn Féin demands. However, it had to accept unionist demands for reforms to the Parades Commission.[178] Again, any changes in the parading issue were perceived by RNU and dissenters to automatically signal a return to nationalist streets for parades and police in another Sinn Féin sellout:

Nationalists were told that Sinn Féin was not playing poker and would not pay the price of Orange feet on the Garvaghy Road, or Ardoyne. Residents of those areas now question whether they have been played like poker chips. Has their right to be free of sectarian Orange parades in their areas been bartered away beneath the political cover of a deal that has satisfied the DUP and Orange Order?[179]

While being present at flashpoints, RNU also used a recognizably traditional repertoire of white line pickets and protests aimed at capturing those disaffected by Sinn Féin's new politics and slick political campaigning, particularly in publicizing the campaign of support for dissident prisoners in Northern Ireland.[180] It did, however, update these methods, claiming that white line pickets had failed to attract wider attention in the mainstream and local media. Noting that, although less active, éirígí received more media coverage, the party became more active in writing press releases and taking photographs of publishable quality.[181] It also learned from éirígí's approaches to guerrilla activism, particularly updating republican traditions like occupations. It did this most successfully in relation to protests surrounding the conditions of republican prisoners which targeted the justice minister David Ford, and which are discussed in chapter six. The prisons issue, like parading, had a twofold effect. It built public awareness of conditions in the jails but it also raised the profile of the organization. This in turn led RNU to play an advocacy role in republican communities and in community restorative justice, including offering welfare advice. In this sense, RNU consciously recreated the radical role that Sinn Féin had played in the 1970s and 1980s.

As the establishment republican project came to co-opt the symbols of republican resistance and sacrifice into the modern partitionist dispensation, RNU railed against the memory of volunteers 'being used as a smokescreen for the ambitions of others. These others are not legitimising our dead but are cynically using the dead to legitimise themselves.'[182] More tellingly, RNU asserted, the leaders of Sinn Féin and their political supporters had benefited financially from the Peace Process while republican communities remained among the most deprived areas in Ireland.[183] RNU's campaign against landlordism and increased rents in West Belfast was partially based on its charges that senior Sinn Féin and former PIRA figures were landlords and owned 'large stakes in property agencies and are complicit in landlord policies that are entrenching poverty in this area'[184] RNU charged that senior Sinn Féin figures were exploitative landlords and were at the centre of a Peace Process 'gravy train' where there were 'jobs for the boys in a junket culture', where 'made-up community jobs are there to keep key Sinn Féin people quiet'.[185]

Ultimately, RNU developed a classic left-wing viewpoint on the Peace Process, seeing the settlement as 'inherently sectarian, inherently partitionist and inherently capitalist'.[186] RNU claimed to be reclaiming the left-wing heart of grassroots republican socialism, campaigning against landlordism and attacks on the benefit system.[187] This was necessary, it argued, because the Good Friday Agreement 'is in fact a sectarian settlement, with sectarian values at its heart and guaranteed sectarian outcome'.[188] The Peace Process and the Northern state, central to the political canon of Sinn Féin, were unreformable and thus the organization sought to stand outside the Peace Process, to find an alternative to a settlement that was sold to the public as inevitable and without an alternative.[189] The alternative, it would eventually argue, was a movement of working-class national liberation, for the control of national territory and the means of production. Again, it ambiguously argued that this would come 'via all available means of struggle'.[190] In this sense RNU became not an exceptionalist project, but one which shared the radical left ground of éirígí, evolving to interpret the Peace Process as part of a wider neo-liberal exploitation of the working class. RNU asserted that the process was an illusion that was built on an artificially created financial recovery and building boom that were created to support the political settlement, 'which saw the population of the six county state groomed into a pool of cheap labour, and in an environment free from republican resistance'.[191]

Notes

1   Dissident republicans, those still committed to armed strategy, are known colloquially in parts of Northern Ireland as 'dissos'.
2   O'Ruairc, 'Defining dissidents'
3   Hall, *Republicanism in Transition 2*, p. 14..
4   Ross, F. Stuart, *Smashing H-Block: The Rise and Fall of the Popular Campaign Against Criminalization, 1976–1982* (Liverpool: Liverpool University Press, 2011), p. 134.
5   'A brief history of the IRSP,' IRSP Internal Pamphlet (author unknown). Available at: www.irsp.ie/Background/theory/historyofirsp.html. Accessed 20 April 2017.
6   'The rise of Fianna Fáil', *Saoirse*, December 1996.
7   'Constitution'. Available at: hwww.32csm.net/p/32csm-policy-documents. html. Not dated. Accessed 20 April 2017. See also the similarly worded Republican Sinn Féin article, 'Historic Sinn Féin declaration', 1986. Available at: http://www.rsf.ie/page17.html. Accessed 10 June 2010.
8   *Twenty First Report of the International Monitoring Commission*, 7 May 2009. Available at: www.cain.ulst.ac.uk/issues/politics/docs/imc/imc070509.pdf. Accessed 18 May 2010.
9   Moloney, Ed, 'Crackdown on the CIRA has begun', *Sunday Tribune*, 27 September 1998.
10   'Republican Sinn Féin: about/Faoi', *rsf.ie*. Available at: www.rsf.ie/page1.html. Accessed 10 June 2010.

11 Frampton, Martyn, *Legion of the Rearguard: Dissident Irish Republicanism* (Dublin: Irish Academic Press, 2011), p. 70.

12 O'Hagan, Dessie, quoted in Sanders, Andrew, *Inside the IRA: Dissident Republicans and the Battle for Legitimacy* (Edinburgh: Edinburgh University Press, 2011) p. 244.

13 Ó'Brádaigh, Ruarí, '99ú ard fheis of Republican Sinn Féin poblachtach 2003', *Saoirse*, December 2003.

14 The *Irish Left Archive* area on the left-wing political blog *Cedar Lounge Revolution* hosts a scan of the original document. Available at: www.cedarlounge. files.wordpress.com/2009/02/en-1971-go.pdf. Accessed 20 April 2017.

15 Feeney, *Sinn Féin*, p. 321.

16 Feeney, *Sinn Féin*, pp. 320–321.

17 Feeney, *Sinn Féin*, p. 321.

18 Morrison, D., quoted in Frampton, *Legion of the Rearguard*, p. 60.

19 Quoted in Feeney, *Sinn Féin*, p. 321.

20 *Éire Nua – A New Democracy*, 1990. Available at: www.clririshleftarchive. org/workspace/documents/eirenuarsf.pdf. Accessed 20 April 2017. See also: Ó'Brádaigh, Séan, '40 years of the Éire Nua'. Available at: www.rsf.ie/page3. html. Accessed 20 April 2017.

21 Murray and Tonge, *Sinn Féin and the SDLP*, p. 73.

22 Sanders, *Inside the IRA*, p. 242.

23 Frampton, *Legion of the Rearguard*, p. 71.

24 Quoted in Sanders, *Inside the IRA*, p. 243.

25 Sanders, *Inside the IRA*, p. 244.

26 McDonald, Henry, 'Orange march sparks Dublin riots', *Observer*, 26 February 2006. Available at: www.guardian.co.uk/world/2006/feb/26/northernireland. ireland. Accessed 26 February 2006.

27 'The Republic's dissident youth: Ireland's young warriors', vice.com, 23 July 2015. Available at: www.youtube.com/watch?v=UZM9Z0NbQwM. Accessed 25 July 2015.

28 www.saoirse.info/. Accessed 10 May 2011. See also: Whiting, Sophie, '"The discourse of defence": "dissident" Irish republican newspapers and the "propaganda war"', *Terrorism and Political Violence* vol. 24, no. 3, 2012, pp. 483–503.

29 Dalton, Des, interview, 20 May 2011.

30 Dalton interview. See also: www.saoirse.info/ for a partial archive of the Irish Republican Information Service. Accessed 20 April 2017.

31 '1.75m Facebook users in Ireland', *rtenews.ie*, 22 February 2011. Available at: www.rte.ie/news/2011/0222/297948-facebook/. Accessed 23 February 2011.

32 Dalton interview.

33 World by Storm, 'Irish left archive: Provisional Sinn Féin, Éire Nua, Jan 1971, Appendix 1972', *Cedar Lounge Revolution*, 9 February 2009. Available at: www.cedarlounge.wordpress.com/2009/02/09/irish-left-archive-provisional-sinn-Féin-eire-nua-january-1971-appendix-1972/. Accessed 9 February 2009.

34 Dalton interview.

35 See: 'Republican Sinn Féin explains position on EU constitution', Indymedia. com, 31 May 2005. Available at: www.indymedia.ie/article/70051?userlangu age=ga&save_prefs=trueand. Accessed 1 June 2005.

36 'Statement from the leadership of the Republican Movement', *Saoirse*, April 2006.

37 'Dissident republican Gary Donnelly takes Derry and Strabane super council seat and faces IRA bomb motion', *Belfast Telegraph*, 12 June 2014. Available at: www.belfasttelegraph.co.uk/news/northern-ireland/dissident-republican-gary-donnelly-takes-derry-and-strabane-super-council-seat-and-faces-ira-bomb-motion-30348381.html. Accessed 29 March 2017.

38 'Free Derry: the IRA drug war', *Vice News*, 14 March 2014. Available at: www. youtube.com/watch?v=gsAHGu-Z-VA. Accessed 17 March 2014.

39 'The truth about Alan Ryan and his funeral', *Irish Independent*, 16 September 2012. Available at: www.independent.ie/irish-news/the-truth-about-alan-ryan-and-his-funeral-26898251.html. Accessed 17 September 2012.

40 '32 County Sovereignty Movement: who we are', *Sovereign Nation*, August–September 2004.

41 McIntyre, Anthony, 'Silent but lethal', *Blanket*, 11 August 2002. Available at: http://indiamond6.ulib.iupui.edu:81/silentbut.html. Accessed 20 August 2013.

42 'The futile path of militarism', *An Phoblacht/ Republican News*, 20 August 1998.

43 See: *Sovereign Nation*, June/July 2010.

44 'Irish Democracy: a framework for unity', *32CSM*, www.32csmdocuments. webs.com/aframeworkforunity.htm. Accessed 20 April 2017.

45 Early policy documents and statements from 2004–2006 are available at: www.web.archive.org/web/20051118212832/http://www.32csm.org/   . Accessed 20 April 2017.

46 'IRSP: who are we?'. Available at: www.irsp.ie/Background/whoweare.html. Accessed 20 April 2017.

47 Hanley, Brian, and Millar, Scott, *The Lost Revolution: The Story of the Official IRA and the Workers' Party* (Dublin: Penguin, 2009).

48 'Workers' Party response to Programme for Cohesion Sharing & Integration'. Available at: http://www.workerspartyireland.net/id533.html. Accessed 20 August 2013.

49 Ruddy, Gerry, 'Where to now comrades?', *Fourthwrite*, Issue 12, Spring 2003.

50 Publication of *Starry Plough* had been infrequent and had no fixed home online, perhaps reflecting a deeper commitment to the hard-copy format but also the smaller financial resources at the party's disposal. It had a presence at: www.theploughblog.blogspot.co.uk/ as well as www.starryplough.net/ and the IRSP website. Accessed 20 August 2013.

51 www.theredplough.blogspot.co.uk/. Accessed 20 August 2013.

52 One respondent to the *Sluggerotoole* article by Carrie McIntyre noted that initial signatories to the group that would become RNU were, 'irps [IRSP] and rira'. Available at: www.sluggerotoole.com/2007/03/06/ex-pows-endorse-independent-republicans/. Accessed 6 March 2007.

53 Walsh, Jason, 'The decommissioning of Marxism', Guardian.com, Comment is Free, 14 October 2009. Available at: www.guardian.co.uk/commentis-free/2009/oct/14/irish-national-liberation-army. Accessed 14 October 2009.

54 www.lookleftonline.org/. Accessed 20 May 2009.

55 'DCTV and Looking Left: the Irish people', *Irish Left Review*, 26 May 2009. Available at: www.irishleftreview.org/left-tv-series/. Accessed 26 May 2009.

56 www.cedarlounge.wordpress.com/about-us/. *Cedar Lounge* is named after a pub in Raheny in North Dublin where the activists involved in the site would meet.

57 Garibaldy, interview, 25 November 2012.

58 Garibaldy interview.

59 Garibaldy interview.

60 www.gaskinbalrog.blogspot.co.uk/. Accessed 9 June 2009. Chris Gaskin, a Sinn Féin activist, was a regular blogger and was nominated for Irish blog awards. After a break from blogging for several years, he resumed in 2013. See also: www.1169andcounting.blogspot.co.uk/. Accessed 20 April 2013. The blog has moved to three separate sites, but has in a little more than five years had more than 500,000 unique page users.

61 M. Fealty, 'Total politics: top 20 NI blogs ...', *Sluggerotoole.com*, 1 September 2010. Available at: www.sluggerotoole.com/2010/09/01/total-politics-top-20-ni-blogs/. Accessed 2 September 2010. The *Total Politics* magazine annual ranking of blogs is seen as one of the marks of quality in the political blogosphere.

62 Wade, K. *et al.*, 'Identifying representative textual sources in blog networks', International AAAI Conference on Web and Social Media, Fifth International AAAI Conference on Weblogs and Social Media, 2001. Available at: http:/ https://www.aaai.org/ocs/index.php/ICWSM/ICWSM11/paper/view/2756/3306. Accessed 20 August 2013.

63 World by Storm, interview, 20 September 2012.

64 Garibaldy interview.

65 Bloggs, Joe, 'Who is the blogosphere?', *Sunday Tribune*, 17 April 2006.

66 World by Storm interview. He noted, 'Many people would not know what we were talking about. This conversation would be esoteric to the point of incoherence.'

67 www.sinnféinkeepleft.blogspot.co.uk. Accessed 1 June 2011. See also: 'Councillor's defection smacks of political careerism', *An Phoblacht*, 14 January 2010.

68 'Sinn Féin Keep Left site is closing down', *SinnFéinkeepleft*, 1 June 2011. Available at: http://sinnfeinkeepleft.blogspot.co.uk/2011/06/sinn-fein-keep-left-site-is-closing.html. Accessed 1 June 2011.

69 'C4 invests in political blogger Slugger O'Toole', *Guardian*, 24 November 2009. Available at: www.theguardian.com/media/pda/2009/nov/24/c4-invests-in-political-blogger-slugger-otoole. Accessed 25 November 2009.

70 For an example of this 'story' see: 'Gulladuff: more heat than light', *Sluggerotoole*, 19 June 2009. Available at: www.sluggerotoole.com/2009/06/19/gulladuff-more-heat-than-light/. Accessed 20 June 2009. A full catalogue of

articles on the issue appears on the website www.longkesh.info, which is maintained by McIntyre herself. Accessed 20 August 2013. For a description of the effects of Rusty Nail's reporting see: O'Rawe, Richard, *Afterlives* (Dublin: Lilliput Press, 2010), p. 151.

71 See: Rusty Nail, 'I will not be attending and will not send a representative', *Sluggerotoole*, 26 May 2009. Available at: http://sluggerotoole.com/2009/05/26/i-will-not-be-attending-and-will-not-send-a-representative/. Accessed 27 May 2009.

72 Fealty, M., 'Net prophets', *Observer*, 4 April 2004. Available at: http://www.guardian.co.uk/technology/2004/apr/04/northernireland.comment. Accessed 10 November 2010.

73 Ó'Broin interview.

74 C. McIntyre interview.

75 Former republican activist and author Deaglán Ó Donghaile, who published in the *Blanket*, noted that *Fourthwrite* was among the biggest selling local magazines in bookshops in Belfast when it was first published. Interview, 4 February 2010. *Blanket* editor Carrie McIntyre noted that articles from the magazine were used for US state department briefings. C. McIntyre, interview.

76 éirígí and 32CSM documents were published by the *Blanket*. See: D. Mac An Mhaistír, 'Address to éirígí's James Connolly Commemoration', *Blanket*, 12 May 2007. Available at: www.indiamond6.ulib.iupui.edu:81/DA150607.html. Accessed 20 June 2009.

77 'James Connolly remembered', eirigi.org, 13 May 2008. Available at: www.eirigi.org/latest/latest130508.html. Accessed 14 May 2008. See also: 'Speech by Anthony McIntyre to an Easter commemoration, Derry City Cemetery, Derry, 23 March 2008'. Available at: www.cain.ulst.ac.uk/issues/politics/docs/rnu/amci230308.htm. Accessed 20 June 2009.

78 McIntyre, Anthony, interview, 12 December 2010.

79 McKearney, Tommy, 'Republicanism in the 21ˢᵗ century', *Fourthwrite*, Issue 1, 2000. McKearney reiterates the radical potential of republicanism in the fractured Peace Process era in *The Provisional IRA*. See also: O'Ruairc, L., 'What is Irish Republicanism?', *Weekly Worker*, 2 June 2005.

80 Ruddy, 'Where to now comrades?'.

81 Nagle, John, 'Potemkin village: neo-liberalism and peace-building in Northern Ireland?', *Ethnopolitics* vol. 8, no. 2, 2009, pp. 173–190. See also: McLaughlin and Baker, *The Propaganda of Peace*.

82 The third way, a central plank of Tony Blair's New Labour in Britain, attempted to reconcile right- and left-wing politics. See: Giddens, Anthony, *Beyond Left and Right: The Future of Radical Politics* (London: Polity Press, 1998). It is an apposite metaphor for reconciling competing republican standpoints in the period.

83 'Fourthwrite', Ulsternation.org.uk, n.d. Edition reviewed was *Fourthwrite*, Issue 8, which dates the review to Winter 2001.

84 Among the loyalists and unionists that contributed to the *Blanket* were David Adams, John Coulter and former Ulster Volunteer Force (UVF) leader Billy Mitchell.

85 Ruddy, Gerry, 'An IRSP alternative', *Forum Magazine*, December 2003.

86 See: 'Up to 300 dissidents working to undermine Northern Ireland peace process, warns Hugh Orde', *Daily Telegraph*, 15 March 2009.

87 'Jonathan Evans' terrorism speech', *Daily Telegraph*, 17 September 2010. Available at: www.telegraph.co.uk/news/uknews/terrorism-in-the-uk/8008252/Jonathan-Evans-terrorism-speech.html. Accessed 18 September 2010.

88 Sheehan, Maeve, 'Republican rebels try a new tactic', *Sunday Times*, 23 February 2003.

89 New Republican Forum is now defunct, but its homepage remains visible at: www.web.archive.org/web/20040924043933/http://www.newrepublicanforum.ie/. Accessed 12 November 2010.

90 'Interview with republican prisoner', *Forum Magazine*, December 2005. The article outlines the reasons IRA prisoners in Portlaoise Prison gave for resigning from RIRA. Declan Carroll, spokesman for the prisoners, argued, 'the continued use of armed struggle was not a viable strategy'.

91 'Interview with Michael McKevitt', *Forum Magazine*, April–May 2006.

92 Morrison interview.

93 See: 'Sinn Féin on the road to nowhere', *Forum Magazine*, August–September 2004; 'End of the line for the Provisionals', August–September 2004; 'Rationalising failure and sacrifice', August–September 2005; 'Provisional's (sic) surrender now complete', August–September 2005; 'The final PIRA humiliation', October 2005.

94 'Sinn Féin prepares for campaign', *An Phoblacht*, 1 March 2001.

95 McDonald, Henry, 'Isn't it time that the double-speak stopped?', *Observer*, 28 December 2003.

96 'Gerry McGeough guilty of 1981 Samuel Brush murder bid', *BBC News Online*, 18 February 2011. Available at: www.bbc.co.uk/news/uk-northern-ireland-12509836. Accessed 18 February 2011.

97 '1916: a Catholic rebellion?', *Hibernian*, May 2006.

98 'God save Ireland!', *Hibernian*, April 2008. 'Libertas: Declan Ganley, the millionaire patriot', *Hibernian*, May 2008.

99 McGeough, Gerry, 'Inside view', *Hibernian*, September 2008.

100 McGeough, 'Inside view'.

101 See: Galvin, Martin, 'Hunger Strikes anniversary', *Hibernian*, September 2006; 'Just say no', *Hibernian*, February 2007, and 'Harknessing back to old ways', *Hibernian*, May 2007.

102 Ó'Floinn, P., 'Themselves alone', *Hibernian*, December 2006.

103 'Ex-Provo gives new life to Irish clerical fascism', *Searchlight*, August 2006.

104 McKearney, *The Provisional IRA*, p. 197.

105 The phrase appears on Oisin Kelly's statue of Larkin which stands on O'Connell Street in Dublin. It also appeared on the masthead of James Connolly's *Workers Republic* newspaper.

106 'The worm is turning – vote NO on May 31st', eirigi.org. Available at: www.eirigi.org/latest/latest300512_3.html. Accessed 31 May 2009.

107 'The worm is turning'.

108 'From socialism alone can the salvation of Ireland come', eirigi.org. Available at: www.eirigi.org/pdfs/socialism.pdf. Accessed 18 May 2009.

109 Cusack, Jim, 'The last republican', *Sunday Independent*, 26 April 2009.

110 World by Storm, 'éirígí – new dawn fades? Or non-Sinn Féin republicanism boldly going where many have gone before ...', cedarlounge.wordpress.com, 23 January 2007. Available at: www.cedarlounge.wordpress.com/2007/01/23/eirigi-new-dawn-fades-ornon-sinn-Féin-republicanism-boldly-going-where-many-have-gone-before/. Accessed 24 January 2007.

111 Mac an Mháistír, Daithí, 'Address to éirígí's James Connolly commemoration', *Blanket*, 12 May 2007. Available at: www.indiamond6.ulib.iupui.edu:81/DA150607.html. Accessed 18 June 2007.

112 MacCionnaith, Breandán, interview, 9 April 2009.

113 MacCionnaith interview.

114 MacCionnaith interview.

115 MacCionnaith interview.

116 Leeson, Brian, 'éirígí: one year on – almost', *Fourthwrite*, No. 28, Winter 2006/7.

117 Robinson, M., 'Interview with Brendan McKenna', *Fourthwrite*, Issue 2, Summer 2000.

118 Fealty, Mick, 'Sinn Féin's flop', *Guardian*, 29 May 2007. Available at: www.guardian.co.uk/commentisfree/2007/may/29/sinnFéinandthefailureofi.

119 McKearney, *The Provisional IRA*, p. 197. See also: Rafter, Kevin, *Sinn Féin 1905–2005: In the Shadow of Gunmen* (Dublin: Gill & Macmillan, 2005), p. 238.

120 Marunchak, Alex, 'SF leader's sister on rise in rival', *Sunday Mirror*, 16 August 2009.

121 'Reclaim the Republic', éirígí.org, May 2006. Available at: https://web.archive.org/web/20060906030716/http://www.eirigi.org:80/campaigns/index.htm. Accessed 18 June 2007.

122 MacCionnaith interview.

123 Mac an Mháistir, Daithí, 'What sort of Ireland do we want?', eirigi.org, 6 March 2007. Available at: www.eirigi.org/latest/latest060307.html. Accessed 9 March 2007. The article is the transcript of a speech given at the Workers' Solidarity Movement's Anarchist Book Fair.

124 Mac an Mháistir, 'What sort of Ireland do we want?'.

125 Kerr, Aine, 'Uncle Sam makes a splash on cross-party canvas', *Irish Independent*, 6 June 2008. Available at: www.independent.ie/irish-news/uncle-sam-makes-splash-on-crossparty-city-canvass-26451898.html. Accessed 7 June 2008.

126 See: interview with Breandán MacCionnaith on the Italian republican website, fivedemands.org, 4 December 2011. Available at: https://thefivedemands.org/2011/04/12/esclusiva-intervista-a-breandan-mac-cionnaith-segretario-generale-di-eirigi/. Accessed 20 March 2015.

127 Ryan, Sean, 'ICTU march – a radical viewpoint'. Available at: www.vimeo.com/17292048. Left-wing blogger and activist journalist Ryan interviewed Mac an Mháistir at the Irish Congress of Trade Unions march in Dublin in November 2010. Accessed 28 November 2010.

128 Morris, Allison, 'éirígí recruits its first elected Sinn Féin politician in the North', *Irish News*, 9 September 2009.
129 'éirígí ard-fheis: Saturday May 10', eirigi.org. Available at: www.eirigi.org/latest/latest090508.html. Accessed 10 May 2008.
130 Belfast Gonzo, 'Ex-IRA leader to address left wing republican party', *Sluggerotoole*, 27 August 2007. Available at: www.sluggerotoole.com/2007/08/27/ex-ira-leader-to-address-left-wing-republican-party/. Accessed 28 August 2007. The left-wing blogger and writer Garibaldy, a Workers' Party activist and frequent contributor to *Cedar Lounge Revolution*, made the point about éirígí punching above its weight in terms of publicity, in the comments on the thread.
131 Belfast Gonzo, 'Ex-IRA leader to address left wing republican party'.
132 *Derry Journal*, 2 February 2007. Available at: www.derryjournal.com/news/an-umbrella-group-led-by-ex-republican-prisoners-opposed-to-backing-the-psni-is-due-to-meet-in-the-gasyard-centre-next-monday-to-plan-a-strategy-ahead-of-the-assembly-elections-in-march-1–2109611. Accessed 3 February 2007.
133 'Why we oppose the PSNI', *republicannetwork.ie*. Archived at: www.web.archive.org/web/20090620162351/http://www.republicannetwork.ie/opposePSNI.aspx. Accessed 20 April 2017.
134 McIntyre, Anthony 'The Foreman', *Blanket*, 12 February 2007. Available at: www.indiamond6.ulib.iupui.edu:81/AM130207.html. Accessed 20 February 2007. See also: O'Ruairc, L., 'Policing', *Blanket*, 7 February 2007. Available at: www.indiamond6.ulib.iupui.edu:81/LOR130207.html. Accessed 12 February 2007.
135 'Why we oppose the PSNI'.
136 Cunningham interview.
137 Cunningham interview.
138 Cunningham interview.
139 Galvin, Martin, 'RNU Easter commemoration speech', 12 April 2009. Available at: www.cain.ulst.ac.uk/issues/politics/docs/rnu/mg09.htm. Accessed 20 June 2010.
140 Cowan, Rosie, 'He did the IRA's dirty work for 25 years – and was paid £80,000 a year by the government', *Guardian*, 12 May 2003. See also: Friel, Laura, 'Donaldson admits role as British agent', *An Phoblacht*, 5 January 2006.
141 McBrearty, Danny, 'RNU Bodenstown address', *Blanket*, 20 June 2007. Available at: www.indiamond6.ulib.iupui.edu:81/RN070707.html. Accessed 4 July 2008.
142 McBrearty, 'RNU Bodenstown address'.
143 McBrearty, Danny, 'Ex POWs' name change', *Blanket*, 20 June 2007. Available at: www.indiamond6.ulib.iupui.edu:81/DMCB070707.html. Accessed 4 July 2008.
144 Rowan, Brian, 'Dissidents deny issuing death threat to Belfast republican', *Belfast Telegraph*, 19 February 2013. Available at: www.belfasttelegraph.co.uk/news/local-national/northern-ireland/dissidents-deny-issuing

-death-threat-to-belfast-republican-28590471.html. Accessed 20 February 2013.

145 For a detailed breakdown of the various dissident organizations and factions, see: *Twenty-first Report of the Independent Monitoring Commission* (London: The Stationery Office, May 2009) and *Twenty-second Report of the Independent Monitoring Commission* (London: The Stationery Office, November 2009). Available at: www.cain.ulst.ac.uk/issues/politics/docs/imc/imcreports.htm. Accessed 10 May 2010.

146 See: 'CFAD activist to be "charged" with drug possession'. Available at: www.cfadardoyne.blogspot.co.uk/2010/11/cfad-activist-to-be-charged-with-drug.html. Accessed 10 May 2010.

147 McBrearty, D., 'We reject the term "no hopers", say Republican Network for Unity', *Derry Journal*, 15 February 2008. Available at: www.derryjournal.com/news/your-community/letters/we-reject-the-term-no-hopers-say-republican-network-for-unity-1-2120436. Accessed 16 February 2008.

148 Mooney, John, 'Terror groups unite in "new IRA"', *Sunday Times*, 13 December 2009.

149 '2011 RNU ard fheis', *Indymedia Ireland*, 2 June 2011. Available at: www.indymedia.ie/article/98860. Accessed 3 June 2011.

150 'Two Londonderry men accused of having rifle', *BBC News Online*, 5 August 2011. Available at: www.bbc.co.uk/news/uk-northern-ireland-14421746. Accessed 6 August 2011.

151 Tonge, Jonathan, 'Dissidents, ultras, militarists or patriots? Analysing the strategies, tactics and support for "dissident" republicanism', Political Studies Association of Ireland conference paper, 8 October 2010.

152 Edwards, Aaron, 'When terrorism as strategy fails: dissident Irish republicans and the threat to British security', *Studies in Conflict and Terrorism* vol. 34, no. 4, 2011, p. 323.

153 Cunningham interview.

154 Cunningham interview.

155 Cunningham interview.

156 See: www.republicanunity.blogspot.co.uk/. Accessed 13 December 2008. The Irish Republican Forum for Unity would remain active until Christmas 2008, whereupon RNU would go to establish itself as a separate presence in the republican sphere.

157 *Standing Outside of the Peace Process*, RNU position paper. 2012. Available at: www.cain.ulst.ac.uk/issues/politics/docs/rnu/2012–11–05_rnu.pdf. Accessed 18 January 2013.

158 McBrearty, 'Ex POWs' name change'.

159 'No more lies', *Blanket*, 31 May 2004. Available at: www.indiamond6.ulib.iupui.edu:81/nomorelies.html. Accessed 20 January 2013. McIntyre and McKearney were among the signatories of a letter urging greater engagement in bringing anti-agreement republicans together. McIntyre would provide the oration at an RNU commemoration in 2008 and McKearney spoke at an internal RNU lecture series in 2011.

160 McGregor, Mark, interview, 3 January 2010. It was alleged that Catney had been denied membership of éirígí because it feared him as a Sinn Féin entryist. See also: '"Dissidents"– they mostly didn't think so'.McWilliams was involved in the high-profile killing of Loyalist Volunteer Force leader Billy Wright in the Maze Prison in December 1997.

161 Price, Dolours, 'Get on with it', *Blanket*, 14 September 2004. Available at: www.indiamond6.ulib.iupui.edu:81/getonwithitdp.html. Accessed 8 January 2010. An archive of Dolours Price's writing for the *Blanket* is available at: www.thepensivequill.am/2013/01/dolours-price-archive.html. Accessed 20 August 2013.

162 Cunningham interview. The undemocratic nature of leadership in these organizations was a familiar motif in the writing of both McIntyre and McKearney, as noted previously.

163 McBrearty, Danny, 'Why label disillusioned republicans as criminals?', *Guardian*, 13 August 2010. Available at: www.guardian.co.uk/commentisfree/2010/aug/13/northern-ireland-criminalisation-republican-dissent. Accessed 14 August 2010.

164 'Revolutionary republicanism', RNU Internal document, 2012. Available at: www.indymedia.ie/attachments/mar2013/core_principles_of_revolutionary_republicanism._1.pdf. Accessed 30 March 2013.

165 Cunningham interview.

166 Cunningham interview.

167 RNU regularly used the *Blanket* in its early phase as a means of communicating to a wider public. It began using *Indymedia* from 2009 and has had a very active presence in social media, especially Facebook, since 2010.

168 Cunningham interview.

169 Cunningham interview.

170 Cunningham interview.

171 www.ardoynerepublican.blogspot.co.uk/. Accessed 20 August 2013.

172 Morris, Allison, 'Drugs haul worth £40k destroyed', *Irish News*, 10 October 2010. CFAD also issued threats to drug dealers in Derry. See: 'Dealers warned', *Sunday Journal*, 2 June 2008. Available at: www.derryjournal.com/news/local/dealers_warned_1_2125759. Accessed 3 June 2008.

173 Cunningham interview.

174 'Ardoyne riot row continues', *Irish Republican News*, 24 July 2009. Available at: www.republican-news.org/current/news/2009/07/ardoyne_riot_row_continues.html. Accessed 25 July 2009.

175 'Ardoyne riot row continues'.

176 McDonald, Henry, 'Youths attack police in Ardoyne over Orange Order', *Guardian*, 13 July 2009. Available at: www.guardian.co.uk/uk/2009/jul/13/police-ardoyne-orange-order-parade. Accessed 14 July 2009.

177 'Use of plastic bullets condemned', *Irish Republican News*, 17 July 2009. Available at: www.republican-news.org/current/news/2009/07/use_of_plastic_bullets_condemn.html. Accessed 20 July 2009.

178 McDonald, Henry, 'Northern Ireland agrees power sharing deal', *Guardian*, 5 February 2010. Available at: www.guardian.co.uk/politics/2010/feb/05/

northern-ireland-power-sharing-deal1. Accessed 6 February 2010. See also: 'DUP backs Sinn Féin power sharing deal', *C4 News*, 5 February 2010. Available at: www.channel4.com/news/articles/politics/domestic_politics/dup%2 bbacks%2bsinn%2bfein%2bpowersharing%2bdeal/3526937.html. Accessed 6 February 2010.

179 Meehan, Martin Óg, 'Has deal opened roads for Orange parades? – RNU', *Indymedia Ireland*, 6 February 2010. Available at: www.indymedia.ie/article /95718?userlanguage=ga&save_prefs=true. Accessed 7 February 2010.

180 McBrearty, Danny, 'RNU support Maghaberry rally', Indymedia.org, 10 April 2010. Available at: www.indymedia.ie/article/96315?search_text=RNU+PRO. Accessed 20 April 2010.

181 Cunningham interview.

182 McIntyre, Anthony, 'RNU Easter commemoration, Derry City Cemetery, Derry, 23 March 2008'. Available at: www.cain.ulst.ac.uk/issues/politics/ docs/rnu/amci230308.htm. Accessed 25 May 2009.

183 Eight of the ten most deprived areas of Northern Ireland were in nationalist West and North Belfast and Derry. *Northern Ireland Multiple Deprivation Measure*, Northern Ireland Statistics and Research Agency, Belfast (2010). Available at: https://www.nisra.gov.uk/statistics/deprivation/northern-ire-land-multiple-deprivation-measure-2010-nimdm2010. Accessed 20 August 2013.

184 Cunningham interview. The case of landlordism in republican areas, although not specifically linked to members of Sinn Féin or PIRA, was also highlighted by a former IRSP ard comhairle member on the *Blanket*. See: O'Ruairc, L., 'Landlordism and the housing question' *Blanket*, 25 September 2002. Available at: www.indiamond6.ulib.iupui.edu:81/landlordism.html. Accessed 20 January 2012.

185 Cunningham interview. See also: McAnulty, John, 'Adams routed on police', *Fourthwrite*, No. 28, Winter 2006–2007. McAnulty notes in the debate about party members leaving over policing and justice reforms: 'It is widely known that many who are still members are on the pay roll as community workers and dependent on the leadership for their livelihood.'

186 'Standing outside the Peace Process'. Available at: www.cain.ulst.ac.uk/ issues/politics/docs/rnu/2012–11–05_rnu.pdf. Accessed 9 January 2012.

187 Cunningham interview.

188 'Standing outside the Peace Process'.

189 'Standing outside the Peace Process'.

190 'Standing outside the Peace Process'.

191 'Standing outside the Peace Process'.

4

Sinn Féin and the life and death of the republican newspaper

A community will evolve only when a people control their own communication.

Frantz Fanon[1]

Irish republican newspapers and their roots

The tradition of republican newspapers that stretches back to the United Irishmen remains active, despite the rapid spread of the Internet and mobile phones that has impacted on the mainstream media markets. *An Phoblacht* remains the highest-profile paper in the republican sphere, continuing an almost unbroken run of publication stretching back more than thirty years. This, in the face of government censorship and the turmoil of the 1970s and 1980s, signified a deep and continued commitment to the belief that a party newspaper could have a cultural and ideological effect in the face of official sanctions and government propaganda. The paper's editor, John Hedges noted, 'There's still that grá for it and that began for a lot of people because we were in a conflict situation and we were censored – *An Phoblacht/Republican News* was the only place you could get uncensored news of the conflict from a republican perspective.'[2]

In the intervening years, *An Phoblacht*'s profile has dropped, along with its sales, with Sinn Féin involved in regular debates about its future.[3] However, in this respect it simply reflects the changing culture of news consumption among modern readers. Its function as the primary space for official news, party information or as an organizing hub for activists has been replaced by social media, and in particular Facebook.[4] Its publication is now monthly rather than weekly, and its website carries a large amount of information on its pages for free. The website is also a multi-media hub, where video is seen as a vital tool in the activist repertoire and has been an area in which Sinn Féin has invested a lot of time and money.[5] The paper, which effectively led the party's agenda, is now a secondary concern within the overall media strategy, which is overseen from the party's press offices

in Leinster House and at Stormont in Belfast, now the central sites for the
direction of media policy. Yet, despite the falling sales and the increasing
centrality of social media to the new digital natives of the wireless communication era that make up the party's young membership, Sinn Féin
maintains monthly publication of a paper that is well written and professionally designed and among the best political periodicals produced in
Ireland. Hedges says:

> The *Irish Times* once wrote that we were the best-subbed paper on the island
> – that was a real badge of pride to our proof-readers. We always wanted it
> to look good and be presentable and easy on the eye. We didn't want it to be
> like the Marxist Leninist Weekly where it was like wading through treacle to
> get the message.[6]

Covering less news and now focused on features and analysis, including more increased coverage of sport and popular culture than at any
period of its history, *An Phoblacht* has changed enormously in appearance
and content since its merger with *Republican News* in 1978. That merger
between papers based in Dublin and Belfast symbolized a shift in power in
the Provisional movement towards Gerry Adams and the Northern-based
leadership of PIRA, and signified their readiness to assume full control.[7]
Sinn Féin re-launched the republican magazine *IRIS* in November 2006
after a gap in publication of thirteen years. Its appearances would be sporadic, but were more frequent between 2010 and 2012. It has not appeared
since the August–November 2012 edition. The fact that Sinn Féin has
maintained publication of hard-copy newspapers and magazines, which
were at the heart of the Provisional movement's blueprint for building a
community and constituency in the 1970s, illustrates a commitment to the
power of activist journalism as a means of developing a consistent, public
political platform.

As noted in the previous chapter, in the rest of the republican activist firmament, Republican Sinn Féin continues with the monthly publication of
Saoirse, while 32CSM has effectively ceased publishing *Sovereign Nation*.
However, neither paper had the same depth of writing or commercial
nous as *An Phoblacht*, and their content was remarkably similar. Whiting,
in a study of seven years of publication of the newspapers, concluded the
most covered topics, outside of party notices and statements, were stories
of republican victimization, critiques of Sinn Féin and restatements of the
historic mandate they each had as the 'true republican party'.[8]

As also noted previously, the Workers Party-aligned *Look Left* is a
modern features-based magazine which shares some republican preoccupations and leftist ideological roots, but is an attempt at broadening the
argument towards a more global perspective. In this sense it owes much

more to the tradition of British left or global left publications. However, it is worth noting that in late 2010, a few short months after its initial run of publications, Sinn Féin's rebranding of both *An Phoblacht* and *IRIS* bore some similarities to *Look Left* in the tone and expanded horizons of their content.

All of these papers owe their existence, to some extent, to the more than 220-year history of Irish republican publishing. At junctures of crisis and contestation in republican history, strands of the movement have turned to journalism and publishing as a means to make meaningful contributions to the political public sphere. They were, from the outset, an effective means of counteracting censorship and marginalization. The *Northern Star*, the newspaper of the United Irishmen, was the first and became an ideologically sustaining influence on the tradition of republican pamphleteering. Brian Inglis noted, 'the odds against the opposition press were overwhelming; but the *Northern Star* ... survived long enough to demonstrate ... that polemical party newspapers could exercise considerable influence when allied to a popular cause.'[9] Marianne Elliott described it as an 'effective mouthpiece'.[10] The *Nation*, the newspaper of the Young Irelanders, established by Charles Gavan Duffy, Thomas Davis and John Blake Dillon, and the *United Irishman*, established by John Mitchel, were militant vehicles of agitation in support of 'an Irish republic which would destroy landlordism and secure the "land for the people" '.[11] Mitchel, a controversial figure who was transported to Australia and later escaped to the USA, where he supported the South and slavery in the Civil War, was described by Lyons as 'among the two or three most forceful and effective journalists to write for Irish newspapers in the nineteenth century'.[12] The *Nation* and the Young Irelanders had been central to the political development of the Fenians, and it was James Stephens who decided that 'the movement needed a newspaper if it was ever going to reach the mass of the Irish people and it was ever to raise enough funds to keep afloat'.[13]

Time and again for revolutionary movements, the newspaper is a means to spread the doctrine of the cause and to raise the money required to buy the tools of the revolution, either arms or political campaigning. Anderson's evocation of the Imagined Community, the post-Enlightenment new nation states and peoples, bound together in the era of emerging nationalisms, was profoundly affected by the development of the mass media and the ideological mobilized press. The printed word 'made it possible for rapidly growing numbers of people to think about themselves, and to relate themselves to others, in profoundly new ways'.[14] Legg notes that the Irish provincial press emerges and develops at a time of the reaffirmation of nationalism through the nineteenth century, including in the early years of what became the revolutionary era in the later Victorian period.[15] The period from 1890 onwards, which had a profound influence on the publication of republican newspapers for more than a century, was a template they would follow for more than thirty years and had an influence on the commitment to publish a party newspaper within modern Sinn Féin. These newspapers were not simply speaking to internal publics but to external audiences, particularly the security forces and the media. Just as *An Phoblacht* was read by almost every journalist during the Troubles, the *Irish Bulletin* was sent to British newspapers at times of censorship during the War of Independence, and 'did much to create a sympathetic public opinion towards the Irish cause'.[16]

Arthur Griffith and James Connolly's forays into newspaper publication said much for the need to produce propaganda materials, as well as the ideological schisms in the movement at the turn of the twentieth century. Griffith was a trained printer and gifted journalist, and his editorship of William Rooney's weekly paper, the *United Irishman*, would see it become as potent a force as the *Nation* had been for the contemporaries of Thomas Davis'.[17] Lyons noted, 'Griffith was an inspired journalist who combined style and temper in a way that no-one else could match'.[18] His work was said to contain the 'savagery of Jonathan Swift and the ruggedness of John Mitchel', although more intense.[19] The paper would be renamed *Sinn Féin* in 1907 and be joined by a number of separatist papers, W.P. Ryan's *Irish Peasant*, the Irish Republican Brotherhood's *Irish Freedom* and Bulmer Hobson's *The Republic*, the paper that modern *An Phoblacht* sees as its progenitor.[20]

Connolly's activism also took him into journalism, founding the *Workers' Republic* paper for the Irish Socialist Republican Society and the *Harp* for the Irish Socialist Federation.[21] P.S. O'Hegarty said *Irish Freedom*, founded and edited by Tom Clarke, a signatory of the 1916 Proclamation with Connolly, 'gave to the separatist movement in Ireland unity and philosophy'.[22] This period of the Irish Ireland cultural revival was the heyday of the republican newspaper. Although the *An Phoblacht* of the 1930s and the mosquito press expanded the repertoire of the republican newspaper, it was in this period that the major themes of modern republicanism were established. Mac Donncha, a former editor of the modern *An Phoblacht*, signified their importance to contemporary Sinn Féin: 'these papers reflected the rebirth of the Irish language, the growth of the labour movement, the emergence of feminism and the renewal of militant Irish republicanism.'[23]

The roots of the republican newspapers of the modern age also lie with the mosquito press as pioneered by the republican dissidents, Frank Ryan and Peadar O'Donnell and their work on *An Phoblacht* in the late 1920s and 1930s, as well as de Valera's establishment of the *Irish Press* in 1931. Ryan, an officer in the Dublin brigade of the IRA, was a committed propagandist and journalist, and had edited an Irish-language prison journal while in jail in Limerick. O'Donnell, another IRA figure, was a novelist and journalist, who would also edit the literary journal, the *Bell*. *An Phoblacht* was a radical counterweight to the propaganda of de Valera and united what the paper described as 'the two wings of the revolutionary movement, the IRA and the communists'.[24] The editorial content of Ryan's *An Phoblacht* set a template for radical republican writing that was anti-authoritarian and had literary designs. On the other hand, the establishment of the *Irish Press* by de Valera in 1931, under the editorship of Frank Gallagher, has enormous parallels with the Belfast Media Group's attempts at launching *Daily Ireland* in 2005–2006. Recognizing the need to control as much as possible of the narrative in the public space, the *Press* was a 'crucial communicative medium'.[25] Implicit through the years of censorship, clampdowns and imprisonment was the deep cultural value of a newspaper, as both an instrument of power and of dissent.

The IRA continued to produce newspapers throughout the twentieth century until the outbreak of the Troubles in 1969. These included the *Wolfe Tone Weekly*, which ran until 1938, and the re-launched *United Irishman* in the 1960s, which is probably the template on which the new paper *An Phoblacht* was based when it resumed publication in 1969. Initially *An Phoblacht*, produced in Dublin, was published in tandem with *Republican News*, which was established in Belfast. The Dublin paper was more professionally produced and had veteran newspaper journalist and historian Eamonn Mac Thomais as editor from 1972–1973. His changes in style and design led to increased circulation for the paper.[26] There was competition between the papers – but the Belfast paper had better access to PIRA simply given its geographic location and the fact that some staff were also PIRA members. *Republican News*, as a result, 'got all the coups'.[27] Tom Hartley noted that, from the outset, *Republican News* was competitive with *An Phoblacht*: 'we got very imperious, we wanted to take over the world; we were very bolshie.'[28] The paper had its first office at 170 Falls Road, premises that would be central to directing Provisional policy until the GFA. The establishment of the paper played a symbolic cultural role in the community in the minds of activists:

> What was important was it was the first time since partition that republicans had established an office inside the state. They had an office for elections in Divis Street in 1964, but this was the first time that they had decided to have an office that would be open permanently, where they could give their view of the conflict that was raging around them at that time.[29]

Republican News and *An Phoblacht* were also a means of making deliberative contributions to the public sphere at the time of the Section 31 broadcasting ban in the Republic of Ireland and sustained periods of police intimidation.

Counterculture, community and the Press Centre

Wider traditions of republican writing were also displayed in the early Troubles period in Belfast and Derry, where there was an explosion of news sheets and news bulletins informing communities of events. The *Andersonstown News* came directly out of the first free sheet of the Andersonstown Central Civil Resistance Committee in November 1972.[30] Hartley, the first office manager of *Republican News* and the Press Centre said, 'pamphleteering was very strong at the time and how you wrote was important to us. The *Andersonstown News* is a continuation of that tradition.'[31] Other information sheets circulating in the early 1970s, and designed to convey information during the curfews and internment, included *An Firinne* from the Falls Road (1971–1977) and the *Banner* from Ballymurphy (1971–1972). Hartley noted,

> There was a real cottage industry in information sheets at the time, there was the *Volunteer* in Andersonstown. Each area had its own sheet produced on Gestetner machines. It is wonderful what you can see with hindsight, but we were denied a voice, it was called censorship, so we thought of other ways of letting our voice be heard.[32]

This style of activism was centrally implicated in the narratives of counter hegemonic struggle and had its roots in anti-colonial thinking that was central to republicanism's countercultural position. Hartley says their activism was influenced by a diverse range of thought; from the Black Panthers, George Jackson and the Soledad Brothers, and the North African anti- and post-colonialists Albert Memmi and Frantz Fanon.[33] The Algerian War and the liberation conflicts of Palestine and South Africa were also key influences.[34] Hartley notes that, having processed often quite diverse influences, they realized that the underpinning of the media battle was about contesting the daily battles of language that go on inside a conflict: 'Language is the battleground of ideas where we translate the concepts and ideas inside our heads.'[35]

This was both an internal project of re-education and of political evolution as well as having an external face. Gerry Adams's Brownie columns, written while he was in Cage 11 in the internment camps and published by *Republican News*, reflected the post-colonial radicalism that Hartley identifies, asserting the need for a republican shadow state which imitated the structures of the British state but outside of its control. *Republican News* was also engaged in producing anything that was going to raise the profile of the movement. The office, which was staffed by volunteers, produced calendars, Christmas cards and candles. Its 'Freedom 74' posters were so effective, said Hartley, that the British Army responded with its own counter propaganda campaign of posters on the Falls Road.[36] *Republican News* was an attempt at taking control of communications in the manner suggested by Fanon at the start of this chapter. Adams centralized republican media activism as implicated in the cultural and ideological development of the movement and party; 'the importance of republican politics leading to a structured approach can be found in the production and availability of republican literature.'[37] The republican newspaper was at the centre of a new revolutionary 'state' that was organized around alternative community councils.[38] The defiant resistance community was 'also characterized by a strong sense of place', and *Republican News* certainly had the sense of being a local newspaper.'[39] Centrality to the community meant that if someone was harassed by armed forces, the Press Centre would hear about it first.[40] The *Andersonstown News*, a paper with revolutionary origins, did become *the* local newspaper in this area and a significant supporting voice to the Sinn Féin cause.

The community centrality of the Press Centre meant that *Republican News* also became the focus of prisoner welfare during and after internment. The first man lost in the system that they were asked to find was Kieran Nugent, who was also the first man to join the no wash, no work blanket protests.[41] Members of the Press Centre had seen the blanket men on prison visits, and arranged marches and developed a range of propaganda materials to highlight the situation in jails. It was another means of extending the cultural relevance of the struggle and developing resonance within its own communities.[42] Republican activist media, of which the papers were a central focus of internal information and organization, gave the movement cohesion. Adams said *An Phoblacht* was 'a radical weekly in as full a sense as one would wish … its weekly production as a centralized expression and platform of republican politics is a great achievement.'[43] When the Belfast leadership of PIRA started the process of undermining Ruari Ó'Brádaigh and the Southern leaders of Sinn Féin in the late 1970s, one of their first acts was to depose Gerry O'Hare, the editor of *An Phoblacht*, merge it with *Republican News* and instal Danny Morrison as editor of the new operation. They realized the media was an apparatus with which to control the narrative and focus dissent.[44] Morrison chose to revise the details of the Northern takeover, and with some years' distance perhaps romanticizes the new aims of the combined *AP/RN*:

Of course, it was seen and depicted as a takeover (which it actually wasn't). We were anxious to cover all the struggles taking place in the south, supporting the trade union movement, giving a voice to women, to gays, to the demands for the right to divorce for example (incredible though that backwardness of Irish society seems now to a modern audience).[45]

Sinn Féin's talent for propaganda, forged in the Press Centre and *AP/ RN*, led one observer to note, 'the PR skills of such as Gerry Adams and Danny Morrison are so highly regarded that the Sinn Féin press office is widely regarded as the Saatchi and Saatchi of "terrorist" publicity departments.'[46] However, the dynamism of the Press Centre was also famously deconstructed by Richard McAuley in an interview with a journalist: 'Do you know the sum total of the famous Republican propaganda machine that everybody talks about? ... I'm it.'[47] As Hartley noted, what the party learned in the Press Centre was to be aggressive and set the agenda. Later, during the Peace Process, the central team of strategists would have daily meetings to 'rudder' the mediated public debates as they took place in a media sphere expanded by radio phone-in programmes like Radio Ulster's *Talkback* and the nascent online communities.[48] That it was able to have a deliberative effect in the mainstream media space was a testament to the shifting terrain of establishment republican activism and its constitutional standing in the political space. This was a result of commitment to a long-term cultural project that broached difficult decisions of divergence from ideological absolutes and which was forged in the Press Centre. In the initial phase *AP/RN* was a space for those decisions to be aired.

The subaltern countercultural publics of radical republicanism became revealed through media activism as discourse. Maillot notes the *An Phoblacht/Republican News* was at 'the height of its influence during the Hunger Strikes.'[49] The paper, which printed special editions after the deaths of each of the ten men, had been the only space that those in the jails could use to communicate with the wider public sphere. The Hunger Strikes provided a potent political opportunity not just to cover republican sacrifices for the cause, but to communicate the broader narratives of reforming the British state as it affected republicans. Hedges says,

> What we realized about the H-Block struggle was that it wasn't going to be won by hardcore republicans, it was a bigger issue than that. The thing about the Northern state was bigger than the Republican Movement, it was about partition and gerrymandering and the sort of society that we had then and about the sort of society that we wanted to see.[50]

The Hunger Strikes was also the last time that *AP/RN* and the Press Centre were the primary space for the republican movement to liaise with journalists and the mass media. As the party moved towards constitutional politics, inevitably Sinn Féin's political figures would come to interact with the media in council chambers and the established spaces of modern political journalism. In one respect, the decentralization of media and exterior relations from Belfast was a major break in strategy and organization. However, the experience of having an office in Enniskillen during the victorious campaign to get Bobby Sands elected in the Fermanagh South Tyrone constituency in 1981 had persuaded the press office and Belfast leadership that decentralization could be achieved without major problems for the overall grand narrative.[51] This began with decentralization in the period after the Hunger Strikes, when the famous propaganda machine in Belfast ceded day-to-day control to local branches.[52] Hedges notes that what has developed are highly evolved and localized patterns of political engagement, particularly in Belfast and Derry, within which local cumann free sheets and information sheets are now, perhaps, rivals of *An Phoblacht*.[53]

The complete shift of the production of *AP/RN* to Dublin in 1979 with the merger of the titles, in part to diminish the chances of being shut down by frequent security forces raids, also saw the diminishment of the Press Centre as the central space for establishment republican media activism. Hedges notes that period was a constant strain, even just in terms of production: 'We had printers getting shut down and our offices were being raided. During Danny Morrison's time in Belfast they made the pages up in different houses to frustrate raids by British soldiers and the RUC just to get the paper out.'[54] It became a *de facto* press office for the armed campaign and the nascent electoral machine. With the later absorption of the party into the Assembly and its growth in the Dáil, the press offices are now largely centred in the parliaments.[55] This produced a gradual recentralization of press and political PR teams which was structured, not for internal communications, but for influencing the daily news agendas. As such *An Phoblacht*, as it was renamed in 2003 after a dispute with a former employee who now owns the *Republican News* title and publishes online, has become an internal party magazine with which to primarily frame the discourses of cumann meetings.

In the years of integration into the mainstream media environment and increased exposure in that sphere, the need for an all-encompassing organ of party policy has become questioned, particularly when the expense of producing it has become questioned in the age of the Internet. *An Phoblacht* has undergone several redesigns and re-imaginings. The first, in 2003, saw it now become a fully functioning online newspaper with parallel hard-copy format publication, but with the online sphere holding equal status to the hard-copy format.[56] In this respect, the paper was ahead of many mainstream corporate media outlets that initially resisted the move to simultaneous or digital-first publication.[57] This re-launch with a new website and extended archives also threw up a conflict that restructured the Irish republican sphere. The new Sinn Féin website was designed by a new team, and Fergus O'Dea, who had built and maintained the original *Republican Media* online presence since 1994, was no longer employed to do so. However, O'Dea, a computer programmer who had initially run the original pages from the University of Texas where he was a PhD student, 'reclaimed' the logo of the United Irishmen which had been used in the masthead of *Republican News*, established a separate web presence and continued to publish *An Phoblacht* material.[58] The *Republican News* name had been one that the Northern leadership maintained even after the merger with *An Phoblacht*. Morrison said that after all the harassment they had received producing the paper, they would never allow anyone to take that off them.[59] The party threatened legal action against O'Dea, who responded, 'I have devoted much of my life to supporting Sinn Féin and the Peace Process and continue to do so. Our news service is almost nine years old and is neither new nor controversial. This is censorship, they are shooting the messenger.'[60] There was resolution of the case with a link from the *Republican News* site still taking users to a Sinn Féin official link.[61] O'Dea has continued to publish *Republican News* as an alternative news space on a weekly basis and publishes material gathered from established news outlets and copy from other republican groups.

An Phoblacht's second re-launch in 2005 saw the paper rebranded and an updating of content to become more features oriented and analytical, as opposed to leading with a news agenda. However, Adams saw the paper's primary function unreduced, 'a progressive, radical weekly paper', an 'invaluable tool of struggle' and 'an organiser of the party, an educator, a means of internal communication and a paper of record'. In April 2010, the decision to take the paper to monthly publication saw a dramatic over-haul and extension of the media offering of the party, in a way that the old, print-only version could never achieve.

> [T]he print edition of the republican paper will become a monthly publica-
> tion and a brand new *An Phoblacht* website will be launched, including an
> online daily news service; up-to-the-minute videos featuring interviews; his-
> toric film footage; and an archive section with access to thousands of pho-
> tographs and historic republican material including back issues of *An
> Phoblacht/Republican News*.[62]

This was a major recalibration of the centrality of the Irish republican newspaper to the activist canon and redefined its potential range and scope, reflecting the increased opportunities of the online age. Falling internal sales (rather than the commercial sense of wider commercial cir-culation) were also part of the party's decision to utilize the online space. The *Irish Independent's* Jim Cusack noted that declining sales, and the

increased presence online, suggested that *An Phoblacht*, despite its historical importance to the party, may be closed in the future.[63] The party,
however, has regularly ridiculed his anti-Sinn Féin agenda, and in particular his reporting the party's 'imminent' demise in the Republic of Ireland
and his attacks on *An Phoblacht*.[64] Hedges said the change in focus to more
features-based material signalled 'the ability to delve deeper into the issues
that affect Irish society. The new monthly format for the print edition will
lend itself much more to in-depth features, interviews and political analysis.'[65] On *Sluggerotoole*, McGregor noted:

> Given SF's already excellent online offering it is hard to see how transforming
> *An Phoblacht* into a competitor will work. I'd suggest we could be seeing the
> death throws [sic] of 'Ireland's biggest selling political weekly' as it goes
> mainly digital and then is inevitably consumed by a party website that will
> attract more hits.[66]

The shift in editorial focus signalled a new era for *An Phoblacht* and a
restructuring of the Irish republican sphere. The spheres of republican
media would not simply be defined by people clustering around parties or
organizational units signified by hard-copy newspapers, but in an extended
online environment. Ó'Broin, a columnist for the paper, noted that *An
Phoblacht* had played an invaluable role during censorship, particularly in
the 'publication of material that you could not get into the mainstream
media pre the existence of the Internet'.[67] Now, in the Internet age and in
the time of the changing profile of Sinn Féin membership,

> Its purpose has changed and the ideological and policy building capacity
> potential among activist and core Sinn Féin supporters has changed. We are
> able to get into all the other forms of media to get the day-to-day politics
> out to the electorate and broader public. What you are seeing with *An Pho-
> blacht* is less news and more analysis, more detailed articles, more features
> and much more about talking to ourselves as activists and immediate support
> base who assist the party in our on going political work.[68]

Hedges observed that the paper is a victim of the party's integration into
the mainstream media politics public sphere, where party members are
seen regularly on television on both sides of the Irish border, where once
the paper, particularly during the broadcasting ban, was their only outlet.
'We are suffering, to some extent, from Sinn Féin's success – the growth
of republicanism, the spread of social media and because of the strong
standing Sinn Féin has established in the national and local media.'[69]
Ó'Broin was reluctant to implicate the development of *An Phoblacht* along
purely technological determinist lines; technology was an addendum to
the offline work, but did not 'virtualize' political activism. Instead, it was
the latest development of political activism:

You can do it quicker, cheaper and more effectively than having a big, old inky Gestetner machine to produce your pamphlets. But focusing on production is missing the point – the most exciting thing about the United Irishmen was the popularizing of political discourse and literature in their day. That's something that progressive movements, republicans, socialists and feminists have continued doing, using whatever technology that is available at the time. New technology allows for the mass production and circulation of material, but the Internet is just the latest phase of that. Is it something qualitatively different from what was before? No, it's not. But, it does allow you to do things in quicker and different ways.[70]

There is a further, more interesting point to be made about the worth of online activism and whether it delivers the kind of deliberative results that street-level engagement does. The Internet and social media are voracious, even insatiable consumers of content, but at what point do they become ineffective? Hedges is keen to recognize the centrality of social media to the lives of vast numbers of activists, but says,

> We cannot ignore the challenges posed by social media and that's why we continue to run our website, Facebook and Twitter channels. The problem we have is there is such a demand on activists who could spend all their time blogging, so it's a matter of striking a balance. If you have enough people to devote to producing a communications vehicle it's fine, but there is a danger that activists can find themselves sitting in their bedsit like TV's 'Citizen Smith' just churning out a blog and there's no activism, there's no politicization. People might feel pleased with themselves but have they changed anything?[71]

An Phoblacht's gradual move towards digital-first production signalled that circulations and influence were diminishing across the print sector, reflecting a broader trend towards digital engagement and social media. For Sinn Féin specifically, learning the lessons of the power of media ownership would see an attempt at taking on the producers of dominant ideology in their own environment – a mainstream media company. *Daily Ireland*, a republican daily launched into the mainstream newspaper market, was to be an attempt at demonstrating the power of the resurgent republican identity and capitalize on the growing Catholic middle class. It also tested the commitment to the voracity of whether 'a community will evolve only when a people control their own communication'. For Sinn Féin the battle remained the same:

> While overt state censorship of Sinn Féin is long gone, the party is still at the receiving end of incredibly distorted and biased coverage in the establishment media. This means that it is just as important as it ever was that we have our own means of getting the republican message out, unmediated and direct.[72]

Towards *Daily Ireland*: the Northern Irish and Irish media landscape

For a minority section of the Irish and Northern Irish political landscapes, the republican sphere is a crowded sector in itself. All these publications vie for readership and position, inside and outside of their party circles, with a high density of mainstream media publications and broadcasting outlets. When *Daily Ireland* launched in early 2005, it jostled for position and attention in the most crowded marketplace in the mass media history of Ireland and Northern Ireland. For example, Northern Ireland, with a population of 1.8 million people, counts more than sixty daily and weekly newspaper titles. The fierce degree of competition in the marketplace made the perceived financial viability of the launch of *Daily Ireland* more difficult to understand, especially at a time of Internet-derived fragmentation.

Northern Ireland has three home-produced 'national' dailies: the *Irish News*, the *Newsletter* and the *Belfast Telegraph*, the readerships of which are largely a product of the historic religious and political divides of the state. The *Irish News*, privately owned by the Fitzpatrick family, has deep roots in the Northern Catholic community, and particularly in Belfast, where it is produced. Locally famed for its death notices, which are a mainstay of Northern Catholic life, Rolston highlighted its historical reputation for religious conservatism, saying it was, 'once the dullest, stuffiest daily in Ireland', known for printing 'every syllable uttered by bishops in the Irish hierarchy'.[73] The *Irish News* has built a reputation for excellent news reporting, the aforementioned daily double-page spread of death notices, and a long-established commitment to covering gaelic sports. The GAA's cultural position in the Catholic community has become ever more elevated since the early 1990s and is an important cultural signification of identity. As such, extensive local and national coverage of the games by the *Irish News* was seen as one of the reasons why the paper temporarily eclipsed the *Belfast Telegraph* as the best-selling paper in Northern Ireland in late 2011.[74] Morrison noted of the demise of *Daily Ireland*, that people refused to place death notices in it, preferring the *Irish News*, and in that respect the *Irish News* was described as an 'idiosyncratic service for the Catholic community'.[75] Investment by the *Irish News* in increased edition sizes and extended coverage, as well as a refusal from the late 2000s onwards to give away all its copy for free online, has meant that the paper's rate of circulation decline has been less rapid than either the *Telegraph* or *Newsletter*.

The aggressive presence of British tabloids and qualities in the Irish marketplace offers significant competition to local dailies of every shade. The *Daily Mirror*, the *Sun* and the *Daily Mail* have strong presences in both Northern Ireland and the Republic of Ireland, with the *Sun* and the *Mirror* recording the best circulations. Added to these, in Northern Ireland, are forty weekly titles, including the *Derry Journal*, which has a historically prominent role in the life of the city. The Dublin-produced *Irish Times* and *Irish Independent* may have a disproportionate political influence locally as they represent less than 2 per cent of total daily sales, and the salacious Dublin tabloid, the *Sunday World*, has a dedicated Belfast edition office and revels in exposés of dissident republican and criminal gangs on both sides of the border. When taken in totality, the crowded marketplace for papers was a difficult one to successfully infiltrate when *Daily Ireland* emerged in 2005.

Broadcasting is a huge presence in the marketplace, with the BBC's Northern Ireland services among the most trusted and popular regional services in the corporation. BBC Radio Ulster takes the largest share of the local audience.[76] Ulster Television, with regional television and commercial radio interests, is an important presence. There are also a number of online media news aggregators and newsgathering services which have sizeable audiences. This media proliferation, along with historic anti-republican bias, has made it difficult for republicans to gain a foothold with which to develop a platform. History has told us that when that has occurred, they have turned to publishing their own journals and papers, and this era would be no different.

Andersonstown News and *Daily Ireland*: 'the voice of banana republicanism' and 'the ghost of Grizzlyism future'[77]

The *Andersonstown News* is a perfect touchstone to the political and social mobility of Sinn Féin, an active symbol of the cultural transition from resistance and countercultural force to a central element of the establishment mainstream. The first edition in 1972 showed the concerns of the nationalist community in Belfast at a turbulent period of history, urging abstention from the Northern Ireland Parliament elections and calling for rates and rent strikes.[78] Established then as a community newspaper by photographer Basil McLaughlin with the profits he made from distributing the best-selling anti-internment song, 'The Men Behind the Wire', it has since 1972 developed into one of the most successful newspaper groups in Belfast.[79] Its archive, particularly of McLaughlin's photographs taken during some of the most violent episodes of the Troubles, captures the history of West and North Belfast during the 1990s–2000s. O'Ruairc noted, 'The *Andersonstown News* was very much the product of a disenfranchised, disaffected and unofficial subculture, strongly reflecting the socio-political location of the Nationalist underclass.'[80]

The paper has always had a close relationship with Sinn Féin, especially in the period when both came to be dominant players in local political and economic life. This was strengthened in 1997 when Máirtín Ó'Muilleoir bought a controlling share of what would become the Belfast Media Group. In every sense, the Belfast Media Group is a modern mainstream media company which has diversified beyond print titles. The core paper, the *Andersonstown News*, is a bi-weekly title and has satellite titles in North and South Belfast. The group also owns the *Irish Echo* newspaper in New York. It took over the Irish-language paper *Lá*, which closed in 2008, and in the wake of this and the failure of *Daily Ireland*, it has diversified its platforms away from traditional print formats to include television production and events management. Its Irish-language documentary company, Bóthar Ard has produced programmes for the Republic of Ireland's public service Irish-language channel, TG4 and its media management company hosts events in Belfast and New York. The company also ran the online news site *Irelandclick.com*, but has also since shut it down through a failure to develop a sufficient revenue stream. If the Fanon model was to take control of the means of communication, the *Andersonstown News* and the Belfast Media Group have done so.

However, rather than being a simple ideological or propagandist exercise, this represented the mainstreaming of republicanism ideologically and economically, the move from the social and economic margins to being a symbol of the risen people. The new prosperous Catholic middle-class entrepreneurial sector is represented by a home-grown media outlet that is structurally central to its community. Ó'Muilleoir, a former lord mayor of Belfast and Stormont finance minister, is one of the pioneers of Sinn Féin electoral politics in the city, and is individually emblematic of Susan Herbst's model for the political and economic transformations of former counterpublics who contest power politically in a long-term structured fashion. Her study of Chicago's black community from 1930 to the 1960s makes note of the changing function of the counterpublic as a political and social organizing structure for Western political movements in pursuit of equality. When leaders of the excluded black community 'gained access to the city's official public sphere, that community's counterpublic sphere was no longer needed.'[81] In Belfast, the radical newspaper of the 1970s was not required in the 2000s, when the political and economic influence of the republican community had become more mainstream.

The *Andersonstown News* has remained profitable in the early twenty-first century, despite the economic downturn. It still circulates around 25,000 newspapers a week across a range of Belfast postcodes in which there are significant Catholic populations. The bi-weekly main edition still has an average circulation of more than 10,000 sales.[82] The range of advertising reflects its centrality to life in West and North Belfast, with a large number of local retailers and estate agents prominent. It has also been a barometer of political feeling in the Catholic community and a leading opinion former in that space: 'it is a source of information and identity for the local community. If you want to know how the Nationalist community feels, the Andytown News is a good place to start.'[83] The paper's long-term editor, Robin Livingstone said, 'if West Belfast really is the cockpit of the North, the Andytown News has become its instrument panel.'[84] Since the mid 2000s, the paper has absorbed the dominant discourses and aesthetic tropes of corporate mainstream media. Senior editorial staff have worked with external consultants to modernize its design, and Ó'Muilleoir cited the *Daily Mail* and European tabloids as influences on production.[85] O'Rourke noted, 'The importance of the coverage given to topics like crime or local sporting celebrities in recent years put the paper more in the league of the *Sunday World* than the paper in its early years.'[86]

The paper's close relationship with Sinn Féin has seen it accused of being both an extra arm of the system that suppresses dissent in republican Belfast as well as being a sycophantic space of 'dear leaderism'. O'Rourke and Bean noted both vanity and self-satisfaction in the paper's coverage.[87] Lynch was more brutal in his evaluation of its achievements, saying it 'serves much the same function for Sinn Féin as Pravda once did for the Soviet politburo and that Fox News now does for the Bush administration. It is a dependable organ of banana republicanism, promoting Dear Leadership and attacking dissenters with zeal.'[88] There were attacks on those that satirized and criticized Sinn Féin and Belfast Media Group papers. The Group moved to close the satire site the *Portadown News*, which had repeatedly derided the paper and its Sinn Féin sympathies.[89] On other occasions it had threatened the *Blanket*, which maintained steadfast critiques of the paper and the symbiotic relationship between it and Sinn Féin. McIntyre said of the *Andersonstown News*: 'its love of censorship makes even Conor Cruise O'Brien appear liberal.'[90] Splintered Sunrise was more direct in his situation of the role of the *Andersonstown News*:

> Máirtín Ó Muilleoir and his little media empire are able to fly kites over sensitive issues, thus giving Gerry some plausible deniability while at the same time campaigning among the base for the route Gerry wants to take. It could therefore best be described as the Ghost of Grizzlyism Future.[91]

In this respect the paper serves a similar political role in the presentation of Sinn Féin policy as the *Irish News* column of senior party advisor and *Republican News* alumnus, Jim Gibney, who was also regularly accused of 'dear leaderism'.[92] Gibney's role has often been to 'fly ideological kites to test reaction among activists'.[93] Splintered Sunrise pointed to the *Andersonstown News*'s championing of policing and justice reforms in 2007 as evidence of its role in flying kites.[94]

The final influence on the development of the *Andersonstown News* (and *Daily Ireland*) was a vehement hatred of the *Irish News*'s constitutional nationalist standpoint and regular criticism of republicanism. Morrison described republican frustration with the fact that the *Irish News* remained supportive of the SDLP at a time of Sinn Féin majority.[95] This was a long-term bugbear of the party, with the *Irish News* being described as 'fanatically pro-SDLP' in the *An Phoblacht* commemorating the death of Bobby Sands in May 1981.[96] The depth of antipathy held by senior republicans for the *Irish News* is difficult to overstate and, in part, the development of 'mainstream' republican newspapers was a reaction to this. In one sense, senior Sinn Féin activists viewed the increased vote for Sinn Féin as a direct snub to the *Irish News*'s anti-republican line over three decades. This was the impetus to launch a paper that would reflect this change in the body politic of nationalism. These senior activists did not seem to realize that Sinn Féin had grown despite the critiques of the *Irish News*.

Daily Ireland was a transparent attempt at capturing part of the Northern Catholic nationalist population that also appeared to represent a newly defined demographic with profitable potential that could potentially help sustain a new newspaper's sales. However, this social group already bought regional newspapers like the *Irish News* and was also a significant factor in the growth of local editions of British nationals in Ireland. The mistake of the Belfast Media Group and, by extension, Sinn Féin, was to believe that the relatively recent increase in support for the party and republican politics and affirmation of Irish cultural identity in Northern Ireland, would be clearly linked to the media politics of newspaper readership. The often caricatured left/right divide in media readership in Britain and the Republic of Ireland was never as clear as it was portrayed by some; a significant number of the working class bought the *Daily Mail* in Britain, and the left/right divide in the Republic was much more difficult to discern in newspaper buying habits.[97] Overall, the major mistake made by the Belfast Media Group was the belief that the cultural legacy of the commitment of the *Irish News* to serving the nationalist community could be overhauled and transferred to the readership for a new newspaper in a short period of time, especially at a time when the market was experiencing significant contraction in sales in the English speaking world due to the rapid development and adoption of Internet technologies.

Daily Ireland: 'A new era for nationalism'[98]

Daily Ireland (2005–2006) was the Belfast Media Group's attempt at restructuring not just the republican sphere, but the wider media sphere, with an all-Ireland newspaper that was 'a credible and readable pro-United

Ireland, pro-Peace Process newspaper for a section of the community that has been largely ignored over the years.'[99] A blogger for *Sluggerotoole* defined the experiment as an expression of freedom from media marginalization and also of the shifting realities of the 'battle for the hearts and minds of a nationalist community in flux.'[100] For twenty months *Daily Ireland* sought to cut a new space in the culturally staid world of Irish newspapers, but eventually closed because it failed to build a circulation large enough to attract government and commercial retail advertising. Its circulation has been contested, but a registered ABC circulation figure of 10,000 was half of that required to survive. Its development was born out of the sense of ideological marginalization and dislocation felt by republicans for whom no newspaper was seen to be in any way sympathetic to their cause. Although there has been a thawing of the *Irish News*'s critical stance on Sinn Féin, especially with Gibney being given a column and former SDLP councillor and columnist Brian Feeney becoming less antagonistic towards Sinn Féin, republicans have remained critical of the paper. Morrison noted, 'I see no "greening" of the *Irish News* other than Jim Gibney's column, and that only happened after Máirtín Ó'Muilleoir announced he was planning a daily paper.'[101]

Daily Ireland launched directly into the same geographic heartland of the *Irish News*: the nine counties of pre-partition Ulster along with Sligo, Leitrim and Louth. It also followed the template of papers in the Andersonstown News Group, centrally implicated in further consolidating the post-GFA republican identity: 'a prerequisite of a strong, united, assertive community is a daily paper, which is independent and authoritative, as well as being built around the image of the community it serves.'[102] The paper started life with the working title *Ireland Today*, before Rupert Murdoch's News International took legal action for breach of the Ireland Today trademark that it owned.[103] Rechristened *Daily Ireland*, it was aimed at the 'self-confident constituency emerging from a traumatic period of conflict, yet it has no daily newspaper which gives voice to its concerns and views.'[104] The paper, however much it tried to separate itself from Sinn Féin, was umbilically linked, perhaps solipsistically, to a belief that the success of the party represented a definitive and lasting change in the cultural and political make-up of Ireland. 'Sinn Féin polls very well in border counties. There is a readership with an appetite for it, but they will have to resist being dominated by Belfast,' said Morrison prior to its launch.[105] Gibney described the launch of *Daily Ireland* as the 'most exciting development in Irish journalism' in his lifetime:

> In the current climate of the Peace Process it is obvious that there is not only a niche for *Daily Ireland* across this country; there is also a political

imperative, a demand, that there should be such a paper. The IRA's cessation and the political process that has emerged has created a new reality for republicans and nationalists committed to a united Ireland.[106]

The fact that the Troubles had been told in the mainstream media, to a large extent, through critiques of republicanism and the dominant ideology of the British and Irish states, was a major catalyst for *Daily Ireland*. It was in a mainstream publication, rather than the marginalized activist space, that republicans would assume the next stage of the struggle. Sean Maguire, news editor of the paper, overtly linked its coverage to a republican sense of grievance against the state, saying some

> [j]ournalists refused to ask tough questions about collusion, plastic bullet deaths, shoot to kill policies and torture. The media had failed to cover the conflict in any even-handed manner. There was a failure to examine the causes of the conflict, or by doing that or engaging in that process begin to tease out solutions to the conflict. We are trying to create a media prepared to ask tough and searching questions.[107]

Daily Ireland was a legitimate commercial journalism attempt at developing a cogent, mainstream republican voice. It employed established and prominent figures from the Irish journalism milieu, including Danny Morrison, Jude Collins, the academic Damien Kiberd, Tom McGurk and the dramatist and former Hunger Striker Dr Laurence McKeown. It also had voices from outside of nationalism, including evangelical Protestant John Coulter, who also wrote for the *Blanket*, and former Green Party MEP Patricia McKenna. It also developed a significant strength in sports coverage, particularly in GAA, in which it invested heavily, and the paper's staff claimed to have rivalled the coverage of the *Irish News*, which remains the market leader.[108] However, while competing on editorial quality alone was one aspect of the paper's plan, the economic factors were much more important. *Daily Ireland* was an expression of economic confidence in the new Sinn Féin electorate's prosperity and its thirst for news told from the party's vantage point, but this demographic grouping was either not large enough or not committed enough to the political project to sustain the publication of a daily newspaper.

Strong economic factors underpinned the launch of the paper. First, bucking the trend of plunging revenues in the rest of the Western mainstream media space, advertising revenues in Northern Ireland, linked particularly to the overwhelmingly dominant public sector, remained buoyant. With 60 per cent of the population employed by the public sector, recruitment advertising was a staple of the local print media industry. This was also supplemented by the newly ubiquitous presence of British high street retailers and supermarket chains in Ireland, which had increasingly colonized Northern Ireland since the end of the conflict and the signing of the GFA. These had remained the cornerstone of display advertising revenues in the British national and regional news market, even in the period of diversification online. The Belfast Media Group hoped to take a small section of this market to keep *Daily Ireland* open, and grow. Ó'Muilleoir said, 'The profit levels of all the newspapers in the North are in rude health. There is a clear business opportunity for a newspaper that's more nationalist in flavour.'[109] However, *Daily Ireland* launched at a time when large amounts of revenue, not associated with these sectors of the print advertising market, began to migrate to the Internet, including non-public sector recruitment advertising. Although the Belfast Media Group would portray its failure as being linked to the Northern Ireland Office and the British government not spreading its public sector advertising to a republican-supporting news organization, evidence suggests that this was a more deep rooted problem affecting the wider print media sector. Perched between the economic downturn of the early 2000s and the most recent recession since 2008 and the collapse of the markets that sustained older print media, *Daily Ireland* represented a failed attempt at launching a legacy media product in the digital era, and not simply another example of anti-republican British discrimination.

The second financial factor that framed the establishment of *Daily Ireland* was the availability of government subsidies and start-up grants for businesses. This came with a precarious business model, if it had one at all, and was at the whim of changes in government policy. The Belfast Media Group had been built in some part on accessing government grants and was perhaps the highest profile example of a new manifestation of public/private financing. When it operated the Irish-language daily *Lá*, it did so based on a subsidy, rather than on the market-based model of commercial media organizations. After it took over *Lá*, it received £357,000 a year from Foras na Gaeilge, the body set up after the GFA to promote the use of the Irish language across the island.[110] When the subsidy was withdrawn in 2008 due to insufficient sales and circulation, and linked to cuts in budgets post-Celtic Tiger, *Lá* was closed with the loss of eight jobs. In this there is an interesting correlation between *Daily Ireland* and *Lá*, with both shutting partly because they failed to build large enough circulations to attract subsidies.

The Belfast Media Group, in the years prior to the establishment of *Daily Ireland*, received more than £550,000 of funding from the Department of Social Development, most of which was used in development of Teach Basil, the group's headquarters and printing hub.[111] Unionist politicians, including Lady Sylvia Hermon, described it as 'outrageous' that 'an avowedly republican newspaper' should receive public funding.[112] The *Irish*

News was more bullish, noting that, 'in the last five years no daily newspaper in Northern Ireland has received any public funding while Mr Ó'Muilleoir's group has been handed in excess of £500,000 from the British exchequer during this period.' Noel Doran, the *Irish News* editor, questioned why a newspaper group, reputedly worth £10m, was receiving public funding:

> Newspapers stand on their own two feet. The idea that the government should provide money to help fund a daily newspaper seems a little curious. Should somebody else be handed large chunks of government money to compete with us? It's difficult to see how that could be justified.[113]

Daily Ireland did not receive any revenue from the British government in the shape of recruitment advertising, although the *Andersonstown News* did after it suspended a ban on security forces advertising in the 1990s.[114] When it pitched for this advertising, it was asked to provide an official Audited Bureau of Circulation figure, to attain the revenue. Despite providing an ABC figure of 10,800, *Daily Ireland* never received the advertising and closed on 8 September 2006, with the loss of fifteen jobs. Ó'Muilleoir said, 'during this crucial period in *Daily Ireland*'s development, we were the only local daily denied job advertisements.'[115] He noted to the UK trade paper, *Press Gazette*,

> *Daily Ireland* played a vital role in promoting the nationalist case at a time when McCarthyism and anti-nationalist voices were in the ascendancy. We are very proud of the achievements of the *Daily Ireland* team over the past 20 months. We hope we have inspired others to take up where we have left off and that this is more a time-out than an ending.[116]

If *Daily Ireland* was an attempt at cutting a traditional republican alternative in the mainstream media market, in the manner of the *Irish Press* of the 1930s, Anthony McIntyre was perhaps more realistic: 'Up against the *Irish Independent* and *Irish Times* there was space for a newspaper saying something radically different. Perhaps had *Daily Ireland* been launched to fill the vacuum created a decade ago when the *Irish Press* folded it may have proved a much more successful venture.'[117] Other figures on the *Blanket* were harsher in their evaluation: 'We've recently heard a lot from Sinn Féin about how it's following in the footsteps of Che Guevara. Imagine Che filling in the forms to fund a revolutionary newspaper?'[118]

In the end, sources close to *Daily Ireland* acknowledge that the £3m start-up capital it received from outside investors was never going to be a big enough war chest to sustain it in an era of contracting circulations and changing news consumption.[119] Danny Morrison stated, 'It would have taken ten years to have started and sustained the paper and to have attracted investment.'[120] His rueful paean to the paper's unrealized propagandist potential was, 'It would only have worked if there was a change in circumstances and it was bought by a philanthropic Friedrich Engels who moved me in as editor. It was an important experiment.'[121]

Notes

1 Cited in Kellner, Douglas, 'Globalisation, technopolitics and revolution', in Foran, John (ed.), *The Future of Revolutions: Rethinking Political and Social Change in the Age of Globalization* (London: Zed Books, 2003), p. 180.
2 Hedges interview.
3 Ó'Broin interview.
4 Ó'Broin interview.
5 Ó'Broin interview.
6 Hedges interview.
7 Moloney, *A Secret History of the IRA*, p. 180.
8 Whiting, ' "The discourse of defence" '.
9 Quoted in O'Brien, Gillian, ' "Spirit, impartiality and independence": "the Northern Star, 1792–1797', *Eighteenth-Century Ireland /Iris an dá chultúr* vol. 13, 1998, p. 7.
10 Elliott, Marianne, *Wolfe Tone: Prophet of Independence* (London: Yale University Press, 1989), p. 135.
11 Lyons, S.F.L., *Ireland Since the Famine* (London: Fontana, 1973), p. 109.
12 Lyons, *Ireland Since the Famine*, p. 109.
13 Lyons, *Ireland Since the Famine*, p. 127.
14 Anderson, Benedict, *Imagined Communities: Reflections on the Origin and Spread of Nationalism* (New York: Verso Books, 2006), p. 36.
15 Legg, Marie-Louise, *Newspapers and Nationalism: The Irish Provincial Press 1850–1892* (Dublin: Four Courts Press, 1999).
16 Lyons, *Ireland Since the Famine*, p. 415.
17 Lyons, *Ireland Since the Famine*, p. 248.
18 Lyons, *Ireland Since the Famine*, p. 248.
19 Lyons, *Ireland Since the Famine*, p. 248.
20 Lyons, *Ireland Since the Famine*, pp. 258–259 and p. 316. For Sinn Féin's claims of kinship with the *Republic*, see: 'About us', anphoblacht.com, undated. Available at: www.anphoblacht.com/about. Accessed 10 November 2010.
21 Lyons, *Ireland Since the Famine*, p. 280.
22 Quoted in Mac Donncha, Mícheál, 'Centenary of "Irish Freedom" newspaper', anphoblacht.com, 28 October 2010. Available at: www.anphoblacht.com/contents/404. Accessed 10 November 2010.
23 Mac Donncha, 'Centenary of "Irish Freedom" newspaper'.
24 Ó'Drisceoil, Donal, *Peadar O'Donnell* (Cork: Cork University Press, 2001), p. 53.
25 English, Richard, *Irish Freedom: A History of Nationalism in Ireland* (London: Macmillan, 2007), p. 330.

26 'About us', anphoblacht.com.
27 Morrison, Danny, 'Where are the Luddites when you need them?', *An Phoblacht*, 2 June 2010. Available at: www.anphoblacht.com/contents/21713. Accessed 4 July 2010.
28 Hartley interview.
29 Hartley interview. The 1964 British general election in which Liam McMillan of Sinn Féin lost his deposit is also important, as it served as Gerry Adams's introduction to the party. See: Adams, Gerry, *The Politics of Irish Freedom* (Dingle: Brandon, 1986), p. 2.
30 *Andersonstown Central Civil Resistance Committee*, vol. 1, no. 1, November 1972.
31 Hartley interview.
32 Hartley interview.
33 Hartley interview.
34 Hartley interview.
35 Hartley interview.
36 Hartley interview.
37 Adams, *The Politics of Irish Freedom*, p. 163.
38 'Brownie', 'Active abstentionism', *Republican News*, 16 August 1975.
39 Bean, *New Politics of Sinn Féin*, p. 55.
40 Hartley interview.
41 Hartley interview.
42 Hartley interview.
43 Adams, *The Politics of Irish Freedom*, p. 163.
44 Moloney, *A Secret History of the IRA*, p. 180.
45 Morrison, 'Where are the Luddites when you need them?'.
46 McNair, B., *Introduction to Political Communication* (London: Routledge, 2011), p. 171.
47 Quoted in Curtis, *Ireland: The Propaganda War*, p. 273.
48 Hartley interview. See also: Spencer, 'Sinn Féin and the media in Northern Ireland'.
49 Maillot, *New Sinn Féin*, p. 77.
50 Hedges interview.
51 Morrison interview.
52 Curtis, *Ireland*, p. 273.
53 Hedges interview.
54 Hedges interview.
55 Ó'Broin interview.
56 'About us', anphoblacht.com.
57 Sweney, Mark, 'Trinity Mirror to double digital staff', *Guardian*, 3 July 2013. Available at: www.theguardian.com/media/2013/jul/03/trinity-mirror-double-digital-staff. Accessed 3 July 2013. The major mainstream newspaper companies in Britain, particularly those with large regional and local papers that had suffered most from the Internet's siphoning off of readers and advertisers, had resisted a 'digital-first' policy because of the effects it would have on revenue from hard-copy sales. *An Phoblacht*'s largely internal audience

did not pose the same problems, especially from the standpoint of satisfying shareholders.

58 Millar, Scott, 'Republicans battle online', *Sunday Times*, 14 December 2003.

59 Morrison interview.

60 Quoted in Millar, 'Republicans battle online'.

61 See: www.republican-news.org/current/news/. Accessed 20 August 2013.

62 '*An Phoblacht* to take major step forward', *An Phoblacht*, 1 April 2010. Available at: www.anphoblacht.com/contents/21454. Accessed 4 July 2010.

63 Cusack, Jim, 'Ireland's oldest Provo newspaper in danger of falling on its sword', *Sunday Independent*, 9 April 2006. Available at: www.independent.ie/opinion/analysis/irelands-oldest-provo-newspaper-in-danger-of-falling-on-its-sword-26410403.html. Accessed 9 April 2006.

64 'Media view', *An* Phoblacht.com, 5 July 2007. Available at: www.anphoblacht.com/contents/17097. Accessed 4 July 2010.

65 '*An Phoblacht* to take major step forward'.

66 McGregor, Mark, '*An Phoblacht* – expanding through consolidation or going digital, then gone?', *Sluggerotoole*, 2 April 2010. Available at: www.sluggerotoole.com/2010/04/02/an-phoblacht-expanding-through-consolidation-or-going-digital-then-gone/. Accessed 3 April 2010.

67 Ó'Broin interview.

68 Ó'Broin interview.

69 Hedges interview.

70 Ó'Broin interview.

71 Hedges interview.

72 '*An Phoblacht* to take major step forward'.

73 Rolston, Bill, 'News fit to print: Belfast's daily newspapers', in Rolston, Bill (ed.), *The Media and Northern Ireland: Covering the Troubles* (London: Macmillan, 1991), p. 161.

74 Greenslade, Roy, '*Irish Times* sale falls by 9% and *Irish News* overtakes the *Belfast Telegraph*', *Guardian*, 22 August 2013. Available at: www.theguardian.com/media/greenslade/2013/aug/22/ireland-abcs. Accessed 22 August 2013. See also: Alan in Belfast, '*Irish News* now sells more full price copies than *Belfast Telegraph*', *Sluggerotoole*, 24 August 2012. Available at: www.sluggerotoole.com/2012/08/24/irish-news-now-sells-more-full-price-copies-than-belfast-telegraph/. Accessed 24 August 2012.

75 Morrison interview.

76 'Most popular radio stations, by total share', *mediauk*, June 2013. Available at: http://www.mediauk.com/radio/data/total-share. Accessed 2 July 2013.

77 Lynch, E. '*Andersonstown News*: voice of banana republicanism?', *Irish Echo*, 11 June 2003. See also: Splintered Sunrise, 'Preas Na Poblachta', *Splintered Sunrise*, 31 January 2007. Available at: www.splinteredsunrise.wordpress.com/2007/01/31/preas-na-poblachta/. Accessed 31 January 2007. The blogger playfully refers to Gerry Adams as 'Grizzly Adams' in reference to the bearded American outdoors man popularized by a 1970s TV series. The official Sinn Féin line is therefore known on the blog as 'Grizzlyism'.

78 O'Rourke, Liam, 'From alternative press to corporate mainstream: the case of the Andersonstown News', *Vacuum*, No. 14, n. d. (2004?). Available at: www. thevacuum.org.uk/issues/issues0120/issue14/is14artandnew.html. Accessed 4 July 2010. This is O'Ruairc writing under his anglicized surname.

79 '*Andersonstown News* founder, Basil McLaughlin dies', *BBC News Online*, 28 January 2010. Available at: www.news.bbc.co.uk/1/hi/northern_ireland/8484650.stm. Accessed 2 February 2010.

80 O'Rourke, 'From alternative press to corporate mainstream'.

81 Hauser, Gerard R., 'Prisoners of conscience and the counterpublic sphere of prison writing: the stones that start the avalanche', in Asen, Robert, and Brouwer, Daniel, C. (eds), *Counterpublics and the State* (Albany, NY: SUNY Press, 2001), p 37.

82 Linford, Paul, 'ABCs: only three paid-for weeklies increase print sales', *Hold the Front Page*, 25 May 2015. Available at: www.holdthefrontpage.co.uk/2015/news/abcs-only-three-paid-for-weeklies-increase-print-sales/. Accessed 25 May 2015.

83 O'Rourke, 'From alternative press to corporate mainstream'.

84 Quoted in O'Rourke, 'From alternative press to corporate mainstream'.

85 Quoted in O'Rourke, 'From alternative press to corporate mainstream'.

86 O'Rourke, 'From alternative press to corporate mainstream'.

87 Bean, *New Politics of Sinn Féin*, p. 102.

88 Lynch, '*Andersonstown News*'.

89 '*Andersonstown News*'.

90 McIntyre, Anthony, 'Volunteer Robin Livingstone', *Blanket*, 7 June 2004. Available at: www.indiamond6.ulib.iupui.edu:81/volsycophant.html. Accessed 4 July 2010. Writer and journalist Conor Cruise O'Brien was a long-term critic of Sinn Féin and PIRA.

91 Splintered Sunrise, 'Preas Na Poblachta'.

92 McIntyre, A., 'The Bogeymen', *Blanket*, 19 November 2006. Available at: www. indiamond6.ulib.iupui.edu:81/AM3191106g.html. Accessed 4 July 2010.

93 Bean, *New Politics of Sinn Féin*, p. 185.

94 Splintered Sunrise, 'Preas Na Poblachta'.

95 Morrison interview. For the use of *Daily Ireland* as a vehicle for denouncing dissidents, see: Morrison, Danny, 'When one does not mind being called a Provo', *Daily Ireland*, 6 September 2006.

96 Delaney, Sean, 'Dublin press worried', *An Phoblacht*, 9 May 1981.

97 For a breakdown of the readership of British newspapers, the last reliable source is Tunstall, J., *Newspaper Power* (Oxford: Oxford University Press, 1996).

98 Máirtín Ó'Muilleoir quoted in 'Ambitious plans for new daily launched', Irelandclick.com, 31 May 2004.

99 'More Daily Ireland staff take up posts in West Belfast', Irelandclick.com, 6 January 2005.

100 Belfast Gonzo, 'Daily Ireland causing a stir in the media', *Sluggerotoole*, 31 January 2005. Available at: www.sluggerotoole.com/2005/01/31/daily_ireland_causing_stir_in_media/. Accessed 31 January 2005.

101 Morrison interview.
102 'Ambitious plans for new daily launched'.
103 Timms, Dominic, 'Newspaper not going to appeal Murdoch', *Guardian*,11 June 2004. Available at: www.theguardian.com/media/2004/jun/11/newsinternational.pressandpublishing. Accessed 5 July 2010.
104 Friel, Laura, 'Planned nationalist daily hits set back', *An Phoblacht*, 3 June 2004.
105 Quoted in Walsh, Jason, 'New Irish newspaper draws fire', *Great Reporter*, 14 February 2005. Available at: www.greatreporter.com/content/new-irish-newspaper-draws-fire. Accessed 17 July 2017. The article was originally written for the *Independent*, but was spiked. Information from author.
106 Gibney, Jim, 'Failte Daily Ireland', *An Phoblacht*, 3 March 2005.
107 Quoted in 'News they like', *Fourthwrite*, No. 23, Autumn 2005.
108 Morrison interview.
109 'Nationalist daily for all of Ireland', *Brand Republic*, 1 June 2004. Available at: www.brandrepublic.com/news/515932/Nationalist-daily-Ireland/?DCMP= ILC-SEARCH.
110 'Irish language newspaper to close', *Belfast Telegraph*, 16 December 2008. Available at: www.belfasttelegraph.co.uk/news/local-national/irish-language-newspaper-to-close-28461318.html. Accessed 5 July 2010.
111 'Anger at funding for newspaper', *Irish News*, 8 July 2004. See also: Twomey, Carrie, 'Fury at community newspaper funding', *Blanket*, 8 July 2004. Available at: www.indiamond6.ulib.iupui.edu:81/atn.html. Accessed 5 July 2010.
112 Cusack, Jim, 'Funding row erupts over republican newspaper', *Sunday Independent*, 18 July 2004.
113 Quoted in McNamee, Paul, 'New kid on the nationalist block', *Guardian*, 31 January 2005. Available at: www.theguardian.com/media/2005/jan/31/mondaymediasection5. Accessed 6 July 2010.
114 O'Rourke, 'From alternative press to corporate mainstream'.
115 Quoted in McCaughren, Samantha, 'Nationalist paper closes in Belfast', *Irish Independent*, 6 September 2006. Available at: www.independent.ie/business/irish/nationalist-paper-closes-in-belfast-26363908.html. Accessed 6 July 2010.
116 '*Daily Ireland* newspaper to close', *Press Gazette*, 7 September 2006. Available at: www.pressgazette.co.uk/node/35566. Accessed 6 July 2010.
117 McIntyre, Anthony, 'Dreary Ireland', *Blanket*, 24 April 2005. Available at: www.indiamond6.ulib.iupui.edu:81/am2404056g.html. Accessed 6 July 2010.
118 Adams, G., 'Bye bye Daily Lies', *Blanket*, 10 September 2006. Available at: www.indiamond6.ulib.iupui.edu:81/GA10090618g.html. This author is Geraldine Adams, a Belfast contributor to the *Blanket*.
119 Morrison interview.
120 Morrison interview.
121 Morrison interview.

5

A republican digital counterculture?
Fourthwrite and the *Blanket*

The republican leadership had for long made much of the concept of 'community as one'. There would be no alternative voices. Sean Russell rather than Peadar O'Donnell being the role model that suited best.[1]

If Sinn Féin's response to the changing political landscape and the rise of the Internet was to dynamically restructure its own activist media output and the internal dynamics of the Irish republican sphere in the process, then the online world was a space that would also inspire and partially sustain two magazines that would contest the line of 'official Provisionalism'. Within the context of definitions of activist journalism, *Fourthwrite* and the *Blanket* are significant artefacts of republican activist media in the post-GFA era because they remain two of the best-quality republican magazines produced at any time in recent republican history, and were sustained examples of committed, high-quality activist journalism. They deserve to be analysed in greater depth for no other reason that, unlike many party and organization papers and websites which struggled to sustain momentum in the same period, they ran for significant lifetimes, and their influence can be measured by traditional means, through sales and influence. *Fourthwrite* in its initial phase was selling hundreds of copies in Belfast bookshops, and more than Belfast's then highly regarded current affairs magazine, *Fortnight*.[2] The *Blanket*, after being picked up by the Irish news-related aggregation service *Nuzhound*, had more than 15,000 hits daily and achieved a significantly higher readership in its later years, particularly when it ran a series of articles controversially addressing Islam and free speech.[3] The *Blanket* had achieved more than 22 million total unique page views even before courting controversy in 2006 by publishing cartoons of the prophet Muhammad.[4] Both magazines were also significant enough contributions to the period to have been cited in key academic and political examinations of republicanism since the GFA, including those of Bean, Frampton and McDonald.[5]

Within the confines of the development of the public sphere and activist journalism since the development of the Internet, *Fourthwrite* and the

Blanket also reflected the transformations in political communication for grassroots and activist political movements. These magazines were the first spaces in which the new counterpublics of Irish republicanism found a space to exist and develop. They were spaces which represented political opinion away from the state and the highly controlled republican sphere. These magazines captured the existential crisis of those former Provisionals left behind by the process, dissident and dissenting republicans, unionists and loyalists willing to start dialogue with republicans, and associated members of the Irish American political diaspora. It was perhaps in the inclusion of loyalists that the magazines diverged most from the polarized space that is republican activist media.

The *Blanket*, an online magazine without the fixed costs of printing and distribution that previous generations relied upon for exposure, was able to publish prolifically and without constraints or censorship. This allowed it to circumvent the traditional challenges faced by marginalized groups. Its editor, Carrie McIntyre said:

> The Internet is so freaking easy, I did this while I had a baby and we had no money. I had a friend who had a server and very kindly hosted it for free. It wasn't about making money or making a name for anyone. It was about debate and discussion and fighting against censorship and giving voice to the voiceless pushing against the [Provisional] narrative that was going at the time. It was important to highlight intimidation and the attacks on people outside the Sinn Féin machine, to give them an outlet.[6]

Both the *Blanket* and *Fourthwrite*'s sustainability was also remarkable at a time when the explosion of the blogosphere saw a high attrition rate for activist journalism projects not linked to political parties. *Fourthwrite* published in hard-copy format for more than eleven years (2000–2011, and concurrently online to 2010), and the *Blanket* ran for more than six and a half years (2001–2008). These were magazines that moved away from the specifically republican hinterlands and correspondents from political organizations, and often featured senior academics and mainstream political writers.[7] In the *Blanket*'s case, it gave a platform for anyone who wanted to offer a political analysis on most political issues. Neither magazine was afraid to take on difficult issues in the area of free speech – the *Blanket* encountered the anger of many when it published the controversial cartoons of Muhammad and profiles of the artists behind them in 2006, thus alienating a significant number of its own left-wing writers and readers.[8] If one of the key attributes of activist or alternative journalism in the online period is the contestation of hegemony and dominant ideology, then *Fourthwrite* and the *Blanket* were the foundation for a new means of seeking another republicanism away from both the establishment and the dissident. They contested the immediate dominant narrative and control of Sinn Féin in their own communities and the wider mediated propaganda of peace, while gathering attention in the macro-political sphere. They were, as previously noted, deeply committed to peace, if not the process, and whether they were successful in finding another way or a solution to the GFA's failure to deliver the aims of republicanism remains moot. However, that perhaps misses the point of both magazines, which were primarily organs of dissent which saw their primary functions as fostering alternative debate as a process of circumventing internal establishment republican censorship. However, it must be noted that while these magazines hosted and encouraged debate, as will be noted later, they rarely provided solutions to the problems presented by the internal crisis caused by establishment republicanism's compromise. What is vital to any examination of the magazines is that they came out of a very specific set of social and political circumstances in Belfast and Northern Ireland. It is necessary to foreground the direct events of the post-GFA period and the power and dominance of Sinn Féin, and its administration of this power in all levels of the republican community.

These endeavours have to be seen as a collective approach to an overall project that began with a small number of writers and activists in the pre-1998 period and which had its roots in the prisons, and that tried to contest the pervasive social and political control that Sinn Féin had wrested in the post-1998 period when it began to supplant the SDLP as the majority nationalist party in Northern Ireland. To those that were part of the Bobby Sands Discussion Group, which begat the Irish Republican Writers Group, which in turn spawned *Fourthwrite*, the gradual move of the Provisionals away from separatism towards post-GFA constitutionalism was scant reward for the years they had spent in prison, sometimes after being involved in blanket protests and hunger strikes. For some of those that would write for the magazines, their dissatisfaction with the Provisionals began while in jail, along with their first forays into activist publishing. Tommy McKearney, the editor of *Fourthwrite*, resigned from PIRA in 1986 after the abolition of abstentionism. He began publishing *Congress '86*, the quarterly journal of his new group, the League of Communist Republicans, while in jail, often producing it by himself.[9] His commitment to the Do-It-Yourself ethos of activist and alternative media, while within the kind of counterpublic discussed in chapter one, was remarkable. The journal was initially financed by fundraising efforts by his sister, and it was able to run from 1987–1991, with the fourteen editions being between twelve and twenty pages in size. Print runs ran between 500 and 1,000 copies and O'Ruairc notes that *Congress* (as it was named after Issue 9) was innovative enough to have inspired the PIRA titles *Iris Bheag* and later *An Glór Gafa*.[10]

McIntyre had been a contributor to *Iris Bheag*, and continued his journalism after his release from jail.

The Northern Ireland Assembly and the deepening of partition were not what they had fought for. However, these issues were secondary to the perception that the establishment republican movement was guilty of silencing any sign of criticism within its own community, whether that was the jail community or that on the 'outside'. It is in this period that the initial contest of hegemony occurred. Outside of the jails and in the post-1998 timeframe, *Fourthwrite* and the *Blanket* emerged specifically because Provisional power in this period pervasively expressed itself in Gramscian terms, as both hard and soft power.[11] The party, through the rump of PIRA, continued to 'enforce' the peace, while it had extended its influence in the political and community sector which further enhanced its social control. This power manifested itself in many ways: in the murders of Real IRA man Joe O'Connor in 2000 and Robert McCartney in late 2004; in the closing of the spaces for debate in republican society or in direct picketing of those that would seek to offer alternative voices, like the editors of the *Blanket*.[12]

The frequent denunciations of the *Blanket* by the *Andersonstown News* was held by the former to be another insidious form of this social control. Both magazines were based upon a contestation of this power, and spoke often of Sinn Féin's 'Stalinist' tendencies in offering no space for alternative republican voices and 'Orwellian' patterns of thought control.[13] While the magazines were also striving for a republican 'third way', they were doing so as Sinn Féin apparently denied that such an option was possible. It was also enforcing this view rigidly in its own communities. McIntyre, in the first article for the *Blanket*, concluded a piece on censorship saying, 'in an era where the repression of difference is a strategic objective of the powerful, it is imperative that republican writers do not succumb to the temptations of a quiet life. Silence is complicity.'[14] After the pickets on the homes of McIntyre and his fellow dissenter Tommy Gorman in 2000, *Fourthwrite* launched a campaign, 'Democracy – a campaign for freedom for political expression'. Its editorial noted:

> Irish republicanism is not a fixed canon. *Fourthwrite* is beginning the search for a new republican programme and policy. As the IRWG has often said before, this is not something that can be obtained tailor-made from the Oracle nor should it be handed down to us on tablets of stone from 'wise men on mountain tops'.[15]

Fourthwrite and the *Blanket* were important and visible vehicles predicated on contesting there was only one republican way. McKearney, in an unpublished piece submitted later to *Daily Ireland*, drew a direct parallel between the Catholic Irish and traditionalist strands of republicanism in arguing for the extension of the republican sphere to all voices: 'Republicanism always draws its mandate from its contemporary situation, that there is more than one republican movement and disparate though many of us are, none can be excommunicated from the republican community by any or several republican papacies.'[16]

It is impossible to speak of the magazines separately because their genesis and development are so closely tied from before the period under examination. McKearney and McIntyre knew one another from jail, with the latter offering the former a home after his release in 1994.[17] Both were critics of Sinn Féin, although McIntyre remained in the party until 1997/98. With Brendan Hughes and Tommy Gorman, they were founder members of the Bobby Sands Discussion Group in late 1994 prior to the first PIRA ceasefire. Although established to 'throw about ideas generated from whatever quarter and to stage public debates', the Group soon faced opposition from the Sinn Féin leadership:[18]

> It effectively shut down the Bobby Sands discussion group by telling party and army activists that participation in public discussion facilitated by the group was contrary to movement policy and would no longer be tolerated. Republican activists were in fact prevented from intellectually engaging in their own community in collective democratic forum to give the autocratic arrogance of leadership a free run.[19]

After the dissolution of the Bobby Sands Discussion Group they established the Irish Republican Writers Group, with a 'commitment to freedom of political expression and a determination to avoid at all costs the Stalinisation of organisational forms and ideas'.[20] McIntyre more specifically noted:

> The Irish Republican Writers Group emerged at a crucial time in the history of republicanism. The Good Friday Agreement had just been accepted by 96% of the Sinn Féin membership. It seemed, in Foucauldian terms, that the anti-systemic soul of Provisional republicanism was being erased as easily as a face in the sand at the edge of the sea.[21]

McIntyre and McKearney established *Fourthwrite* as an online presence in 1998 in a bid to disseminate their own positions on the GFA and the direction of republicanism.[22] McKearney said, 'Anthony might be more libertarian than I am and I might be a bit more orthodox left. Neither of those terms are perfectly accurate, but we wanted to get a broad range of opinion.'[23] At a time when the online world was growing thanks to the development of the mass market Internet, they gathered a small degree of momentum, with Carrie McIntyre (née Twomey) coming in contact with them from California via various Irish political message boards.[24] They had also been using the letters page of the *Irish News*, as a non-Sinn Féin-supporting newspaper, and that of the *Andersonstown News*, to offer their critiques.[25]

The politically dissenting countercultural online space was central to the development of the *Blanket*. It was there that the McIntyres met and where they fixed the libertarian approach to freedom of speech that the magazine stood for. It was also in this zone where alliances with key media figures, such as Mick Fealty of *Sluggerotoole.com*, were forged.[26] These spaces were interesting as counterpublic spaces in themselves but also within the confines of the Peace Process – in the days before the mass Internet, it was often on the sites of diametrically opposed groups that debate took place. Carrie McIntyre, while still living in California, used the guest book of a unionist website called Peace Book to debate with people posting from across the political spectrum.[27] The libertarian 'wild, anything goes' ethos of spaces like *DebateCentral.com*, which was initially self-moderated then had a policy of light-touch moderation, allowed a multiplicity of voices denied public airing by dominant media and political actors.[28] Developed in 1994 by American postgraduate students Julie Brown and Alan Bond to investigate the Peace Process, the community was established along ideological lines of the countercultural ethos, collectively adopting 'an uncensored, free speech approach' moderated lightly by Brown.[29] However, two factors saw many of the republican posters move on. In an interesting microcosm of the process itself, the community became split along politically sectarian lines and dominated by the contributions of unionists. Secondly, a libellous allegation about a Sinn Féin councillor and his wife, posted in 2001, led to legal action, which saw the site go down for a concerted period of time. The cross-community aspect of both *DebateCentral.com* and *Sluggerotoole*'s earliest incarnation would prove the inspiration for the *Blanket*.[30] Although relatively small counterpublics, their persistence in making themselves visible in this period was important and proved that there was a hinterland that would at least listen and read. They were, of course, tangible evidence of the digital homesteaders of the counterculture in the unlikely setting of the Peace Process:

> People are more savvy about the Internet now, but then it was still quite internal, the behaviour was very Id, it was wild. But it was a community. There was a time that there was a community of unionists and republicans and we got on together – but it has scattered now.[31]

Republicans like Carrie McIntyre naturally emigrated to the safety of republican-specific boards, specifically Sinn Féin's website, run by Fergus O'Dea – which was the most advanced of its kind and had the most extensive email address book – as well as the *Irish Republican Bulletin Board*. This was to be an experience in censorship that was instrumental in the establishment of the *Blanket*. Just as the new republican bloggers and writers sought out these new spaces, Sinn Féin activists quickly moderated them. Dissenting opinion became marginalized or disappeared. The denial of space in which to interact, which also coincided with offline world intimidation of groups of Irish republican dissenting writers, would serve as the catalyst for pockets of dissidence online:

> The Sinn Féin bulletin board was called the Republican Bulletin Board and I had started the *Alternative Republican Bulletin Board* because I had been banned so many times and the discussion had been censored so much. A Sinn Féin member who is a councillor in Derry now had been the *de facto* policeman of the Sinn Féin board, they and their cronies shut down discussion.[32]

Condemnations of the IRWG had seen Carrie contact McIntyre to offer her support and to help in designing the *Fourthwrite* website, and from there their relationship grew. She eventually moved to Belfast in early 2000.[33] The tight group of the IRWG would, along with Liam O'Ruairc and a number of other activists, establish *Fourthwrite* as a hard-copy publication in spring 2000. The development of a hard-copy magazine represented the differences in the group. McKearney, by his own admission, was unconvinced that the Internet was a space that was conducive to their message, while the McIntyres were more evangelical about the medium.[34] Sinn Féin made several attempts at shutting the magazine down, particularly after Gorman and McIntyre accused PIRA of the murder of Joe O'Connor via the letters page of the *Irish News* in September 2000. Carrie McIntyre had also been threatened for revealing details of the murder on the *Alternative Irish Republican Bulletin Board*, which she was still editing. As the pickets and intimidation were stepped up, Danny Morrison offered an official Provisional reaction, damning with faint praise in the *Andersonstown News*:

> [M]any of the articles and analyses in the new magazine have been written by deeply committed republicans who fought and suffered for their convictions, and whose families also suffered. The magazine cannot be ignored – but neither are its views to be specially weighted because of the people from whom they originate. That their opinions might be thoroughly outnumbered by the diametrically opposed views of other ex-lifers, ex-blanketmen or ex-hunger strikers, in support of Sinn Féin policy, does not invalidate the arguments expressed in *Fourthwrite*. Everyone else might be wrong.[35]

Fourthwrite's editorial in edition four, in which the campaign for democracy was launched, referred to the Morrison review, complaining of 'undemocratic efforts made to silence IRWG members and denigrate their magazine'. The climate of fear and reprisal for speaking out against PIRA was a pervasive motivation for those that would establish and run the magazines as well as those that would submit articles. Theirs was activist journalism as protest. Anthony McIntyre said, 'on one level it was about republicanism, but on another it was about censorship, about people telling you what to think.'[36] Within the closed off public sphere space, which was being controlled by Sinn Féin as a means of guarding its own revised republican narrative, the IRWG saw itself as involved in counter hegemonic praxis; the magazines were an activist journalism counterbalance to this climate. Another contributor, who had also left Sinn Féin and been involved in anti-GFA groups, said, 'People were being threatened in their own homes and in public meetings. Ex-prisoners were being threatened. The thought control was immense. Sinn Féin had a McCarthyite vision, they were Stalinist in their thought.'[37]

By the end of 2000, in the midst of ongoing attacks on republican dissident groups which saw the O'Connor murder, McIntyre and Gorman's condemnation of PIRA forced the group to continue their publication in the face of mounting opposition from Sinn Féin. McIntyre noted, 'I said to Tommy Gorman, "the die is cast – the chips are down here, we have no place to go. We have to see it through no matter what the cost, we have to stay firm." '[38]

Towards *Fourthwrite* and the *Blanket*: the mosquito press

The Internet was a natural home for republican dissidents in the early years of the Good Friday Agreement because it was, partially, beyond the influence and control of both the state and establishment republicanism, and because it offered a space in which to interact with ideologically congruent, and disparate, activists. However, while *Fourthwrite* and the *Blanket* appeared through the visibility afforded them by the Internet, and in the offline spaces in which they existed, they were also profound inheritances of an older anti-establishment republican tradition of dissent. As an immediate influence, *An Phoblacht/Republican News*, in its countercultural 1970s/ 1980s period, represented the continuation of a tradition of similar anti-establishment organs from the 1930s to the 1970s. The mosquito press of the 1930s developed a deeply held tradition of high-quality activist journalism which also occasionally broke out of the narrow confines of the republican sphere and found its way into the mainstream. This was the case for some of the content of the seminal 1940/50s literary journal the *Bell*, which was edited by veteran anti-treaty republicans, Seán Ó'Faoláin and Peadar O'Donnell. The term 'mosquito press' was coined first for the Irish separatist papers of the Home Rule period, after a Tory minister noted that he 'would take no more notice of them than of the buzzing of so many mosquitoes'.[39] Also applied in wider studies in anti-colonial literature in Ireland, as well as anti-Marcos-era publications in the Philippines, mosquito press perfectly encapsulates the role of anti-establishment activist journalism, which exists as a less powerful, but still vibrant, counterbalance, or annoyance, to the dominant ideological structures.

O'Donnell and fellow anti-treaty republican Frank Ryan were responsible for the apotheosis of the dissenting Irish republican mosquito press publication, when they resurrected and transformed the fortunes of *An Phoblacht* in the 1930s. The paper became the definitive voice of this strand of anti-treaty republicanism in the period, selling more than 40,000 copies weekly before being closed by de Valera.[40] The description of Ryan's paper as a mix of 'pictures, cartoons, and make-up as they had never seen before in this country, with witty captions in Irish, French, German as well as English', is strikingly similar to the spirit of *AP/RN* in the 1970s under the editorship of Danny Morrison, and the satiric iconoclasm of the *Blanket*.[41] Ní Bheachain's explanation of the editorial content of the anti-imperial papers of the 1930s illustrates deeper republican interests in international issues that also directly correspond to both the 1970s and the contemporary period, particularly that of *Fourthwrite* and the *Blanket*. The 1930s generation focused on the visit of a Basque activist to Dublin in 1933 and had acquired 'a definite unease with the development of global capitalism'.[42] Even the 1930s *An Phoblacht's* highest circulation figure of 40,000 directly corresponds to that of *AP/RN*, which achieved the same sale in 1981 during the Hunger Strikes, when the momentous events of the time allowed it to temporarily break out of its marginalized space as the voice of PIRA.[43]

An Phoblacht in the 1930s was considered 'the most significant paper in post-Independence Ireland'.[44] While neither *AP/RN* nor the *Blanket* could be described as the most significant publications of their time, they were vital contributions to their contemporary republican sphere and allow us a much deeper understanding of its developments and its schisms. If there is a need to categorize *Fourthwrite* and the *Blanket*, it is that they were the continuation of the mosquito press in the Internet age, rather than products of the Internet. Ó'Donghaile situated the *Blanket*, in particular, in the space comparable to that of communist dissent: 'The *Blanket* was samizdat. I always thought that it was like the little journals of the 1970s, the *Volunteer* and *An Fiorscéal* [the *True Voice*), which also opened up debate in the 1970s.[45] Anthony McIntyre was less sure about that reference, but confirmed that they saw this work as samizdat:

The mosquito press was knocking about the republican environment in the 1970s, but they were heavily controlled. We entered a different sphere with the Internet and the *Blanket*. I'm not sure that we were mosquito press, but we performed functions that were very similar to what people in Russia would have done.[46]

Whether samizdat or the mosquito press, the new magazines were buzzing around the dominant narrative of Sinn Féin. McIntyre, in rebutting critiques of *Fourthwrite* in 2000, indicated this apparent reversal of roles. Senior republicans who had used *An Phoblacht/Republican News* in the 1970s to savagely denounce nationalists who had been willing to participate in the Stormont government in the 1970s were publicly advocating the same course of political action just over twenty years later. McIntyre noted: 'The accusation from the pen of Danny Morrison, writing under the pseudonym Peter Arnlis, was that they were collaborators, traitors and opportunists.'[47] The satiric edge of the *Blanket* and *Fourthwrite*, particularly through the latter's often satiric covers, was a direct inheritance from the often anarchic approach of *AP/RN*. The scabrous 'Brigadier' column in *AP/RN*, a satire of the British military establishment written by the anarchist John McGuffin, was a direct predecessor and inspiration for Anthony McIntyre's wickedly satiric anti-Sinn Féin 'Jimmy Sands' and 'Angrytown News' articles in the *Blanket*.[48] The witty subversive streak of the 1930s mosquito press, exemplified by the cartoons of Frank Ryan's *An Phoblacht* of the 1930s, had modern equivalents in *AP/RN*'s 'Cormac' cartoons by Brian Moore, and those of Brian Mór and John Kennedy in the *Blanket*.[49]

Fourthwrite was less overtly satiric in its content beyond the occasionally humorous covers which borrowed from *Private Eye* and the tradition of British and Irish satiric magazines. By and large, its editorial content was more serious and analytical and rarely strayed towards the countercultural spirit of the *Blanket*, which, through the sheer volume of the articles that it published and its online situation, had significantly more space and opportunity to publish satiric material. *Fourthwrite* had an average of twenty-four pages in each edition and was a conventionally left-wing magazine in content and tone, eschewing a lighter tone to pursue regular features on Israel–Palestine, the war in Afghanistan, the growth of the left in Germany with Die Linke and other left-wing-friendly issues. Under McKearney's editorship, *Fourthwrite* sought to articulate republicanism's place within both local and global left-wing concerns, but which also covered issues that affected the working class as central to developing a coherent worldview.[50] Certainly, as the Peace Process progressed, the magazine became less republican focused and developed further into specifically left and left international issues.[51] Splintered Sunrise identified this lack of republican focus, but noted, '*Fourthwrite* is essential reading nonetheless. *Fourthwrite*'s strength, I would say is its weakness – while its openness is to be commended, its lack of a well defined line means it has trouble really taking the lead in a 'recomposition' project.[52]

The *Blanket* had a more flexible anti-ideological stance to the Peace Process which made it a more suitable space in which to destabilize the dominant narratives and fevered egos of politicians of its time. Gerry Adams and Ian Paisley were frequent targets of the Brian Mór and John Kennedy cartoons. Without the need for any agenda other than publication of any material that was submitted, it was not required to develop a cogent worldview in the way that *Fourthwrite* did. McKearney noted that this reflected the personal political perspectives of those producing the magazines: he was a Marxist and ultimately in pursuit of a political project; the McIntyres were libertarian in outlook and not interested in any project other than publishing.[53] This would be the fulcrum around which the *Blanket* would eventually emerge from the *Fourthwrite* project. As McKearney sought to develop a position on the Peace Process and to develop an organization that would become active at some level of republican politics, a schism developed:

> On the crest of a wave the Group suddenly malfunctioned. The old spectre that had long haunted the main body of republicanism had weaved its way into the IRWG – a committee would examine writers' contributions for their suitability. The game was up. Those long time believers in the concept that nothing is impossible until given to a committee called it a day.[54]

McKearney, noting that 'hindsight is not a precise science', said that had a progressive republican left project like éirígí existed in 2000, he probably would have supported it, but there was no left-wing, non-militarist group involved in the Irish republican sphere that was suitable for the political aspirations of either him or others involved in *Fourthwrite*. Of establishing a republican alternative, he noted, 'the conditions weren't favourable at the time. A lot of people maintained a lot of faith in Sinn Féin that they aren't doing now.'[55] For the McIntyres, the situation was more fundamentally about a threat to freedom of speech and closing up the space that they had forged:

> Tommy had proposed it should be anti-agreement and have a mission statement, make it more activist. We were aghast because the whole thing was about freedom of speech – once you start declaring a position it shuts down freedom of speech. It was about teasing out all the views and you can't shut out the pro-agreement people, we have to hear their views. We weren't against activism, the act of writing and act of analysis *was* activism to our minds. In the end the more left leaning went to *Fourthwrite*.[56]

The people behind both magazines would remain closely tied, with deep interpersonal relationships and regular shared content, but *Fourthwrite* and the *Blanket* became independent media projects in late 2000/early

2001. *Fourthwrite* perhaps never regained the public prominence that it did in its first year of publication, when it was the focus of criticism from Sinn Féin and Morrison. Carrie and Anthony McIntyre's establishment of the *Blanket*, with its more regular, higher-profile criticism of the party, would see the magazine become the focus of Sinn Féin attack: The regular critiques of it by Sinn Féin and the *Andersonstown News* would sustain it as a protest project, while its commitment to publishing any materials submitted saw it as a space where éirígí and RNU became public. *Fourth-write* became a more marginalized influence after its early successes, despite publishing until 2011. Within the confines of an analysis of the development of the Internet as a space of activist journalism, the *Blanket* is the dominant example. However, without the impetus of *Fourthwrite*, and the shared hardships of personal threats and censorship, the *Blanket* would perhaps never have existed.

The *Blanket*: a journal of protest and dissent

The *Blanket* came to represent two strands of republicanism: an older tradition of literary, journalistic republican dissidence that was present in journals like the *Bell*, as well as an anti-authoritarian, libertarianism emblematic of the Internet or countercultural generation. Carrie McIntyre had little knowledge of the earlier traditions or of the recent history of republican publishing and pamphleteering, because her background was in the American musical and cultural underground. Her inspiration was primarily the style and spirit of the Southern Californian punk fanzine *Flipside* rather than *An Phoblacht*: 'I was introduced to this world through fanzines and free information sheets at record stores and I soon started doing my own fanzine. The Do-It-Yourself ethic, that anyone could make their own media was always important to me.'[57] However, it is remarkable that her vision for her magazine instinctively drew on a culture of dissent which sought to highlight inconsistencies within mainstream republican dogma as the older mosquito press had done sixty years previously. Anthony McIntyre, fully cognizant with this period of cultural republican history, noted:

> The republican leadership had for long made much of the concept of 'community as one'. There would be no alternative voices. Sean Russell rather than Peadar O'Donnell being the role model that suited best. The idiocy of the Green Book ultimately came to be preferred to the intellect of The *Bell*.[58]

The *Blanket* would seek to redress this intellectual disparity, and perhaps the online world was the only place that it could at this time. Despite being produced with virtually no financial resources, the magazine built its reputation thanks to both the regularity of publication and the standard of much of the writing, drawing contributions from beyond the republican activist milieu. Initially publishing weekly, it attracted high-quality contributions from the academic community, thanks to McIntyre's contacts through having completed a PhD at Queen's University Belfast. Having written for *Fortnight* prior to his release from jail, and, later, various national and international newspapers, he also had contacts in the closely knit journalism and cultural communities in Belfast. Through this period, the *Blanket* published work by writers like Malachi O'Doherty (editor of *Fortnight* at the time), and national newspaper journalists and authors such as Suzanne Breen, Henry McDonald and Eamonn McCann. Noting the *Blanket*'s passing with some regret, O'Doherty recognized one of the key qualities of the magazine: 'it was a pressure valve, a place where republicans could let off steam in much the same way as the *Sunday Independent* did for unionists.'[59]

Cutting a position critical of the Peace Process and which also attracted mainstream journalists and political figures, including senior unionists, legitimated the *Blanket*, giving it an intellectual credibility that other magazines and activist media outlets did not. The McIntyres were already newsworthy because of their stance on the O'Connor murder, and the subsequent Sinn Féin picketing of them attracted the attention of US and European media.[60] Anthony McIntyre was a gifted writer and a prolific one from his time in jail, and was published widely by the *Guardian*, the *Los Angeles Times*, *Irish Times* and *Parliamentary Brief*. The quality of his writing, plus that of the other central core of activists, meant that the *Blanket* stood out from the party magazines which remained guilty of continuing to use the leaden republican activist prose of *An Phoblacht*'s old 'War News' column and its constant reference to the British Army as 'the crown occupying forces of oppression'. The *Blanket* also became legitimated further because of media interest in AGFARs in the post-1998 period, particularly those like McIntyre and Brendan Hughes, who were highly articulate in their opposition to Sinn Féin. The influence of the magazine grew. Carrie McIntyre discovered articles and analysis from the pages of the *Blanket* were used by the US State department and the British Home Office, while TDs were moved to quote it on the floor of Dáil Éireann.[61] The *Blanket*'s was an important space in the work of journalists for traditional media outlets, such as Suzanne Breen and Henry McDonald, who were able to mine the dissenting seam of protest which the magazine had cut for itself. The *Blanket* was remarkable by virtue of the media space that it developed for itself in the contemporary public sphere, and thus represented a successful application of the potential of the Internet while also adhering to an extant tradition of radical republican writing.

The *Blanket* was launched with the tagline 'a journal of protest and dissent', and its name served as a reference to the men and women who had taken part in the no work, no wash, 'dirty' protests of 1976–1981. The jails, and the dirty and blanket protests were the dominant experiences in the lives of most of those that formed the IRWG and *Fourthwrite*, especially Hughes and McKearney, who had been on the first Hunger Strike in 1980. While its name referred to the republican past, it was the present, and the possibility of the online world, that would sustain its reputation. It published online for six years, going twice weekly soon after its launch to accommodate the sheer volume of contributions, and had a light touch when it came to an editorial stylebook or rules for publication. It subverted the online convention of the use of anonymity for posters: writers had to put their names to whatever they wrote; only once was anonymity allowed, and in that case there was extreme danger of violent reprisal. Also subverting the modern tendency for Internet 'handles' or pseudonyms, the *Blanket* only published a handful of contributors working under pen names. Although it published very accomplished writers like Anthony McIntyre, the *Blanket*'s outlook was ultimately libertarian rather than literary, and it included articles by less practised authors. Its sole aim, beyond critiques of Official republicanism, was to give a voice to those denied a space to speak in the mainstream media in a contemporary political landscape dominated by Sinn Féin. The *Blanket* echoed its contributor Henry McDonald, who sought 'to challenge an entirely fake orthodoxy ... that the IRA's bombs and bullets expended during that period were done so in order that somehow Ulster's Catholics could become equal citizens in the North of Ireland'.[62] McIntyre's critical analysis of the 'journey' of Provisionalism was that: 'for the Provisional Republican Movement, the long, slow one-way journey away from the core tenets of republicanism, which sustained it throughout its struggle, will at some point be completed. ... The only destination that awaits them is the establishment sea of constitutionalism.'[63]

These writers reflected the experiences of mid twentieth-century republican dissenters, in both symbolizing and articulating the sense of loss and a political landscape of post-struggle disillusionment. As with their predecessors, traditional tactics of marginalization were used to demonize them, with Gerry Adams accusing McIntyre and Gorman of being 'fellow travellers with the Real IRA'.[64] McIntyre had gone to some pains to emphasize the fact that although the space was open to any that wanted to contribute, he consistently denounced 'a futile armed campaign' of dissidents:[65]

> Republican dissidents such as Tommy Gorman and myself have stood firm against any suggestion that republicanism should engage in violence. At one point we argued that never again should it take life in pursuit of its goals. Two nights later our homes were picketed by Sinn Féin, who took exception

to that line of thinking. It seemed to us that while we supported the peace Sinn Féin only supported the process. Hardly a recipe for a lasting stability in society.[66]

Interviewed by Liz Curtis about the dissident violence of CIRA and RIRA, he said: 'I would prefer Gerry Adams' strategy to that, because it's not leaving body bags in the street.'[67] Critics of the magazine accused it of a problematic and ambiguous relationship with dissident groups, pointing to the fact that it provided a platform for groups still actively engaged in an armed campaign or supportive of one.[68]

There was indeed an intellectual gap inherent in the *Blanket*'s stance of being both supportive of peace but critical of the abandonment of core ideological tenets of the republican armed struggle. Dissidents pointed out that republicanism had aimed to forcibly coerce the British from Ireland and to discredit the notion that unionist consent was needed for the British to leave. That remained their *raison d'être*, yet the *Blanket* occupied a more morally ambiguous space by providing no plan of its own for the future. Brendan Hughes said, 'I don't have an alternative, people keep saying to me if your [sic] going to criticize put up an alternative. I don't have an alternative, the alternative is within the republican movement.'[69] The editors of the *Blanket* did not offer an alternative: out of all the articles posted over the period, only a few discussed a blueprint for the future or for arriving at a means of protest that would force a united Ireland back onto the agenda. One writer suggested rejecting the new states, perhaps missing the point that there was little support for such a course of action either in the Republic of Ireland or among Northern unionists and middle-class nationalists:

> Radical rejection in the form of boycotts and a general refusal to engage with the invader anywhere would have prevented further factionalism and fostered a far better culture of Irish independence than the usual Brit tit dependence we are seeing now making 2016 no nearer than 3016.[70]

American correspondents were important in the early years, including Karen Lyden-Cox who saw the *Blanket* as being the centrepiece for a significant group of people, both within and outside of Ireland, to resist the status quo and rethink the 1998 peace agreement.[71] Another frequent American contributor in the early years, Paul A. Fitzsimmons, regularly advocated independence for Northern Ireland and detailed his plans on several occasions.[72] The relative paucity of definitive plans for the future of Ireland which satisfied the competing strands and sub-strands of dissenting opinion is, however, symptomatic of the magazine's resistance to being part of a reconstructionist programme and existing as anything other than a space of dissent for those marginalized from the mainstream political milieu. This simple role of offering a space, where the marginalized may recognize each other through dialogue, allowed it to be seen as one of the new activist media milieux of counterpublics.

The *Blanket* was perhaps most successful, within the political ambit, as critique and counterbalance to the establishment republican leadership's *volte face*, from being dedicated to smashing Stormont and resisting the Brits and the security forces to getting elected to the Assembly and leading reforms of the once-hated RUC. Dissenting republicans articulated that their fight had not been for a rebranding of the police force and reforms to the justice system that incarcerated them, but for the establishment of a new system of policing beyond the 'sectarian' security forces republicans opposed.

The *Blanket*'s early years would reflect this bitter ideological division in the republican movement. In 2002, when Gerry Adams stopped just short of suggesting there was a unionist veto on achieving a united Ireland, saying, 'I don't think we can force upon unionism an all-Ireland which does not have their assent or consent and doesn't reflect their sense of being comfortable',[73] ideological tremors were sent through dissenters and dissidents alike. This was the final and ultimate betrayal of one of the centrepieces of the armed struggle and the core republican tenets that had offered ideological sustenance inside jail. In one statement, Sinn Féin was doing what it had vowed never to do: to assume the position of the constitutional nationalist SDLP it had so lambasted for collaboration in the 1970s. It also reinforced the SDLP deputy leader Seamus Mallon's assertion that the Good Friday Agreement had been built on his party's analysis and on the principles of consent and non-violence, and that it was Sinn Féin who had made substantial moves to support SDLP strategies. This point was made by two senior *Blanket* correspondents.[74] Eamonn McCann's *Belfast Telegraph* column on the statement was reproduced by the *Blanket*:

> Some will remember the deluge of derision which Sinn Féin poured on the SDLP in the 1970s and 80s for signing up to the principle of consent. It was this which, in republican nomenclature, earned the SDLP the alias, 'Stoop Down Low Party'. The dismay of some who stood up for the Republic and gave years of their lives to the fight to achieve it is natural.[75]

McIntyre was much more savage in his critique of the final piece of evidence that Sinn Féin were doing more than going slightly constitutional:

> A revolutionary body that settles for and then seeks to legitimise the very terms it fought against simultaneously de-legitimises and arguably criminalises its own existence. Consequently, historians of the conflict, now armed with the present Sinn Féin logic will in all probability come to view the IRA campaign much more negatively than may previously have been the case. A sad denouement to an unnecessary war in which so many suffered needlessly.[76]

The New York-based Northern Irish journalist Eamon Lynch decried the cognitive dissonance of Sinn Féin now being able to simultaneously accept the principles of constitutional nationalism and the rigours of the Peace Process, while also using the rump of the IRA as a policing force in republican communities:

> While claiming to have entered a new phase in its war of liberation against the British, the reality is that the IRA is now engaged in little more than a territorial scuffle. ... This may constitute community defence of a sort, and many nationalists clearly tolerate or welcome it as both necessary and justified. But it is not republicanism. Perhaps when that fact is acknowledged we will be spared the now-familiar spectacle of Sinn Féin conducting a chorus of 'A Nation Once Again' when they know the band is actually playing 'Rule Britannia'.[77]

Lynch's article would have further implications for the *Blanket* when Máirtín Ó Muilleoir attacked the posting in a column in the *Andersonstown News* the following week, and threatened legal action on Nuzhound for posting it. He also threatened legal action against Anthony McIntyre, and the episode would be satirized in an 'Angrytown News' column on the *Blanket* by McIntyre.[78] Lynch, who also claimed that there had been censorship of his work by the *Irish Echo*'s owner Sean Finlay, under pressure from Ó Muilleoir, resigned from the paper.[79]

The *Blanket* and loyalism

The *Blanket* sought to offer a space for dissenting voices but it also sought to escape the narrow corridor of identity politics in which both establishment and dissident republicanism were now situated. If Sinn Féin's Armani suit generation were launching an assault on taking power they did so on the basis of a new, updated brand of Catholic defenderism with little outward focus on addressing the nature of the ethno-religious divides. They did so as dissidents had refused to move from a position of Brits out. It was against this background that the *Blanket* would offer a platform for loyalists as a matter of principle and not simply as an editorial or commercial decision. There were no commercial imperatives to the editorial process anyway, with the magazine never seeking to derive income from publication. The only revenue stream would have been from advertising, and it eschewed that. Carrie McIntyre said, 'we didn't make a decision not to go corporate, we didn't need to because it wasn't what we were about. It wasn't about making money or making a name for anyone.'[80] Anthony McIntyre stated that to complain about being silenced by mainstream republican leaders, yet not give an opportunity for loyalists and unionists to write about their position, would be an act of hypocrisy.[81] American correspondent, Seaghán Ó'Murchú wrote,

> The Internet allowed the broadcasting of voices beyond Belfast or Derry. Loyalists, Sinn Féiners (a couple, perhaps), constitutional nationalists, and physical-force advocates could all add their opinions. The editors allowed and encouraged this discussion in the noblest example of how thoughtful suggestions might advance a more equitable version of republicanism than the one offered to the island's voters.[82]

Reflecting the McIntyres' commitment to the promise of freedom and accessibility that the early Internet and its message boards offered, the *Blanket* was a natural home for former loyalist commander Billy Mitchell and other evangelical Protestants. The *Blanket* sought to escape the identity binaries ingrained into Northern Ireland political life and the political system that was in the process of becoming dominated by the mutually exclusive ambitions of Sinn Féin and the DUP. This reflected a conscientious decision, by Carrie McIntyre, to resist sectarianism and censorship. Anthony McIntyre's relationship with Mitchell, fostered producing the *Other View* magazine, meant that the latter became a thoughtful contributor to the *Blanket*, submitting some of the most literary and engaging articles it published. Former leader of the Ulster Defence Association, David Adams, who was also a former senior member of the Ulster Democratic Party, wrote for the magazine and became a weekly columnist for the *Irish Independent* and the *Irish Times*. These columns were re-published by the *Blanket*. The evangelical Protestant Orangeman and journalist, Dr John Coulter was perhaps the most intriguing unionist/loyalist who wrote on the *Blanket*, due to his natural bent towards controversial political positions however disliked they were. Coulter had a background in journalism and contributed to the *Irish Daily Star* and later *Tribune* magazine, having also written for *Daily Ireland*. Coulter later continued to contribute columns to McIntyre's blog, *pensivequill.com*. The work of all three men was of high journalistic quality.

Mitchell is an important figure in the development of the *Blanket* because he represents the opening up of such a supposedly republican space to a man who was responsible for the murders of many Catholics while a paramilitary. Mitchell, while UVF chief of staff, had also met with Official Republican leadership in the early 1970s, at a period when he, and the organization, were still advocating a far right, National Front position.[83] However, having been sentenced to two life sentences in the late 1970s he became a born again Christian in jail. It was from his period of reflection as a prisoner that he developed a vision of Northern Irish identity and how it could embrace the panoply of political and religious traditions. McIntyre remarked that his vision of Christianity and Marxism resembled the Catholic liberation theology of South American radicals.[84] After release from jail, Mitchell was the founder of the North Belfast reconciliation group Intercomm and wrote a column for the *North Belfast News* which was 'an attempt to reach out to nationalists without compromising his own belief in the value of the union with Britain'.[85]

The series of articles published in the *Blanket* demonstrate the journal's commitment to publishing a more progressive voice from loyalist circles, much like the *Bell* did, but also in attempting to circumnavigate the pitfalls of identity politics which were a clear barrier to reconciliation. For Mitchell, the binary polarities of the two identities, Irish Catholic and British Protestant wilfully ignored the commonalities of experience that might provide the foundation for a new, less contested identity. He contended that this isolation perpetuated a narrow sectarian identification structure which amounted to a nihilistic self-harming. Despite being an unapologetically proud Protestant, he identified and yearned for common ground in the *Blanket*. For him, reconciliation would only come when cultural catechisms of ethnic difference were abandoned and Northern Ireland discovered its own narrow diversity. Mitchell identified four cultural strands in modern Ireland: 'indigenous Irish Gaelic culture, Anglo-Irish culture, Ulster-Scots culture, and the cultures of those ethnic groups who have settled in the Province in more recent times'.[86] Echoing the American Declaration of Independence, he wrote:

> Each citizen of Northern Ireland has an inalienable right to watch over, promote, protect and enjoy the cultural tradition with which he or she chooses to identify. It is incumbent upon all of us to validate each of these cultures, together with the modes of expression and celebration associated with them.[87]

Writing in 2001, Mitchell used the friendship of Protestant Thomas Carnduff and republican socialist Peadar O'Donnell as a symbol of the friendship and forgiveness that were possible for loyalists and republicans open enough to respect opposing traditions. Carnduff, an Ulster Volunteer Force gun runner during the Home Rule Crisis in 1912–1914 later became the Worshipful Master of Sandy Row Independent Loyal Orange Lodge; but he also became a valued contributor to the Irish literary magazine the *Bell* when O'Donnell, a radical socialist, 1916 Easter Rising veteran and former IRA commander, was the magazine's editor. The two men became firm friends.[88] For Mitchell, this friendship was a template for the public compromises required in Northern Irish society. Two men who had advocated the rights of their respective classes and traditions were interesting touchstones for the forgiveness required between warring communities. Mitchell said:

> The friendship between O'Donnell and Carnduff reminds us that political adversaries need not dehumanise one another. On the contrary, they should have the capacity to respect each other's political integrity and dedication to a cause. It reminds us too that those who have worn the uniform of opposing forces need not live in a state of perpetual hatred, base recrimination and ongoing demonisation. As in the case of Carnduff and O'Donnell, dedicated political opponents are very often kindred spirits who share similar passions and, but for an accident of birth, could have been on 'the same side'.[89]

The road travelled by Mitchell, from the far right of loyalism, to socialism based in evangelical Protestantism, allowed him to take aim at those who refused to see the solution to Northern Ireland's problems with sectarianism, other than from their own well-defined positions, and who failed to recognize those who had made compromises themselves:

> The potential for the development of class politics that is being cradled within a number of loyalist and nationalist communities should be validated and supported by socialist groupings. Some have been very supportive while others have put out a tentative hand of friendship. Sadly there are too many elitist socialists who refuse to believe that anything good can come out of the loyalist community and are dismissive of the work of loyalist political and community activists.[90]

Mitchell was, however, realistic enough to note that, 'some socialists have a tendency to lecture nationalists and unionists for daring to be what they are – unionists and nationalists. But nationalism and unionism are facts of life.'[91]

Coulter was more provocative than Mitchell in more than a hundred columns for the *Blanket*, deploying a populist tabloid instinct to outrage. His political manifesto was diametrically opposed to the republican belief system of the magazine. Coulter's blueprint for the future of Northern Ireland was 'left-field': a popular evangelical Protestant revival coinciding with a thirty-two-county reunited Ireland which returned to being a British territory under the Commonwealth. Coulter did not see recognition of the rights and political cultural aspirations of all the communities of Northern Ireland as holding the solution to the Peace Process, because neither partition nor the existing British state institutions and traditions were the root cause of the Troubles. In his vision, Northern Irish Protestants were not the architects of partition, and therefore his solution was that all Irish nationalists needed to embrace further integration of a United Ireland with Great Britain under the auspices of the British Commonwealth:

Many Southern Catholics and Northern Prods could be attracted to a pro-Commonwealth Unionist movement – driven by an evangelical radical Presbyterianism – which guaranteed their middle class lifestyles would not be threatened by the ever expanding European Union. Revolutionary Unionism would take the British islands – including Ireland – out of the EU and into the global economic security of the Commonwealth.[92]

Unwittingly, Coulter had encapsulated the nostalgic and patriotic vision of the benevolence of the British Empire that was a central tenet of the return to populism that the 2016 Brexit-supporting vote represented. It certainly did not take into account Irish and nationalist views of the Empire. His view of the golden age of colonialism and crown as a bulwark against modern globalization severely misunderstood what the imperial era did to kickstart globalization in the first place.

Coulter never deviated from a position that the IRA had been defeated in the conflict and that Britain remained the best place to offer the people of Northern Ireland political sanctuary and economic opportunity. In his penultimate column for the *Blanket*, as the magazine was closing in 2008, he outlined a revolutionary vision for a new Ireland. The final editions ran in February and May 2008, and much of the final weeks of content commemorated the life of Brendan Hughes, as well as tributes to the *Blanket* from a broad spectrum of writers, including loyalists like Coulter and David Adams, who said of the magazine:

[T]he real strength lay not in the finding of or even the searching for harmony, but in the agreeing to differ with good grace. Freedom of speech is a powerful, frightening thing. Invariably far more dangerous to those who make full use of it than to those who oppose it most. But it is a necessary thing. Without it, freedom of any kind does not exist.[93]

But Coulter remained ever the arch agent provocateur by conflating modern republicanism with the seventeenth-century ideals of the Protestant revival, which he saw as the panacea to all of Northern Ireland's ills. It only confirmed the fearlessness with which the *Blanket*'s editorial impulse to publish intellectually challenging material acted:

Unionists should remember Brendan Hughes; a republican who realised the pitfall into which Sinn Féin had tumbled. So my fellow Unionists, forget the feuds – when Paisley is gone, we can formally begin the process of reclaiming our ultimate birthright bequeathed to us by King William III in the Glorious Revolution. Ironically, it may well have been IRA OCs [Officers Commanding] such as the late Brendan Hughes who pointed the way. Now that's one of the ironies of Irish politics.[94]

The idea that more than a handful of his fellow unionists were reading a magazine called the *Blanket* was naïvely optimistic, but nevertheless, for an evangelical Protestant to be given a platform to do so on a magazine published by avowed Irish republican atheists is remarkable in this time period. What is most interesting and instructive about the nature of the space that *Blanket* cut for itself, is that the most challenging articles it published and most effusive tributes it was paid came from loyalists, for whom its ultimate ideals should have been anathema.

The *Blanket* and satire

The *Blanket*'s commitment to publishing a wide variety of materials meant there was a varying degree of both quality and tone. However, as noted before, it displayed a consistently witty and vicious satiric bite which was inherited from both *AP/RN* and older traditions of republican letters. This was an example of republican eclecticism in practice, in its ability to draw universal satiric critiques from often very specific circumstances. The targets of this satire were invariably Sinn Féin, other politicians and, in particular, the Sinn Féin-supporting media including the *Andersonstown News*, which was frequently referred to as the 'Angrytown News'. Journalists were also a target, their names twisted: the *Irish Times* writer Daeglán de Breádún was renamed Barney de Breadbin; Eamonn Mallie's moniker was Eamonn Codswallop. Their names often appeared as a joint by-line on pieces which lampooned Sinn Féin revisionism. The cartoonists Brian Mór and John Kennedy were frequent contributors, which is all the more noteworthy given that all of the work done for the *Blanket* was *pro bono*.

However, the most regular satiric voice in the magazine was Jimmy Sands, a fictional republican figure, who was used to destabilize the double-think of establishment republican positions at times of crisis during the Peace Process. Sands was a playful reference to loyalist graffiti during the Hunger Strikes. Danny Morrison noted, 'shortly after Bobby died in 1981 some idiot, in an attempt at irony, wrote on a gable wall in loyalist East Belfast, "We'll never forget you, Jimmy Sands." '[95] Although Bobby Sands and the Hunger Strikers remained sacrosanct figures in the *Blanket*, the alleged exploitation of their memory by Sinn Féin as a means of political advancement was the underlying basis of the 'joke'. This expanded the repertoire and tone of activist journalism of this period and perhaps took it closer to the destabilizing Situationist-influenced spirit of culture jamming used by éirígí which is addressed in the following chapter. Satire was not the sole preserve of the *Blanket*. Sinn Féin maintained the Fifth Column section in *An Phoblacht*, which also poked fun at public figures, but it lacked the satiric depth of the 'Jimmy Sands' and 'Angrytown News' missives. Jimmy Sands had no fixed identity; he did not represent one singular Sinn Féin figure, and was used to fit the individual circumstances of specific episodes of conflict of policy. The 'Angrytown News' articles appeared at periods when the *Blanket* had published denunciations of the *Andersonstown News*, particularly after Lynch's 'voice of banana republicanism' column.

Jimmy Sands was a key 'figure' in the *Blanket's* coverage of the Colombia Three case, in which Sinn Féin was linked to a party representative and two former PIRA members arrested apparently training socialist guerrillas of the FARC in Colombia. Two of the men were allegedly former members of PIRA's engineering department, with particular expertise in explosives, and another man, Niall Connolly, was revealed as the Sinn Féin representative in Cuba. The case was damaging, particularly at a time when the Northern Ireland Assembly was suspended because of an alleged Sinn Féin spying ring at Stormont, with PIRA being seen to internationalize at a time of ceasefire and decommissioning, angering the US government.[96] When the case came to trial, after a Sinn Féin campaign to free the Colombia Three led by Catriona Ruane (or Catriona Ruin as she was known in the columns), 'Jimmy Sands' became the 'ceann comhairle' (chairperson) of the Caribbean Sinn Féin cumann. He noted of his 'visit' to South America, 'there is a real bond that unites revolutionaries across the globe. We listened to their stories of battles against the Colombian army while I tried, in my schoolboy Spanish, to explain the Private Finance Initiative to them.'[97]

In the same year, when Sinn Féin attempted to news manage the revelation that Freddie Scappaticci was the double agent 'Stakeknife', the *Andersonstown News* ran an 'exclusive' interview with him. This gave Anthony McIntyre, who wrote the majority of the 'Jimmy Sands' columns, an opportunity to target both Sinn Féin and the *Andersonstown News*. Playing on the money that the paper had received from government grants and advertising, the editor Robin Livingstone, who has written the Squinter column for many years and is an ardent Adams loyalist, was by-lined both 'the Squealer' and 'Sir Robert Squintingstone'. Scappaticci, the British spy, became 'Jimmy Sands O.B.E.' and rubbished claims that he had been paid £80,000 a year for being an informer, retorting, 'I'm not getting out of bed for £80,000.' The article's conclusion said much about the *Blanket's* abhorrence of Sinn Féin's double standard over Stakeknife and, later, the Denis Donaldson case:

> According to the press I am guilty of forty murders. But I am telling you this now: after this has settled, I want to meet the families of the people that they said I murdered. And when I do I will stand in front of them and say, 'I didn't do it. I had no part in it.' And I will keep a straight face when I do it. As soon as I can find the time.[98]

During a period when the International Monitoring Commission noted the persistence of PIRA punishment beatings in West Belfast, and less than a year before the murder of Robert McCartney, the 'Angry-town News' angrily responded to the allegations that PIRA and Sinn Féin were linked: 'everyone to whom we spoke denied being the source, some indeed finding the suggestion so ludicrous that it caused momentary loss of bowel control when one of our community outreach teams visited their homes.'[99] An accompanying graphic purporting to be about raising money for Sinn Féin, headlined 'SinnAid', saw a baseball bat, the weapon most commonly used for punishment beatings, representing the totalizer. The rancorous relationship between the *Blanket* and the *Andersonstown News* led to the latter's relationship with Sinn Féin being satirized further:

> Our titles are rigorously apolitical and independent of almost all political organisations and have more diverse views in their columns than any other newspaper in Ireland (*An Phoblacht, Sunday Business Post*). We cater for Catholic and Nationalist alike. Our columnists include a Sinn Féin councillor, a Portadown loyalist [letter from Mr. Emerson Newton-John, April Fools edition], a Sinn Féin Lord Mayor, a former IRA volunteer, the well known author and writer Mr. Danny Armalite (a leading non-member of Sinn Féin), Fr. Ted Wilsputin, Ireland's leading defrocked cleric, and a woman ... to name just all.[100]

In the same article, the 'Angrytown News' editorial denounced McIntyre: 'for some time, Mr. McIntyre has been running a one-man campaign against the Hanschristianandersonstown News. This has included his recent outrageous claim that we're journalists.'[101]

The revisionism of the Sinn Féin project and the lionization of the leadership that was actively denying its activities in PIRA were at the heart of other satiric jibes. Barney de Breadbin and Eamonn Codswallop were the authors behind the Gerry Adams hagiography, 'Adams nearly quit Sinn Féin – Peace Process hero angered by IRA violence', which had the subheading, 'the news five years from now: Irish Tomes, January 1, 2005.' The piece had been written four years previously, first appearing on the IRWG website, and was a revisionism fantasy that Gerry Adams had joined the IRA by mistake and had never been the architect of the PIRA cell structure or the Long War strategy while jailed under internment:[102]

> Mr Adams spent his time in jail profitably however and he drew up plans to re-organise the IRA into 'peace cells' and formulated a strategy which became known as 'the Long Peace'. After his release from prison he set up a Northern Command to coordinate the 'peace cells' which were given the task of bombarding British security bases with leaflets containing threats to impose 'Stormont power-sharing' on Unionists. When a two ton truck containing the leaflets was discovered in the heart of the City of London, the British government agreed to secret talks with the IRA.[103]

The piece was underpinned with an anger given the frequency of punishment beatings linked to PIRA that were taking place at the time. The article was included that week because of an attack on former INLA member, Bobby Tohill, who had told the *Andersonstown News* that his life was under threat.[104] Tohill was, soon after, beaten by four men in a Belfast bar and kidnapped in a van which was stopped by police.[105] An accompanying cartoon by Brian Mór was more savage – four masked men are seen beating an unconscious man on a pub floor in front of the slogan 'Give peace a chance! Or we'll kill you.'[106]

The depth of inventiveness shown by the *Blanket* in the 'Jimmy Sands' and 'Angrytown News' articles represented a movement away from the perception of dissenting republican publications as dull and full of traditionalist cant. *Fourthwrite* and the *Blanket* made honourable attempts at elevating the content and analysis of republican activist media and were given that opportunity by the new environment of the Internet. But, rather than representing a significant political point in the development of dissenting opinion that would be taken forward and turned into political capital, the *Blanket* and *Fourthwrite* perhaps represent the end of an era – the end of the socialist republican counterpublic that found its voice in the jails but which did not establish itself on the outside. Many of those that found their activist journalism voice in *Iris Bheag* or *An Glór Gafa* joined the establishment republican project and became public representatives. Others, like McIntyre and McKearney, chose a different path, and sought a new means of developing a voice and position in the republican sphere. Both magazines, but particularly the *Blanket*, are worthy of their inclusion in any discussion of the development of the Irish republican activist sphere, because of the quality and long-term commitment to simply making an intellectual and countercultural contribution. Ó'Murchú wrote a fitting eulogy for the magazine:

> Without official or clandestine support for free speech against oppression and censorship, a few principled opponents can only endure so much. The effort had been made with integrity and enthusiasm. When the headlines no longer raged with the latest assault or last night's atrocity, perhaps 'The Blanket' had, however indirectly, done what it had meant to do: get people to act more civilly in their efforts to move forward into a fairer society.[107]

If one subscribes to the belief that the global public sphere was in part democratized by the development of new activist journalism projects, then the *Blanket* deserves analysis because it performed a similar role in the Irish republican context. The *Blanket* and *Fourthwrite* captured a strand of republican thinking in development that is more important to the understanding of the activist journalism milieu in Britain and Ireland than perhaps it is to understandings of republicanism. They had no deliberative political effect, other than to demonstrate that long-term activist projects can play a part in the political process simply as cultural projects. Fealty summarized the *Blanket*'s contribution best, noting:

> More broadly an era of protest has passed. There are still a few who are attempting to carry on the armed struggle the IRA effectively abandoned fourteen years ago. But for many others, The *Blanket* gave another, more civil account of a term that has more commonly been reserved for Republican paramilitaries who refused to follow the lead of the Provisional IRA: 'dissident'.[108]

The activist journalism project of both magazines could be said to have achieved little other than publication, but what would follow would be a period when new forms of republican dissent would replace their keyboard activism. Perhaps the most salient point is that, nearly a decade after the *Blanket* shut, no dissenting groups have come close to producing magazines of such great vision and inventiveness in their writing.

Notes

1 McIntyre, Anthony, 'Dangerous words: the genesis of the Irish Republican Writers Group', *Fortnight: Art and War Supplement*, September 2001.
2 Ó'Donghaile, Deaglán, interview, 4 February 2010.
3 A. McIntyre interview.
4 McDonald, Henry, 'Ex-IRA man to post Muslim cartoon on net', *Observer*, 12 March 2006. Available at: www.theguardian.com/uk/2006/mar/12/muhammadcartoons.northernireland. Accessed 12 March 2006.
5 See: Bean, *New Politics of Sinn Féin*; Frampton, *Legion of the Rearguard*; McDonald, Henry, *Gunsmoke and Mirrors: How Sinn Féin Dressed up Defeat as Victory* (Dublin: Gill &Macmillan, 2008).
6 C. McIntyre interview. See also: Frampton, Martyn, 'The Blanket and the cartoon controversy: Anthony McIntyre interviewed', *Blanket*, 9 May 2006. Available at: www.indiamond6.ulib.iupui.edu:81/MF2206066g.html. Accessed 8 April 2011.
7 *Fourthwrite* featured articles by Northern Irish academics, Henry Patterson, Arthur Aughey and Paul Bew, an interview with Tony Benn and an article by Ulster Unionist Stephen King, David Trimble's special advisor. See *Fourthwrite*, Nos. 1–4, 2000–2001.
8 See: McIntyre, Anthony, 'Profile: Ayaan Hirsi Ali', *Blanket*, 12 March 2006. Available at: www.indiamond6.ulib.iupui.edu:81/AM1203062g.html. Accessed 6 April 2011. Carrie McIntyre noted that left-wing writer Eamonn McCann, who contributed regularly to the magazine, was angered by the publication of the cartoons, and 'fell out' with the *Blanket* as a result.

9 O'Ruairc, Liam, 'The League of Communist Republicans, 1986–1991', *Irish Left Archive*, 2001. Available at: www.clririshleftarchive.org/document/576/. Accessed 24 March 2017.

10 O'Ruairc, 'The League of Communist Republicans'.

11 Bean, *New Politics of Sinn Féin*.

12 Holland, Jack, 'US woman forced from Belfast home', *Irish Echo*, 25–31 October 2000.

13 McIntyre, Anthony, 'Stalinville', *Blanket*, 19 May 2003. Available at: www. indiamond6.ulib.iupui.edu:81/stalinville.html. Accessed 6 April 2011. Brendan Hughes noted Sinn Féin as 'truly Orwellian'. See: McDonald, Henry, 'IRA rebuff for Adams prison ally', *Observer*, 13 October 2000.

14 McIntyre, Anthony, 'Silence is complicity', *Blanket*, 17 June 2001. Available at: http://indiamond6.ulib.iupui.edu:81/silence.html. Accessed 8 April 2011.

15 'Editorial', *Fourthwrite*, Issue 4, Spring 2001.

16 McKearney, T., unpublished article.

17 C. McIntyre interview.

18 McIntyre, 'Dangerous words'.

19 McIntyre, Anthony, 'Republican leadership excludes republicans', *Sunday Tribune*, 14 November 1999.

20 McIntyre, 'The Irish Republican Writers Group'.

21 McIntyre, 'Dangerous words'.

22 A. McIntyre interview.

23 McKearney interview.

24 C. McIntyre interview.

25 C. McIntyre interview. Ó'Donghaile also noted the *Irish News* editor's letters page as a space conducive to critiques of Sinn Féin. Ó'Donghaile interview.

26 Carrie McIntyre contributed regular posts on republicanism, and in particular the ongoing debate over the Hunger Strikes, as 'Rusty Nail'. See: O'Rawe, *Afterlives*, p. 111.

27 C. McIntyre interview.

28 C. McIntyre interview.

29 'History of the Debate Central community', Available at: www. brideofdebatecentralrevisited.yuku.com/topic/875/History-of-the-Debate-Central-community#.UUm0HhcqZTA. Accessed 9 April 2013.

30 C. McIntyre interview.

31 C. McIntyre interview.

32 C. McIntyre interview.

33 C. McIntyre interview.

34 McKearney interview; C. McIntyre interview. The *Blanket* would also publish a hard-copy magazine edited by Liam O'Ruairc in 2002. It is now available digitally. Available at: www.indiamond6.ulib.iupui.edu:81/theblanketwinter. html. Accessed 1 February 2009.

35 Morrison, Danny, 'Too Forthright', *Andersonstown News*, 13 March 2000. Available at: http://www.dannymorrison.com/wp-content/dannymorrisonarchive/133.htm. Accessed 20 April 2013.

36 A. McIntyre interview.

37 Ó'Donghaile interview. See also: McIntyre, 'The Irish Republican Writers Group'. He writes that 'party activists who asked a difficult question of a Movement speaker were "gripped" after the event.' 'Gripped' in this sense means confronted by Sinn Féin 'enforcers'.

38 A. McIntyre interview.

39 P.S. O'Hegarty, 'The mosquito press', *Bell*, vol. 12, no. 1, April 1946. O'Hegarty was a member of the editorial board of the *Republic*, and a propagandist in England for the paper. The first use of the phrase in the context of Ireland is 'British searching suspects in Ireland', *New York Times*, 22 May 1918. It noted, 'The Sinn Féin has no daily newspaper. Its half dozen little papers, known in Dublin as "the mosquito press," appear weekly on Thursday.'

40 Ní Bheacháin, C., ' "The mosquito press": anti-imperialist rhetoric in republican journalism, 1926–39', *Éire-Ireland* vol. 42, no. 1, 2007, pp. 256–89.

41 Ní Bheacháin, 'The mosquito press', p. 261.

42 Ní Bheacháin, 'The mosquito press', pp. 262–263.

43 'An Phoblacht: About us'.

44 Ó'Drisceoil, *Peadar O'Donnell*, p. 44.

45 Ó'Donghaile interview.

46 A. McIntyre interview.

47 McIntyre, 'The Irish Republican Writers Group'.

48 McCann, Eamonn, 'John McGuffin', *Blanket*, May 2002. Available at: www.indiamond6.ulib.iupui.edu:81/johnmcguffin.html. Accessed 6 April 2011. McCann noted of the Brigadier column, 'frequently, the Provos wouldn't print it because they thought their readers would find it offensive. They weren't bad judges.'

49 See: 'RIP "Cormac"; – Brian Moore – cartoonist with *An Phoblacht/ Republican News*', *An Phoblacht*, 13 March 2011. Available at: www.anphoblacht.com/contents/781. Accessed 15 March 2011. See also: McIntyre, Anthony, 'The death of Brian Mór', *Pensive Quill*, 20 February 2012. Available at: www.thepensivequill.am/2012/02/death-of-brian-mor.html. Accessed 21 February 2012. The Cormac cartoons are referenced in Davis, Richard, 'Have the Northern Ireland ceasefires of 1994 ended "zero sum game" and mirrored thinking?', in O'Day, Alan (ed.), *Political Violence in Northern Ireland: Conflict and Conflict Resolution* (Westport, CT: Praeger, 1997), p. 36; and Killen, John, *The Unkindest Cut: A Cartoon History of Ulster, 1900–2000* (Belfast: Blackstaff Press, 2000).

50 For an example of the wide editorial policy of *Fourthwrite*, see Issue 12, Spring 2003. Articles on anti-imperialism and anti-war protests, house price inflation and mental health issues share the agenda with an evaluation of traditional republicanism activist writing. Available at: www.indiamond6.ulib.iupui.edu/cdm/singleitem/collection/Fourthwrite/id/52/rec/5. Accessed 20 April 2011.

51 For an example of the later editorial policy, see: *Fourthwrite*, No. 39, Summer 2010. It contained only one small article on republicans, a piece on the prisons, one article on the Saville Inquiry, and an article on bigotry and the marching season. All the other articles covered were specifically on the

political left, and two international stories, one from Greece and one from Palestine. Available at: www.indiamond6.ulib.iupui.edu/cdm/singleitem/collection/Fourthwrite/id/69/rec/25. Accessed 20 April 2011.

52 Splintered Sunrise, 'Preas Na Poblachta'.
53 McKearney interview.
54 A. McIntyre, 'Dangerous words:'.
55 McKearney interview.
56 C. McIntyre interview.
57 C. McIntyre interview. She cited *Flipside*, an LA underground punk fanzine which published between 1977 and 2000, as an early example of the underground, countercultural fanzines that inspired her work.
58 McIntyre, 'Dangerous words'.
59 O'Doherty, Malachi, interview, 21 March 2011.
60 C. McIntyre interview.
61 C. McIntyre interview.
62 McDonald, *Gunsmoke and Mirrors*, p.iii.
63 McIntyre, A., 'Rivers change their course sometimes but always reach the sea', *Blanket*, 18 April 2003. Available at: www.indiamond6.ulib.iupui.edu:81/riverstosea.html. Accessed 6 April 2011.
64 Moloney, Ed, 'Adams article fuels Republican dispute', *Sunday Tribune*, 29 October 2000.
65 McIntyre, 'The Irish Republican Writers Group'.
66 McIntyre, 'Supporting peace but not the process'.
67 Curtis, Liz, 'A rebel republican', *Irish Post*, 26 April 2001.
68 Frampton, *Legion of the Rearguard*, p. 163.
69 See 'Radio Free Eireann interview with Brendan Hughes', *Blanket*, March 2000. Available at: www.indiamond6.ulib.iupui.edu:81/BH60208.html. Accessed 14 April 2011.
70 O'Suilleabhain, Eoghan, 'Can you hear Ho Chi Minh laughing?' *Blanket*, 1 July 2004. Available at: www.indiamond6.ulib.iupui.edu:81/hochiminheos.html. Accessed 13 April 2011. See also: Ó Murchú, S., 'Magpies nest', *Blanket*, 6 July 2004. Available at: www.indiamond6.ulib.iupui.edu:81/magpiesnestsom.html. Accessed 13 April 2011.
71 Lyden-Cox, Karen, 'The op(posi)tion to the status quo', *Blanket*, 13 March 2002. Available at: www.indiamond6.ulib.iupui.edu:81/opposition.html. Accessed 13 April 2011.
72 Fitzsimmons, Paul A., 'Independence for Northern Ireland: why and how', *Blanket*, 2001. Available at: www.indiamond6.ulib.iupui.edu:81/independence.html. Accessed13 April 2011.
73 'United Ireland will not be a cold house for Unionists', *An Phoblacht*, 7 February 2002.
74 Fanning, Aengus, 'Your problem, Seamus, is you don't have guns', *Sunday Independent*, 28 January 2001. Available at: http://www.independent.ie/opinion/analysis/your-problem-seamus-is-you-dont-have-guns-26246899.html. Accessed 6 April 2011. See also: McIntyre, 'The Irish Republican Writers

Group', and O'Ruairc, 'Ditching republicanism', *Weekly Worker*, Issue 581, 15 June 2005. Available at: http://weeklyworker.co.uk/worker/581/ditching-republicanism/. Accessed 13 April 2011.

75 McCann, Eamonn, 'Green is still the colour', *Blanket*, 14 February 2002. Available at: www.indiamond6.ulib.iupui.edu:81/greenstill.html.

76 McIntyre, A., 'Republicans acknowledging a democratic basis to partition', *Blanket*, 10 February 2002. Available at: www.indiamond6.ulib.iupui.edu:81/partition.htm. Accessed 13 April 2011.

77 Lynch, 'Andersonstown News: voice of banana republicanism?'.

78 'Angrytown News responds', *Blanket*, 22 June 2003. Available at: www.indiamond6.ulib.iupui.edu:81/angrytownresponds.html. Accessed 13 April 2011.

79 'Censorship at the Irish Echo', *Blanket*, 20 June 2003. Available at: http://indiamond6.ulib.iupui.edu:81/censorshipie.html. Accessed 13 April 2011.

80 C. McIntyre interview.

81 A. McIntyre interview.

82 Ó'Murchú, Seaghán, 'Folding up the Blanket', *Blanket*, 18 May 2008. Available at: www.indiamond6.ulib.iupui.edu:81/SOMLB.html. Accessed 17 June 2012.

83 Hanley and Millar, *Lost Revolution*, pp. 226–228.

84 McIntyre, Anthony, 'Billy Mitchell', *Blanket*, 31 July 2006. Available at: www.indiamond6.ulib.iupui.edu:81/AM02080610g.html.   Accessed   14 August 2011.

85 McIntyre, 'Billy Mitchell'.

86 Mitchell, Billy, 'Culture and identity', *Blanket*, February 2002. Available at: www.indiamond6.ulib.iupui.edu:81/culture.html. Accessed 14 August 2011.

87 Mitchell, 'Culture and identity'.

88 Mitchell, Billy, 'The Orangeman's handshake', *Blanket*, 2000. Available at: www.indiamond6.ulib.iupui.edu:81/orangemans.html. Accessed 14 August 2011.

89 Mitchell, 'The Orangeman's handshake'.

90 Mitchell, Billy, 'Is class politics a possibility?', *Blanket*, 4 July 2002. Available at: www.indiamond6.ulib.iupui.edu:81/classpolitics.html.   Accessed   14 August 2011.

91 Mitchell, 'Is class politics a possibility?'.

92 Coulter, John, 'Revolutionary unionism', *Blanket*, 13 November 2006. Available at: www.indiamond6.ulib.iupui.edu:81/JC2191106g.html. Accessed 14 August 2011.

93 Adams, David, 'A genuine platform of free expression', *Blanket*,18 May 2008. Available at: www.indiamond6.ulib.iupui.edu:81/DALB.html. Accessed 14 August 2011.

94 Coulter, John, 'An irony of Irish politics', *Blanket*, 24 February 2008. Available at: www.indiamond6.ulib.iupui.edu:81/JCDARK.html. Accessed 14 August 2011.

95 Morrison, Danny, 'Ireland – Bobby Sands!', *Andersonstown News*, 12 May 2003.

96 Hodgson, Martin, McDonald, Henry, and Beaumont, Peter, 'IRA blunder in the jungle sparks US rage', *Observer*, 19 August 2001.

97 'Bogota diary', *Blanket*, 3 February 2003. Available at: www.indiamond6. ulib.iupui.edu:81/bogotadiary.html. Accessed 14 August 2011.

98 'Jimmy Sands breaks his silence – world exclusive!', *Blanket*, 12 June 2003. Available at: www.indiamond6.ulib.iupui.edu:81/worldexclusive.html. Accessed 14 August 2011.

99 'The Angrytown News presents: SinnAid, a community response', *Blanket*, 13 May 2004. Available at: www.indiamond6.ulib.iupui.edu:81/sinnaid.html. Accessed 14 August 2011.

100 'Angrytown News responds'.

101 'Angrytown News responds'.

102 For an explanation of the Long War strategy see: Moloney, *A Secret History of the IRA*, pp. 148–162.

103 'Adams nearly quit Sinn Féin – Peace Process hero angered by IRA violence', *Blanket*, 25 February 2004. Available at: http://indiamond6.ulib.iupui.edu:81/ kcam.html. Accessed 14 August 2011.

104 Barnes, Ciaran, 'Tohill death threat on website', *Ireland Click*, 23 February 2004. Available at: www.saoirse32.wordpress.com/2004/02/page/2/. Accessed 20 August 2013.

105 McDonald, Henry, 'They just kept telling me they were going to kill me', *Observer*, 22 February 2004. Available at: www.theguardian.com/ politics/2004/feb/22/northernireland.northernireland1. Accessed 20 August 2013.

106 Mór, Brian, 'Try not to forget it', *Blanket*, 12 March 2004. Available at: www. indiamond6.ulib.iupui.edu:81/peaceachance.html. Accessed 20 August 2013.

107 Ó'Murchú, 'Folding up the Blanket'.

108 Fealty, Mick, 'In praise of a journal of dissent', *Blanket*, 18 May 2008. Available at: www.indiamond6.ulib.iupui.edu:81/MFLB.html. Accessed 20August 2013.

6

New forms of republican (in)activism: éirígí and RNU

There are two ways to be wrong about the Internet. One is to embrace cyber-utopianism and treat the Internet as inherently democratizing. Just leave it alone, the argument goes, and the Internet will destroy dictatorships, undermine religious fundamentalism, and make up for failures of institutions.[1]

éirígí and RNU: guerrilla media, propaganda and the public sphere

Situating republican activism within the structural confines of the public sphere and counterpublic structures allows us to conceptualize and map groups of people as they gather in virtual and physical spaces. It tells us much about the changes in how activist groups within the Irish republican sphere use the online space, but this space, as we have noted, lacks any evidence of having a deliberative effect on the overall political sphere. In the Irish republican activist sphere there clearly is little deliberative democratic change with the realignment afforded by the restructuring of the sphere, for the most part because the majority of those activist groups involved in the space were disengaged from the political process in any meaningful sense. This zone may be more democratic, in that it gives opportunity for a wider, more diverse range of actors to make their interventions, but radical change has not and cannot be arrived at in this sphere. Therefore, to evaluate the effectiveness of modern Irish activism it is necessary to further examine the impact that new activist spaces have had on the practice of conventional forms of activism. Developing away from seeing the activist sphere merely as a space of overlapping publics and zones, this chapter evaluates the significant developments in dissenting activist practices in the post-GFA period and their effect on the development of the republican sphere.

There are commonalities in Irish republican activist practice. For example, with the use of the Internet as a space for augmenting new and traditional forms of activism, éirígí has adhered to a long-held canon of republican ideology and activism but has also situated itself within newer countercultural activist communities of practice that in themselves have influences dating back to the New Social Movements of the 1960s and further. éirígí and Republican Network for Unity's shared repertoires of occupations and guerrilla activism events like 'rebranding' Starbucks shops and vandalizing commercial premises of landlords, may fall under the shared practice of modern anti-globalization groups, but are also situated within a longer tradition of republicanism and the British left.[2] Occupations of premises were used in the post-Bloody Sunday period, both in Ireland and in Britain, and were utilized again during the Hunger Strikes.[3]

The media space, both online and in the mass media, has remained the primary site for intervention as an impetus for deliberative action in the political public sphere. The Internet is particularly important because activist media outlets provided greater control over the narratives and discourses individual groups wanted to convey. While éirígí was initially a compound of republican street activism and modern anti-corporate guerrilla activism, it used a variety of online outlets to spread its message. Traditional agitprop materials like street theatre and provocative posters were also utilized – and they were influenced by the development of modern anti-corporate and anti-globalization groups. The Irish republican activist space shared mediated and mediatized practices designed to convey deeper interpretative messages to communities beyond its own. éirígí and RNU may have used the Internet to disseminate their messages, but it was in the physical lifeworld that such activism primarily took place. These parties illustrated the belief of the blogger and political activist, World by Storm, who argued, 'political activity off line is the most important thing'.[4]

The final phase in the battle for hegemony within the Irish republican sphere centred on the control and appropriation of traditional forms of activism and the political messages they communicated. éirígí and RNU sought to re-mould or update extant republican activist media practices reflecting the changing nature of the sphere and the complex relationship between the Internet, social media and the mass media. However, by prioritizing lifeworld activism and linking it to the virtual world, dissenting republican groups, in their nascent state, illustrated that, in this sphere, the Internet was a subordinate zone to physically interrogating issues and gathering support. The direct political factors for gathering online also emerged from the lifeworld, from the specific political realities of the day, rather than emerging exclusively from online activism space in the manner of some anti-corporate groups.

From the earliest days of its founding, éirígí belied a relatively small membership by demonstrating highly engaged internal cultures of activism which were rooted in the belief in the power of the Internet as a useful vehicle for radical and fringe political movements. In these years it seam-lessly integrated a highly mobilized repertoire of pickets, street demon-strations and occupations of buildings, which reflected members' shared background in Sinn Féin's 'in your face street activism' years. It also deftly used the virtual space with a great degree of skill, posting regular updates on its website and using *Indymedia Ireland* and other activist outlets online in the belief that, to stand out in the crowded and highly engaged Irish left space, it had to be more visible and active than the other groups.[5]

éirígí also demonstrated an instinctive talent for attracting mainstream media attention, at least in its early phase, with spectacles and events. Although it attracted figures who would problematically straddle the dissident/dissenter divide, éirígí sat squarely with the ambit of dissent towards the Peace Process, yet retaining an ideological fealty to the core republican values of Sinn Féin before the onset of the peace initiatives: a radical left-wing class-struggle agenda, and opposition to the negative effects of globalization and neo-liberal capitalism and how they impacted upon Ireland and Irish republicans. This initially set it apart from the other dissenters and dissidents for whom Irish sovereignty was still the central plank of their ideological construction and made them rather one-paced, old-fashioned performers in a global resistance community underpinned and constructed by the Internet and the growing presence of social media. For éirígí to build its internal coherence and external distinctiveness, it underpinned street-level grassroots activism with an online media pres-ence that mirrored other left-wing republican organizations. In this context, it mirrored the concerns of the Workers' Party and which RNU would also come to adopt. The Internet provided the opportunity for often radical restructuring of political communities that could be redefined from the grassroots, as a form of 'self-determination and control' from below the political hierarchies that previously dominated.[6]

éirígí built a high profile initially within the republican dissenting milieu, but the question that was never really answered was whether any of this visibility had any real deliberative effect in the wider political world. That éirígí coalesced and mobilized quickly and was able to rapidly spread its message from foundation in 2006 can be attributed to promises of the Internet and growth of new online activist spaces. éirígí successfully bridged the gap between online activity and lifeworld activism's delibera-tive effects, and demonstrated that the online space exists merely as an addendum to the traditional grassroots street-level activism that is central to counter hegemonic activist practice.

Irish politics had been dynamically reframed by the twin impetuses of the collapse of the Celtic Tiger and its economic effects and the near constant tumult at Stormont. New radical political publics emerged in the Republic of Ireland in opposition to the effects of housing boom and bust, water charges, economic uncertainty, political corruption and declining standards of life. In Northern Ireland, the sense that the sectarian carve-up between the DUP and Sinn Féin was hampering both social justice and the progress of republicanism made fruitful ground for éirígí. The Internet was a liminal space in which these oppositional voices could be heard.

Vital to the early momentum that éirígí gained when it launched in April 2006 was the dynamic website which formed the focus for the party's activists, performing the role that a conventional hard-copy newspaper had done for other republican groups. éirígí activists who had experienced the pitfalls of producing and selling *AP/RN* while in Sinn Féin, such as the fixed capital overheads and huge time commitment, noted that these efforts detracted from vital party business and developing policy documents. It therefore made the collective decision to develop a platform with a predominantly digital-first policy.[7] As a nascent party with a relatively low membership and, therefore, lower financial resources, this might also be a case of turning a necessity into a virtue. However, éirígí's media output included a mélange of activist video and photographic essays alongside occasional information sheets and newsletters.[8] MacCionnaith noted:

> Parties that run newspapers never cover their costs. Every year there was a debate over the future of *An Phoblacht*. You have to ask whether people want political newspapers anymore. We decided that the website would be our main media source and it would be updated every day, or every second day at least. But we also decided to use Facebook, Bebo, trying to use the media that people were using.[9]

The *Irish Times* was quick to recognize the changing nature of republican activism, noting that éirígí saw 'little point in broad-based membership if activism is limited to selling ballots and circulating *An Phoblacht*'.[10] Internal Sinn Féin divisions had also emerged when members in Dublin had been chastised by Denis Donaldson for their political performance prior to his being revealed as an informant, this being another reason for the split.[11] éirígí emerged at a time when dissenting former Sinn Féin activists sought to build a platform based on a version of radical Connollyite socialism which many within the republican movement said Sinn Féin had turned its back on in government, despite its continued pretences towards radicalism. éirígí realized that the failure of previous republican dissenting projects was not simply that they were ideologically unappealing but that there was a detachment between lifeworld activism and communicating it to wider publics. It realized that it had to build meaningful synergies between committed street activism which cut a niche online but which also allowed it to reach beyond the narrow confines of traditional republican politics.

It initially did this by rediscovering the aggressive, often agitprop activism of Sinn Féin from the 1980s which allowed it to develop an agenda-setting forum beyond its relatively low human resource base.[12] It deliberately implicated éirígí in the global resistance milieu, taking sustenance from ideologically congruent causes like Palestinian resistance and environmental activism such as Shell to Sea protests in the west of Ireland. Its environmental concerns in Ireland had both a symbolic link globally and in republican history, placing them within a Connollyite tradition of republican socialism and the first Dáil. Its environmental policy borrowed the 1907 Connolly phrase, 'We only want the earth!' and was prefaced by reference to the Democratic Programme of the First Dáil of 1919: 'we declare that the nation's sovereignty extends not only to all men and women of the Nation, but to all its material possessions, the Nation's soil and all its resources.'[13] MacCionnaith said:

> Instead of reverting to armed struggle we look to South Africa and the popular movements which achieved shifts in power, Venezuela for example. Where we would have previously looked towards South America for armed struggle we now see populist movements coming to power without a shot being fired and Republicans should recognise that. Whether we are talking Marx or Connolly, Ireland cannot be divorced from struggles elsewhere in the world, there are similarities and it is only right that we show global solidarity.[14]

The coherence of the éirígí agenda in its early years was remarkably consistent and disciplined, where it did not allow itself to become distracted by fashionable or fleeting causes. About a quarter of its public and media statements concerned Shell to Sea gas pipeline protests, perhaps seeing this as a means to capture modern young republicans for whom environmentalism was a natural adjunct concern to globalization and neo-liberalism. Reflecting MacCionnaith's and senior members' beliefs in the capacity to build coherence with global movements, around another 10 per cent focused on news on popular left-wing regimes, particularly those in Venezuela, Cuba and Latin America. Other key core interests included opposition to policing and justice reform proposals and the St Andrew's Agreement in Northern Ireland, which had been the defining moment in the last catalysing phase of dissidence.

Reflecting the seemingly perennial struggles, éirígí was also involved in active opposition to Orange Order parades, yet it showed enough ideological flexibility to address issues of both racism and homophobia in Ireland, neither of which were necessarily of any concern to more traditionalist forms of republicanism.[15] However, these types of socially progressive causes had become Sinn Féin's hinterland. If one of the mottos of various modern movements has been 'think globally, act locally', then éirígí's pickets of Israeli goods on sale in the Castle Court shopping centre in Belfast were also situated and informed by global anti-Zionist protests.[16] Rather than see media activism within the confines of a conventional and staid party publication, éirígí's enthusiastic embracement of direct action sought to re-energize the radical republican space which had been made docile by the conventional spectacle of mediatized politics. éirígí sought out the same disruptive role in microcosm in Ireland that Occupy did on the global stage.

The highly mediated spectacles that éirígí created belied its relatively resource-poor status and exaggerated its strength. They were designed to influence mainstream media as much as possible but were not simply a result of guerrilla activism or anarchic opportunism. Former publicity director, Pádraig Mackel said these events were conceived by senior members as stunts as a means of aggressively setting the news agenda. These actions would then become press releases and media packages sent to national news outlets, while branches or 'ciorcals' redrafted them for their local media.[17] This model of activism-led events that would force the hand of the mainstream was conceived from a Marxist perspective of the media being a tool of the establishment and political and financial elites. Mackel noted:

> When we first sat down strategically to plan press and publicity we knew the capitalist media was not impartial and we had the mindset that we were going to have to battle on every single issue. We knew that we were going to have to try and set the news agenda, we were going to have to force our way into the news.[18]

There was nothing new about éirígí's repertoire: marches, civil disobedience and the occupying of buildings, utilized by the anti-neo-liberal and environmentalist movements, had deep roots in Irish resistance groups across two centuries. éirígí was also relatively successful in increasing its public profile but it did little to build any real public support.

Traditional activist practices: occupations, social disruption and marches

The essence of éirígí can be seen in the Mansion House protest in Dublin in January 2009 and the anti-Nama protests in May 2010, which were both centrally conceived to be captured on video and distributed online in the manner of anti-globalization activist networks. After activists scaled the

Mansion House to protest against the Good Friday Agreement, éirígí chairperson, Brian Leeson said:

> this country, far from being free, remains occupied by the same British forces that occupied it at the time of the First Dáil. Ninety years on from that historic gathering, no amount of weasel-words can deny the fact that Britain's war machine is still less than one hundred kilometres from the Mansion House, very much entrenched on Irish soil.[19]

Anti-Nama protests, which included the occupation of the Anglo Irish Bank headquarters in April 2010, and further protests in May 2010, were aimed at capturing both the activist and mainstream media agenda. Nama, the National Asset Management Agency, was the government organization which bailed out failing banks while unemployment and poverty grew in the Irish Republic. It became a focus for left-wing groups as the triumph of the inequality of neo-liberal economics and the capitalist banking sector.[20] Although fitting with a pattern of leftist protests at the bailing out of banks across Europe, éirígí also saw activism of this kind as being specifically situated within traditional republican left struggle. At the occupation of Anglo Irish, the bank which contributed most to the collapse of the Irish banking sector, Leeson urged, 'through mass public protest, through civil disobedience, through the withdrawal of labour we can collectively bring the Nama Republic to its knees. And, in its place, we can build a country that will truly reflect the vision of the 1916 Proclamation.'[21]

The party's ongoing commitment to the Shell to Sea Corrib gas pipeline protests also saw it highly active in pickets and occupations at the controversial natural gas refinery in Ballinaboy, County Mayo and elsewhere. From its inception, Shell to Sea was a key issue for the party, an issue it believed would accentuate its bona fides in the radical Irish left space, rather than in the purely republican space. The 32CSM was also broadly supportive, if less visible on the Ballinaboy protests.[22] Former senior PIRA prisoner and ex-Sinn Féin member, Rab Jackson, who had joined éirígí and become Belfast chairman, was arrested along with fellow member Dominic McGlinchey in Ballinaboy in November 2007 as they joined a sit-down protest by environmentalists.[23] éirígí also sent two former prominent Sinn Féin members, MacCionnaith and Gerard Rice, because of their experience in roadblocking protests against unionist marches in Portadown and the Lower Ormeau Road area of Belfast respectively. The party described the activists as 'men with vast amounts of experience in defending the interests of their community'.[24] Jackson and McGlinchey were convicted of obstruction, and fined and given probation orders in February 2008.[25] McGlinchey, the son of the murdered INLA leader Dominic McGlinchey, was also convicted of similar obstruction offences after a protest against Tony Blair and the Iraq war at Stormont in May 2007.[26]

While these protests, which had close alliances with the Irish and British left and a coalition of environmental groups, could be deemed successful because of the numbers that they attracted and the attention that they garnered, in some instances from the mainstream media, the party was less successful with traditional republican protests. éirígí proved it could play an active role in protests focused on social and economic issues, but older republican oppositional issues with the British state and the Peace Process were less fruitful for the party. In the early years of the party's existence and as a result of its highly mobilized activist strategy, it represented, to some sectors of the media, a challenge to Sinn Féin, albeit still a nascent one. In the run-up to a controversial homecoming parade for Royal Irish Regiment soldiers returning from Iraq in November 2008, Sinn Féin called a demonstration against the RIR. éirígí announced a separate march in direct opposition to Sinn Féin's. One journalist captured the stakes:

> One veteran republican dissident from Derry who spoke to the *Guardian* this week succinctly summed up the challenge posed to Sinn Féin: 'If éirígí brings a big crowd to their protest it will unnerve Sinn Féin.' In other words Sinn Féin is trying to hold that part of republican space that could be potentially occupied by its former radical, street-fighting element.[27]

The challenge was met strongly by Sinn Féin's Jim Gibney, who reasserted Sinn Féin's lead on the issue, opining that, 'the insensitivity and indifference of those behind the parade was felt most acutely by those relatives whose loved ones were killed directly by the British crown forces or indirectly by loyalists through collusion'.[28] éirígí's protest did not garner the same support as Sinn Féin's, reflecting the latter's continued hegemony in nationalist Belfast. However, éirígí's highly mobilized activism in protest against the armed forces continued the following year in Belfast with a piece of guerrilla activism that would come to define its strategy in the coming years. At the Tall Ships Festival in Belfast, two party activists visited a British naval vessel docked as a visitor attraction, and distributed DVDs of British military actions in Northern Ireland, Afghanistan and Iraq. The action led to the cancellation of a proposed parade of Royal Marines in the city, and was a propaganda success signifying that the party was capable of staging protests that could capture the media's attention.[29]

The key set piece protest against the visit of Queen Elizabeth II to Dublin in 2011 was a barometer to the changing attitudes, particularly in the Irish Republic, to the British monarchy and British rule in Northern Ireland in general. While it was natural that dissident and dissenting republicans would protest against the visit as a reaction to the continued British presence in the North, historic antipathies towards the monarchy and Britain were not held as deeply in the Republic of Ireland – which in itself was perhaps indicative of the effects of partition and the development of the Irish state. A previous visit to Ireland by the Queen's daughter, Princess Anne, to Croke Park, the home of the 'nationalist' GAA to watch an Ireland v. Scotland rugby union international, had failed to gather more than 'dozens of protestors', but it did capture the mainstream media's attention enough to see party chairman Brian Leeson interviewed on RTÉ television's *Seoige and O'Shea* daytime TV programme.[30] The 2011 visit, the first visit by a reigning British monarch to Ireland since 1911, and which saw the Queen lay a wreath to dead Irish republicans at the Garden of Remembrance, was a strategic focus for both éirígí and RSF, with éirígí most prominent in the weeks prior. The party situated the discourse of protests beyond a simple rejection of the British presence in Ireland and expanded them to encompass critiques of ongoing imperialism as represented by the Iraq and Afghanistan wars and the 'British caste system, a system which is based on sectarianism, inherited privilege and class'.[31] It did not, however, wholly resist a traditional republican angle, and in asking people to join it and play their part in 'the struggle for Ireland's freedom', it pledged: 'as the countdown to the centenary of the 1916 Rising continues éirígí is committed to building popular resistance to British imperialism in Ireland. And that includes opposition to visits by British royals to all parts of Ireland.'[32]

Despite a prolonged campaign of protest by éirígí and a huge amount of time given over to the planning of a march against the visit, the party and RSF failed to gather more than 210 protestors between them according to mainstream news reports.[33] A large security operation by the Gardaí to shut down sections of North Central Dublin close to the ceremony was one reason for the lack of success of the protest. The *Guardian* noted that the protests were 'lacklustre', and captured the central issue in éirígí and RSF's failure to engender more support, asserting that 'the response of the majority of the Irish public, whose attitude veers from a warm welcome to benign indifference, also underlines how isolated the republican dissidents are in modern Ireland.'[34] This visit, and a subsequent one to Belfast in 2012, during which the Queen shook hands with Martin McGuinness, would illustrate the marginalization of traditional republicanism in the period after the GFA and the problems of re-establishing broad-based traditional critiques of 'Brits Out'. The visit to Belfast, which éirígí also protested heavily against, was another step on the progression line of the GFA, and republican dissident opposition was marginalized after the success of the Dublin visit. McGuinness's meeting was greeted in wider political circles, not as a republican sellout, but as another success for the Sinn Féin strategy.

Regardless of the outcomes of these kinds of protest, éirígí established itself as a highly visible and active presence in the republican and wider political spheres. It did so more inventively than other dissenting groups by co-opting the repertoires of the global left. It created activist media opportunities where it would change the shared practices of the republican activist community in a Situationist, guerrilla activism which forced its presence into the mainstream media sphere.

Jamming the republican signal: guerrilla activism

éirígí perhaps represented an Irish republican project that was very much the product of its global times given its close relationship with anti-establishment, anti-neo-liberal and anti-globalization countercultural groups. These groups grasped the potential of the Internet early and utilized its power to bring globally diverse groups together rapidly. In one corner of the anti-globalization movement were the radical left-wing opponents of corporations and the gospel of advertising and market that did much to enslave the West in patterns of consumption which was, in turn, sustained on the exploitation of the global South. Guerrilla artists and activists such as those in the Culture Jammers borrowed the subversive and anarchic humour of the French Situationist movement to subvert the ideology, dogma and dominance of global corporations.[35] By defacing billboards, subverting the slogans of seemingly ubiquitous commercial presences like Nike and McDonald's, they jammed the signal of the corporations and drew attention to the effects of this form of capitalism. Mark Dery described this culture jamming as, 'media hacking, information warfare, terror-art, and guerrilla semiotics, all in one. Billboard bandits, pirate TV and radio broadcasters, media hoaxers, and other vernacular media wrenchers who intrude on the intruders, investing ads, newscasts, and other media artifacts with subversive meanings are all culture jammers.'[36]

The Situationist influence also embraced guerrilla tactics that were well known and had been employed successfully by republicans through their history: modern sit-ins and occupations to draw attention to the effects of neo-liberalism were part of the republican repertoire. In London, anarchist group Space Hijackers targeted Starbucks because the coffee corporation was colonizing British high streets and driving away distinctive local and regional identities.[37] It defaced a coffee shop's sign in East London and encouraged people to stage mock fights in their local branch.[38] éirígí was involved in a similar event, rebranding shops in Dublin and Belfast, although its campaign was erroneously instigated on the basis of the corporation's purported support for Zionist causes.[39] In the Situationist sense, the Culture Jammers were 'literally turning around, *détournement*, re-routing spectacular images, environments, ambiances and events to reverse or subvert their meaning and thus reclaiming them'.[40] These *No Logo* generation activists cleverly cited modern popular culture 'in self-conscious postmodern parodies' to destabilize the pervasive semiotics of modern capitalism.[41] In a piece on the Cuban revolution as an inspiration, one éirígí correspondent situated the party's impulse in such ideological confines:

> The consumerist ideology clouds the possibility of viewing oneself as part of a greater intrinsically valuable whole; like a community, a nation or the human race. The values of the Cuban revolution are a reminder of our humanity and struggle that it takes to realise the full potential of that humanity in a world brutalised by capitalism.[42]

For éirígí, co-opting the visual symbols and slogans of establishment republicanism, of the corrupt political establishment and its implication in the application of the neo-liberal agenda, necessarily had to be rooted in a wider contemporary tradition of defiance globally.

éirígí's media campaigns deliberately reflected the influence of this global movement and repackaged received notions of Irishness. It subverted symbols of Irish identity previously used to drive tourism, and this was achieved by co-opting cultural influences from punk rock. Famous twentieth-century Guinness advertising was retooled to make critical points about the EU by means of Situationist *détournement* and co-option. Guerrilla marketing activist strategies re-imagined the accepted modes of the Irish commercial aesthetic and were redeployed to make alternative republican statements.

Before this, the party showed its adroitness in repackaging media products for its own propaganda aims. In December 2008, when the primetime ITV talent programme *X Factor* released the song 'Hero' in support of a British armed forces charity, éirígí recut its own video, retooling it not as televisual hagiography but as condemnation of what it described as 'military brutality' in Ireland and the Middle East.[43] This action came only a month after the disputed Royal Irish Regiment homecoming protests that had seen the party challenge Sinn Féin.[44] Its rapid response to opportunities presented by popular culture demonstrated a deftness and engaged sensibility for which dissenting and dissident republicans are often given little credit. For example, noting the increasing popularity for guerrilla art pioneered by Banksy, éirígí updated republicanism's historic commitment murals as propaganda, with stencilling campaigns across Belfast.[45] This art has been most prominent around West Belfast and Lenadoon, in particular featuring revered leaders like Connolly and James Larkin.[46] éirígí showed the cultural flexibility of the latest generation of activists who are as likely to turn to punk rock as Patrick Pearse.

By far the most eye-catching and savvy example of the party's deployment of guerrilla media tactics was its appropriation of John Gilroy's era-defining mid-twentieth-century Guinness advertising for use in the campaign against the Lisbon Treaty referendum in 2009, which coincided with the 250th anniversary of the founding of the brewery. The birthday had spawned a year-long series of events to celebrate the beer which had so long been a pervasive symbol of Ireland throughout the world. The famous 1930s and 1940s posters of Toucans bearing the slogan 'Guinness is good for you' were again highly prominent. Co-opting the iconography and subverting the slogan, éirígí posters appeared around Dublin with the toucan birds carrying pints of porter on their beaks, only this time the adverts said, 'Lisbon is bad for you', with the supplementary line: 'Vote No'. Party spokesman Daithí Mac an Mháistír told the media, 'The eyes of the world are on the Guinness celebrations and we decided to inject a bit of seriousness into it. Guinness has been great for Ireland but there's little about Lisbon that's any good for us.'[47] Republican groups were united, as they had been historically, against Ireland's further integration into Europe on the basis of the erosion of Irish national sovereignty and because the EU was perceived as aggressively pursuing the neo-liberal agenda that had imposed privatization and driven deeper control of the state through multi-national banking interests.[48] éirígí's Louise Minihan, former Sinn Féin councillor, said:

> The Lisbon Treaty is designed to bring us one step closer to a federal united states of Europe. A Europe based on a foundation of neo-liberal capitalism. Nama, savage cutbacks, the privatisation of healthcare and education and the introduction of water charges are just a few examples of what we can expect if the Lisbon Treaty is passed.[49]

The party's campaign one year earlier also displayed the Situationist talent for guerrilla street theatre combined with a clever pop cultural reference. Using punk godfathers the Sex Pistols' Jamie Reid-designed garishly coloured album cover for *Never Mind the Bollocks: Here's the Sex Pistols*, the title was reinvented as the arresting slogan, 'Never mind the bollocks: It *IS* the same treaty. No to Lisbon 2.'[50] Showing an eye for jamming the signal and gaining attention far beyond its resources, éirígí activists launched the poster campaign by causing a disturbance outside Leinster House dressed as punks.

The same 2008 campaign saw éirígí capture further headlines and broadcast media attention with another clever poster that was augmented with its first piece of street theatre. Parodying the 1917 World War I American recruitment figure Uncle Sam, the personification of the USA who proclaimed 'We Want You! For the US Army' in a world-famous poster, éirígí satirized EU imperialism as the newly rechristened Uncle EU sternly pointed over the slogan 'I Want You for a United States of Europe', with 'Vote No to Lisbon' as the secondary line.[51] However, displaying éirígí's talent for converting online subversion into street campaigning, this did not remain a static piece of art. Rather, displaying its customary agitprop tendencies, an éirígí activist dressed as Uncle EU confronted high-profile politicians on the campaign trail on busy weekend Dublin shopping streets. In full view of the watching mainstream media retinue, the activist challenged Fine Gael's then opposition leader Enda Kenny, the Labour leader Eamon Gilmore and ruling Fianna Fáil finance minister Barry Andrews as they canvassed for a Yes vote in the upcoming referendum. Uncle EU shouted, 'Vote Yes to Lisbon for a militarized Europe!', 'Vote Yes for a European Defence Agency!' and 'Vote Yes for a United States of Europe!' He asked Gilmore, a centre-left politician influenced by historic Irish socialism, what James Connolly would have thought of a United States of Europe.[52] Speaking to the media, a party spokesperson said an

> éirígí activist made clear the links between the protest and the referendum. Acceptance of the Lisbon Treaty will result in Ireland becoming further entwined in an undemocratic, militarised super-state. Our activists have highlighted this threat today in a colourful and imaginative manner and informed people about how to counter it.[53]

If part of the intention of guerrilla marketing stunts, for resource-poor groups like éirígí, is to make a demonstrable intervention in the mainstream political sphere, then this event was hugely successful. It was reported by both RTE television news and by the *Irish Independent*.[54]

The stunt by éirígí which gained the highest-profile media attention in this period was another piece of agitprop, guerrilla campaigning that could have been borrowed from Sinn Féin in its own agitprop years, or indeed from animal rights activist organization, PETA. Louise Minihan, campaigning against the closure of a respite care ward for Alzheimer's and dementia patients at a West Dublin hospital, poured red paint over the Irish health minister Mary Harney as she was 'turning the sod' to mark the opening of a primary care centre in Ballyfermot. Harney, who was involved in a conventionally staged pseudo event of no real substance, was doing so at a time when the Irish Republic's health service was engaged in cutting the budget which, republican activist groups said, would see more than a fifth of staff accepting voluntary redundancy.

éirígí had been particularly vocal in the debates surrounding the restructuring of the health care system, and this protest was also intended to illustrate the growing privatization of the Irish health system and attacks on the public sector in the Republic during the Post-Celtic Tiger austerity measures in general.[55] The red paint symbolized that, with the closure of hospitals and units in the aftermath of health service rationalization, people would die and Harney would have 'blood on her hands'.[56] Minihan reiterated this point when the event was given widespread mainstream media coverage, including on the national broadcaster RTE's top-rated radio phone-in show, *Liveline*.[57] It further galvanized éirígí's standing as proactive and diligent guerrilla activists whose strategies were aimed at penetrating the mainstream media space while also signifying their countercultural bona fides.

The Dáil's budget of 2010 was deemed the 'blood budget' by left-wing groups because of the effects it would have on the health care system, and protest posters were spread online opposing cuts.[58] However, the guerrilla activist intentions of Minihan's act were deeply rooted in Situationist critiques of the banality of such staged political events, as well as directly linking the economic crisis to the bailing out of banks while the Irish working class suffered. Minihan's actions destabilized the emptiness of the political spectacle and drew the agenda back to éirígí and the Irish left's opposition to extensive public sector cuts in the Republic's budget. As photographs from the event captured Harney left to 'turn the sod' with red paint dripping down her neck, éirígí noted:

> December's blood budget will result in the unnecessary and avoidable deaths of hundreds, if not thousands, of people over the coming years. Irish citizens are literally dying to satisfy the demands of the IMF, the EU and the money markets. The wealth of this country should be used to provide a first class health service that is open to everyone and not to bail out the private banks.[59]

Minihan was found guilty of assault, fined and given a two-year suspended sentence. She refused to pay the fine and was jailed for seven days, saying, 'My protest was a legitimate political action, which should never have been brought before the courts. I never intended to apologise for my actions.'[60]

After running candidates in council elections in Northern Ireland in 2011 and in both states in 2014, with no success, éirígí never again emulated the committed activism of its first five years. The effects of being implicated in the arrest and conviction of activists for possession of weapons in 2014 left a public cloud over its early claims to pacifism and having left the violence of the conflict behind.[61] Some close observers privately suggested to the author that éirígí had tried to form a radical republican movement in reverse, by establishing the political party first before gradually attempting to reassemble an armed wing. Its assumed veneer of bolshie self-confidence also perhaps disappeared as activists became disillusioned with making few electoral gains by not only failing to break into the political mainstream, but also seeing Sinn Féin's popularity continue to rise in the Republic of Ireland. Seven years after its foundation a republican blogger asked under the headline: 'éirígí losing its way' whether the party had replicated the undemocratic, 'Stalinist' leadership-led structures of Sinn Féin which had caused dissent in the first place. He noted: 'it remains to been seen whether éirígí are a progressive republican alternative or just a reincarnation of the left wing Provisionalism dominated by bureaucratic centralism from the centre.'[62] It was also the victim of the rise of the socialist People Before Profit party in Northern Ireland, which took two seats, one in Derry and one in West Belfast, in the 2015 Northern Ireland Assembly election on a radical left-wing platform. There were more deeply held suspicions about the overall foundations of the project, with cynics suggesting that Sinn Féin had choreographed the defection of dissenters by infiltrating éirígí's activist structures soon after its establishment. Certainly, it never got beyond perceptions that it was merely an ersatz version of the dominant party, a 'I Can't Believe It's Not Sinn Féin' facsimile. The *Sunday Tribune* went further, suggesting that, 'The conspiracy theory goes that Sinn Féin knew it would lose people, so it decided to set up a "tame opposition" that would engage in left-wing activities rather than have members defect to dissident paramilitary organisations.'[63] éirígí limps on in 2017, but has a hugely diminished activist base, and former senior figures like Mac an Mháistír who were ideological drivers of the project are no longer as visible or attached.

Regardless of these critiques of the substance of éirígí's ideological canon, the party displayed a greater understanding of the practices of newer forms of political intervention and had learned much from the new era of anti-globalization, post-*No Logo* politics. It was the first attempt by any of the new republican dissenting groups to embrace the new emerging global online counterculture, and it sought to expand the horizons of republicanism beyond the traditional – beyond the party newspaper and conventional forms of protest. It attempted to make its political narrative global and global issues relevant to its locale. With an eclectic set of activist media and the exploitation of popular cultural references it developed the historically narrow remit of republican propaganda by extending its propaganda tools to embrace contemporary practices and global activist movements. éirígí's agitprop standpoint was an aggressive attempt at entering the political agenda which was still dominated by the main political parties. In doing so it developed the repertoire of republican activist practices, or at least updated and extended them.

RNU: guerrilla activism, prisoner rights and landlords

RNU emanated out of quite specific schisms in the republican space in Northern Ireland, yet also had aspirations towards the republican left which was influenced by revolutionary activism globally. However, as noted in chapter three its main concerns were more traditional and closer to home, and were centred in the four Ps: the direction of the Peace Process, policing reforms, protesting at contentious parades, and the welfare of republican prisoners. As a specific challenge to the constitutionalism of Sinn Féin and its pervasive political and social influence in republican areas of Northern Ireland, RNU activist repertoire was limited. Without contesting elections, it has been restricted to street protests, and, with a much smaller activist base, these have rarely been given much attention by either the mainstream media or wider republican sphere. It may have built branches in the Republic of Ireland, but it remains most active and visible in the North.

RNU noted that the traditional means of protest – pickets and white line pickets – were regularly ignored by mainstream media outlets, including those catering for the nationalist community in Northern Ireland, including the *Irish News* and the *Andersonstown News*.[64] It noted that its strategy was underdeveloped and needed to be more aggressive, a conclusion it arrived at while reflecting on the relative success of éirígí in receiving attention with its occupations and mediated stunts.[65] As a response to this, it made a central decision both to professionalize its media strategy – to develop closer relationships with the news desks of nationalist newspapers and provide more professionally written copy and photographs:

> We were much more active than éirígí, in Belfast anyway, but they were able to get headlines doing less than we were. But they were writing the stories for journalists. Journalists are basically lazy and we pretty quickly realised that if we wrote a half decent article and delivered it into their laps with a decent photo, it would get in.[66]

Initially, this had repercussions for activist strategy – seeing that white line pickets gathered little mainstream or activist media attention, it also decided on more attention-grabbing stunts – guerrilla activism like occupations and vandalism of premises.[67] While this was an active response and can be situated in the modern activist ambit, on another level RNU's guerrilla activism had deeper roots in the republican activist strategies of the Troubles. In particular, the question of prisoner welfare and the jails, which had served to galvanize many to the Sinn Féin cause when it had been marginalized by the armed campaign, became a central issue where the old and new elements of RNU's republican activism would converge.

As noted in chapter three, there was very little that was 'new' in RNU's broad adoption of the prisoner welfare question and the establishment of Cogús. The party was once more using these issues as a means to develop a localized infrastructure with which to both gather support and develop ideological positions on which to build more dynamically. The party's mobilized advocacy of prisoner welfare was a reaction to already extant activism within Maghaberry jail, rather than originating from RNU leadership.

Dissident prisoners in Maghaberry adopted structured protests against prison regulations from June 2010 and there had been sporadic periods of conflict since the mid 2000s.[68] The prisoners, many of whom were PIRA and INLA inmates prior to the post-GFA release in 2000, adopted longer-held traditions of jail protest. Dissident prisoners engaged in hunger strikes and dirty protests, both of which had been successful activist practices in building support and publicity during the Troubles.[69] These were echoes or simulacra of previous generations of republican activism, clearly learned rituals of communities of activist practice. Two prisoners, Liam Hanna-way, a relative of Gerry Adams, and the prominent dissident and former éirígí member, Colin Duffy, initiated hunger strikes protesting about the continuation of strip searches, lock-up times and freedom of movement in the Roe House block of the jail.[70] More than thirty dissident prisoners linked to a number of groups were involved in the protests, including those from RIRA, CIRA, INLA and ONH.[71]

Although senior Sinn Féin and SDLP representatives had been to the jails in a welfare capacity, prisoners had refused their help. In this vacuum, RNU became the representative of the prisoners, reflecting its origins as Ex-POWs against PSNI/MI5. This was a natural fit for the organization, as several senior members had been Maghaberry inmates in the post-2000 period. The former prisoner bloc had been the most active bloc in the Forum for Unity from which RNU emerged.[72]

The campaign for prisoner rights, which intentionally aped similar campaigns by Sinn Féin in the 1970s and early 1980s, saw RNU activists engage in protests targeting the Northern Ireland justice minister, David Ford of the Alliance Party, who had become the public face of the states. There were conventional forms of republican protest for RNU, with wall murals in support of prisoner rights and the ending of strip searches in Belfast and Derry.[73] However, the organization now had an opportunity to update its activist repertoire and develop a profile with the mainstream media that it had previously failed to do. Reflecting on the success of the recent re-adoption of occupations by éirígí, RNU repeatedly targeted the Alliance Party HQ. Three protests specifically gathered mainstream media attention – an occupation which was captured by Ulster Television cameras and two acts of vandalism which used the imagery of the dirty protest as a means of raising the profile of the prisoners.

The first occupation, a familiar republican tactic, saw RNU members, including Cunningham, gain access to the Alliance's office demanding a meeting with Ford over prisoner rights.[74] Cunningham noted that the sit-in had been staged to 'shake Ford out of his comfort zone, and we got lucky and barricaded ourselves in'.[75] RNU was also fortunate in the timing of the protest and the closeness of the Alliance HQ to Ulster Television's offices. When activists alerted the station to the situation, it captured those involved in the sit-in being arrested by PSNI officers, and the item appeared on the main evening bulletin.[76] Cunningham was filmed being arrested while wearing a t-shirt with the slogan, 'Ford can end strip searching', a photograph of which accompanied a local evening newspaper's online report of the protest.[77] The increased profile was the catalyst for further examples of non-violent direct action by the organization and the rethink of its strategies: 'We had done several peaceful protests and the media never covered them. We occupied his [Ford's] office to increase media interest in Maghaberry. We were just blatant and shameless and it worked. We have not done a white line picket since then.'[78]

Two further RNU guerrilla protests which had echoes of the aesthetics of Sinn Féin protests of the 1970s also managed to capture the attention of the mass media. In December 2011, four months after the sit-in, two men carrying an RNU banner were caught on camera smearing the Alliance Party offices with excrement.[79] A second 'dirty protest', in October 2012, was a more conventionally staged political stunt – two RNU members, dressed in isolation suits and masks to highlight the treatment of prisoners in the jail, threw horse manure at the premises. Its press statement said, '49 republican prisoners are suffering the serious effects of a "dirty protest", living in excrement filled cells and being forced to inhale toxic fumes in cells which are hosed down with deep cleansing chemicals.'[80] RNU staged pictures of both guerrilla stunts, and these appeared on online and activist media sites in Ireland.[81] Both acts coincided with dissident prisoners continuing no wash 'dirty protests' in Maghaberry over strip searches, a clear echo of the blanket and dirty protests of the 1970s and 1980s.

Both stunts using animal excrement raised awareness of the prisons issue. BBC Northern Ireland's political editor, Mark Devenport, interviewed RNU's Martin Óg Meehan on the prisoners issue on Radio Ulster's 'Inside Politics' programme at a time when the media was under pressure not to cover dissidents.[82] By any measure of guerrilla activism as a means of raising public and media awareness or profile for an issue, this strategy can be deemed a success. However, again, it is cautionary to note that these actions could deliver little deliberative political effect other than raising awareness of the jail campaign and the profile of the organization. The organization also performed an advocacy role for political prisoners in the Republic of Ireland when it raised awareness of what it termed the 'Victorian' and 'squalid conditions' in E Block of Portlaoise jail. Prisoners, it said, were still forced to 'slop out' sanitation buckets in a practice that was condemned by jail advocacy groups.[83] RNU's support for republican prisoners sought to extend the dissident project by making the correlation between a republican alternative to the Peace Process and the legitimacy of opposing British rule in Ireland. This kind of praxis did not emerge out of a vacuum caused by the recalibration of the republican sphere in the Peace Process era, but was about reclaiming those elements of the republican ideological repertoire that Sinn Féin no longer used or required.

Away from seeking the reform of treatment of prisoners in jail, RNU was also heavily involved in the campaign to free Brendan McConville and John Paul Wooton, CIRA prisoners convicted of the murder of Constable Stephen Carroll in Craigavon in 2009. The organization also led calls for the release of dissident figures who had been arrested and kept on remand in Maghaberry, including its ongoing campaign for the release of its senior member Tony Taylor, who had served three years for possession of a rifle in 2011 and whose licence was revoked in March 2016.[84] Despite vowing never to use white line pickets again, it has done so along with the candle-lit vigils during this campaign.[85] The campaign attracted support across the republican sphere, including from Sinn Féin, with party MLA and former prisoner Raymond McCartney speaking on the matter in March 2017 on the first anniversary of Taylor's re-arrest.[86]

It is unfair to explain RNU's activism as simply being implicated in the traditional environs of republican advocacy and localized forms of activism, but this is where it has had its highest prominence in the eyes of both the media and the interested observing publics. It has assumed some of the left-wing issues that éirígí once made mileage with, along with its repertoire of activism. In December 2012 it disrupted the sale of Israeli goods in Castle Court shopping centre, noting that,

> activists dropped 6 paint bombs made from balloons and red paint from the balcony on to the stall, to symbolise the trauma created during Israeli air assaults on Palestinian citizens. A baby doll covered in red paint was also left at the kiosk in reference to the murder of Palestinian children in the latest round of Israeli air strikes.[87]

It was also highly active in left-wing protests around the G8 conference of leading world leaders which was held in Northern Ireland in June 2013, taking part in two pickets moving from West Belfast to the city centre, the second of which was part of a major anti-globalization anti-corporate march against the conference.[88] The organization claims that activists were forcibly pinned into a corner of a street by the PSNI.[89]

The party also led protests against 'draconian Tory benefit cuts' by lobbying social security workers to refuse to implement the measures in their official roles. An accompanying leaflet was distributed in Belfast to raise awareness of the effects the cuts would have in Northern Ireland.[90] It was also involved with anti-austerity cuts in the welfare state in the Republic of Ireland, and sought to confront the justice minister James Reilly on a visit to a hospital in Louth.[91] This branch of the organization was also highly active in civil disobedience protests against water charges in the Republic of Ireland. Three members were arrested in October 2014 as they attempted to block the installation of water metres in the Father Murray Park area of the town.[92] In November of the same year, and again early in 2015, RNU campaigners picketed Topaz filling stations, partly owned by billionaire Denis O'Brien, in protest at his involvement with Irish Water. However, documentary evidence of the protests would suggest that they only attracted very small numbers of activists and failed to influence the mainstream media agenda in any way.[93]

In a real sense these low-level, localized protests represented the 'performance' of activism, of going through the motions because that is what activists do, and without any real expectation of gathering much support or attention. This was activism conceived within the community using the established norms of activist behaviour but which had little deliberative effect other than being visible in online spaces with apparently little Internet traffic.

RNU also used guerrilla activism to link the long-term dissenting and dissident complaint of Sinn Féin members 'profiting' from the Peace Process with increased levels of poverty in nationalist areas. In this instance it embarked on a campaign targeting landlords, particularly in Belfast, which it said were profiting by charging extortionate rents. Although this issue did have clear links with the republican left and the movement's history of rent strikes and civil disobedience, RNU focused on landlords in West Belfast and linked them to Sinn Féin. Cunningham claimed that figures linked to Sinn Féin had large financial stakes in letting agencies and were 'complicit in landlord policies that were entrenching poverty' in West and North Belfast.[94] The party has yet to officially name these figures and appears unwilling to do so, perhaps due to libel and defamation laws. It also claimed that the close links between Sinn Féin and the Belfast Media Group meant that these claims were left unreported. It claimed to have given the *Andersonstown News* reports and photographs of RNU activists vandalizing Northern Properties, one of the biggest letting agents in West Belfast, but said it was repeatedly met with ambivalence by the paper.[95]

Again, whether this is true or not, the style of protest was less subtle and perhaps less newsworthy to a mainstream media organization than that of éirígí and its 'rebranding' of Starbucks. While there was an element of *détournement* in the Starbucks rebranding – including replacing the company's logo with one that echoed the original aesthetic, RNU activists simply defaced letting and estate agencies with slogans like, 'SCUM LANDLORDS' and 'DROP THE RENTS'.[96] This lack of interest, where RNU said that it had 'politically hit a wall', meant that the organization has had to rely upon social and activist media channels to force this issue. In a direct inverse correlation to that of éirígí, RNU has found itself more successful in pushing the agenda with republican-specific issues while those with a wider social connotation, for a variety of reasons, have failed to capture the attention of the mainstream media.

In the years after 2015, Republican Network for Unity maintained a presence in the republican countercultural space in Northern Ireland and parts of the Republic of Ireland, overlapping with Republican Sinn Féin in some matters, including prisoner advocacy. It has turned to social media, and Facebook in particular, as the primary online space of mobilization and discussion, eschewing a website, but this has also failed to raise its profile beyond the marginalized republican dissenting and dissident communities. The increased vote for Sinn Féin in the 2017 Assembly election and the support for People Before Profit in Belfast and Derry suggest that without contesting elections, RNU will continue to perform the role of a grassroots street-level advocacy organization primarily involved in quixotically helping to keep the flame of pre-1998 republicanism alive, while demonstrating occasional aptitude for attention-grabbing guerrilla media actions.

Notes

1 Morozov, Evgeny, 'Why social movements should ignore social media', *New Republic*, 3 February 2013. Available at: www.newrepublic.com/article/112189/social-media-doesnt-always-help-social-movements. Accessed 4 March 2013.

2 'Support the boycott campaign', eirigi.org. Available at: www.eirigi.org/latest/latest180109.html. Accessed 26 March 2012. See also: 'End landlord extortionism', republicanunity.org. Available at: http://www.republicanunity.org/campaigns-3/end-landlord-extortionism/. Accessed 26 March 2012.

3 For the range of protests during the Hunger Strikes, see: 'Abroad', *An Phoblacht*, 9 May 1981.

4 World by Storm interview.

5 MacCionnaith interview.

6 Kahn, Richard, and Kellner, Douglas, 'Oppositional politics and the Internet', *Cultural Politics* vol. 1, no. 1, 2005, p. 77.

7 MacCionnaith interview.

8 See: 'No to Lisbon photo essay', *Indymedia.Ireland*, 24 September 2009. Available at: www.indymedia.ie/article/94196?author_name=PRO&comment_order=desc&condense_comments=false&userlanguage=ga&save_prefs=true. Accessed 24 September 2009. See also: 'Leinster House, 11th May.- Next Protest May 25th', *YouTube*, 12 May 2010. Available at: www.youtube.com/watch?v=k9Zcv8-oLUM. Accessed 13 May 2010.

9 MacCionnaith interview.

10 Keenan, Dan, 'Radical group seek republican ground lost by Sinn Féin', *Irish Times*, 27 July 2009.

11 Private information from party activist.

12 Miller, David, *Don't Mention the War: Northern Ireland, Propaganda and the Media* (London: Pluto Press, 1994), p. 114.

13 See: 'We only want the earth', eirigi.org, undated. Available at: www.eirigi.org/campaigns/naturalresources/index.htm. Accessed 26 March 2012. See also: Connolly, James, 'Be moderate', in *Selected Writings* (London: Pluto Press, 1988), p. 292.

14 MacCionnaith interview.

15 'Homophobia acceptable in anti-rights assembly', eirigi.org, 21 September 2007. Available at: www.eirigi.org/latest/latest210907_1.html. Accessed 22 September 2007.

16 'Protests for Palestine escalate', eirigi.org, 11 January 2009. Available at: http://www.eirigi.org/latest/latest110109.html. Accessed 14 January 2009. See also: 'CLIP0016', *YouTube*, 10 January 2009. Available at: www.youtube.com/watch?v=qgVE0ppM06g. Accessed 14 January 2009.

17 Mackel, Pádraig, interview, 15 April 2010. As Sinn Féin calls local groups cumanns, éirígí uses the Irish word 'ciorcal' (circle) for its branch meetings.

18 Mackel interview.

19 'Dáil Éireann remembered on Mansion House roof', eirigi.org, 20 January 2010. Available at: hwww.eirigi.org/latest/latest200109.html. Accessed 21 January 2010.

20 The protests against the Nama cuts were coordinated by the group United Alliance Against the Cuts, which encompassed members of the People Before Profit party (itself originating in the Socialist Workers Party) and the Socialist Party. It led to the electoral alliance of the United Left in the Dáil, which also included the Workers and Unemployed Action Group. This alliance eroded and recent alliances have been between the Anti-Austerity Alliance and People Before Profit.

21 'éirígí: occupation of Anglo Irish – full report', eirigi.org, 24 April 2009. Available at: www.eirigi.org/latest/latest250410.html. Accessed 25 April 2009. See also: 'Protestors invade Anglo-Irish HQ', *BBC News Online*, 24 April 2010. Available at: www.news.bbc.co.uk/1/hi/northern_ireland/8641640.stm. Accessed 24 April 2010.

22 Siggins, Lorna, *Once Upon a Time in the West: The Corrib Gas Controversy* (London: Transworld, 2010), p. 246.

23 'Shell and their cops are losing ground', eirigi.org, 10 November 2007. Available at: www.eirigi.org/latest/latest101107_2.html. Accessed 11 November

2007. Siggins notes that Derry 32CSM member Gary Donnelly also visited the picket. 32CSM has given less attention to Shell to Sea and environmental matters in general.

24 'Shell and their cops are losing ground'. See also: 'Making Shell feel the heat', *Irish Republican News*, 22 November 2007. Available at: www.republican-news.org/current/news/2007/11/post_6.html. Accessed 24 November 2007.

25 Siggins, *Once Upon a Time in the West*, p. 246.

26 Erwin, Alan, 'McGlinchey son fined on Iraq clash', *Daily Mirror*, 12 February 2009.

27 McDonald, Henry, 'Much at stake for Sinn Féin when army war veterans parade through Belfast', *Guardian*, 30 October 2008. Available at: www.theguardian.com/politics/blog/2008/oct/30/northern-ireland-parade. Accessed 30 October 2008.

28 Gibney, Jim, 'Army parade cannot airbrush murder legacy', *Irish News*, 6 November 2008. See also: Whelan, Peadar, 'Parade of shame was old fashioned unionist coat trailing', *An Phoblacht*, 6 November 2008.

29 'Dissidents linked to parade halt', *BBC News Online*, 15 August 2009. Available at: www.news.bbc.co.uk/1/hi/northern_ireland/8203039.stm. Accessed 15 August 2009. See also: 'éirígí activists board British warship in Belfast', eirigi.org, 14 August 2009. Available at: www.eirigi.org/latest/latest140809.html. Accessed 15 August 2009.

30 'Dozens attend anti-Windsor protest', eirigi.org. Available at: www.eirigi.org/latest/latest230208.html. Accessed 23 February 2008. See also: www.eirigi.org/campaigns/imperialistsoutofireland/British_queen_visit.html. Accessed 21 August 2013. See also: 'Leeson challenges British Royal visits on RTÉ [1/2]', *YouTube*, 21 July 2008. Available at: www.youtu.be/bOV7Zd-zjxo. Accessed 22 July 2011.

31 'No to British withdrawal? – no Royal visits!', eirigi.org. Available at: http://www.eirigi.org/campaigns/ImperialistsoutofIreland/british_queen_countdown.html. Accessed 18 May 2011.

32 'No to British withdrawal? – no Royal visits!'.

33 McDonald, Henry, 'Queens lays a wreath for dead republicans on Ireland visit', *Guardian*, 17 May 2011. Available at: www.theguardian.com/uk/2011/may/17/queen-lays-wreath-republicans-ireland. Accessed 18 May 2011. McDonald noted that there were 150 éirígí protestors and 60 from RSF. éirígí corroborated his estimation of their numbers. See: 'éirígí anti-Windsor protests, May 17 – full report', eirigi.org. Available at: www.eirigi.org/latest/latest190511_2.html. Accessed 19 May 2011.

34 McDonald, Henry, 'Queen's visit to Ireland is test for republicans', *Guardian*, 18 May 2011. Available at: www.theguardian.com/politics/blog/2011/may/18/queens-visit-ireland-test-for-republicans. Accessed 19 May 2011.

35 Klein, Naomi, *No Logo* (London: Picador, 2010).

36 Dery, M., *Culture Jamming: Hacking, Slashing, and Sniping in the Empire of the Signs*, 1993. Available at: www.markdery.com/?page_id=154. Accessed 23 May 2011.

37 Albert, Saul, 'Graffitiing the brain space', *Mute Magazine*, 9 May 2002. Available at: www.metamute.org/editorial/articles/graffitiing-brain-space. Accessed 23 May 2011.

38 'Leicester Square store launch party!', spacehijackers.org. Available at: www.spacehijackers.org/starbucks/html/lsq.html. Accessed 23 May 2011.

39 'Éirígí activists rebrand Starbucks', *Politics.ie*, 17 January 2009. Available at: www.politics.ie/forum/northern-ireland/40529-eirigi-activists-rebrand-starbucks.html. Accessed 17 January 2009. See also: 'éirígí activists rebrand Starbucks', *YouTube*, 17 January 2009. Available at: www.youtube.com/watch?v=6uysPbQRpyA&hl=en-GB&gl=GB. Accessed 18 January 2009.

40 Lasn, Kalle, *Culture Jam* (London: Harper Collins, 1999), p. 103.

41 Strinati, Dominic, *An Introduction to Theories of Popular Culture* (London: Routledge, 2004), p. 243. Strinati was analysing the post-modern impulse in some forms of contemporary cinema.

42 'Revolution in Cuba: propaganda or truth', eirigi.org, 30 August 2008. Available at: www.eirigi.org/latest/latest300808.html. Accessed 1 September 2008.

43 'X Factor heroes', eirigi.org, 14 December 2008. Available at: www.eirigi.org/latest/latest141208.html. Accessed 15 December 2008.

44 'Take the message back to your masters in Downing Street', eirigi.org, 2 November 2008. Available at: http://www.eirigi.org/latest/latest021108.html. Accessed 3 November 2008.

45 Rolston, Bill, 'The War of the Walls: political murals in Northern Ireland', *Museum International* vol. 56, no. 3, 2004, pp. 38–45.

46 See: 'Do your worst', extramuralactivity.com, 27 October 2012. Available at: www.extramuralactivity.com/2012/10/27/do-your-worst/. Accessed 28 October 2012.

47 Carroll, Steven, 'Lisbon outtakes: borrowing from Arthur', *Irish Times*, 26 September 2009. Available at: www.irishtimes.com/newspaper/ireland/2009/0926/1224255280729.html. Accessed 27 September 2009.

48 See: 'éirígí say no to the Lisbon treaty', eirigi.org. Available at: www.eirigi.org/campaigns/no_to_Lisbon.html. Accessed 18 September 2009. Sinn Féin's agenda was strikingly similar; see: www.sinnfein.ie/files/2009/Lisbon2_AlternativeGuide.pdf. Accessed 19 September 2009. See also: 'Sinn Féin's alternative guide to the Lisbon Treaty', *YouTube*, 19 September 2009. Available at: www.youtube.com/watch?v=usCKm-PfD2c. Accessed 19 September 2009.

49 'Republican councillors against the Lisbon Treaty', eirigi.org, 24 September 2009. Available at: www.eirigi.org/latest/latest240909.html. Accessed 25 September 2009.

50 'éirígí launches first wave of No to Lisbon 2', eirigi.org, 25 August 2009. Available at: www.eirigi.org/latest/latest250809.html. Accessed 25 August 2009.

51 'Tackling the liars on Lisbon', eirigi.org, 5 June 2008. Available at: www.eirigi.org/latest/latest050608(02).html. Accessed 6 June 2008.

52 'Tackling the liars on Europe', *Indymedia.Ireland*, 5 June 2008. Available at: www.indymedia.ie/article/87841?author_name=I&save_prefs=true. Accessed 6 June 2008.

53 'Tackling the liars on Lisbon'.

54 Kerr, Aine, '"Uncle Sam" makes splash on cross-party city canvass', *Irish Independent*, 6 June 2008. Available at: www.independent.ie/irish-news/uncle-sam-makes-splash-on-crossparty-city-canvass-26451898.html. Accessed 7 June 2008. See also: 'How would James Connolly have voted?', *YouTube*, 6 June 2008. Available at: www.youtube.com/watch?feature=player_embedded&v=qot0OaSVX7c. Accessed 8 June 2008.

55 'Dublin City councillor Louise Minihan imprisoned in Mountjoy', eirigi.org, 18 July 2012. Available at: www.eirigi.org/latest/latest180712.html. Accessed 19 July 2012.

56 'Harney has blood on her hands', *Irish Republican News*, 1 November 2010. Available at: www.republican-news.org/current/news/2010/11/harney_has_blood_on_her_hands.html. Accessed 1 November 2010.

57 'Councillor who threw paint at Harney released', *Irish Times*, 2 November 2010.

58 'Direct action protest leaves Harney seeing red in cherry orchard', *Indymedia Ireland*, 1 November 2010. Available at: www.indymedia.ie/article/98047. Accessed 1 November 2010.

59 'Mary Harney "blood on your hands" direct action', eirigi.org, 1 November 2010. Available at: www.eirigi.org/latest/latest011110.html. Accessed 1 November 2010.

60 Byrne, Luke, 'Councillor Minihan jailed over Mary Harney attack', *Irish Independent*, 18 July 2012. Available at: www.independent.ie/irish-news/councillor-minihan-jailed-over-mary-harney-paint-attack-26877212.html. Accessed 19 July 2012.

61 'Trinity graduate gets six years for possession of guns', *Irish Independent*, 28 February 2014. Available at: www.independent.ie/irish-news/courts/trinity-graduate-gets-six-years-for-possession-of-guns-30050314.html. Accessed 29 February 2014.

62 Magee, Joseph, 'éirígí losing its way', *Pensive Quill*, 15 November 2013. Available at: www.thepensivequill.am/2013/11/eirigi-losing-its-way.html. Accessed15 November 2013.

63 McMorrow, Conor, 'Éirigí: new kids on the republican block', *Sunday Tribune*, 9 August 2009. Also available at: www.saoirse32.dreamwidth.org/2009/08/10/. Accessed 10 August 2009.

64 Cunningham interview.

65 Cunningham interview.

66 Cunningham interview.

67 Cunningham interview.

68 'Dirty protest at Maghaberry', *Irish Republican News*, 21 June 2010. Available at: www.republican-news.org/current/news/2010/06/dirty_protest_at_maghaberry.html. Accessed 23 June 2010.

69 'Prison "dirty protest" is echo of troubled past', *Newsletter*, 30 July 2010. Available at: www.newsletter.co.uk/news/regional/prison-dirty-protest-is-echo-of-troubled-past-1-1867170. Accessed 30 July 2010.

70 See: McDonald, Henry, 'Ex-prisoner held over Northern Ireland soldier murders on hunger strike', *Guardian*, 23 March 2009. See also: 'Dissident republican Liam Hannaway ends hunger strike', *BBC News Online*, 25 May, 2010. Available at: www.bbc.co.uk/news/10159464. Accessed 26 May 2010.

71 Rowan, Brian, 'Dissidents on lockdown as Maghaberry protest grows', *Belfast Telegraph*, 26 May 2011. Available at: www.belfasttelegraph.co.uk/news/local-national/northern-ireland/dissidents-on-lockdown-as-maghaberry-protest-grows-28620684.html. Accessed 26 May 2011.

72 Cunningham interview. RSF has its own, longer-established prisoner rights organization, Cabhair but represents only CIRA prisoners. RNU was more visible in its advocacy.

73 For examples of RNU murals, see: 'Ardoyne supports Maghaberry POWs'. Available at: www.ardoynerepublican.blogspot.co.uk/2010/05/ardoyne-supports-maghaberry-pows.html. See also: extramuralactivity.com. Available at: www.goo.gl/pFD7cZ. Accessed 21 August 2013.

74 'Lock-on protest at Alliance Party HQ', *Irish Republican News*, 11 August 2011. Available at: www.republican-news.org/current/news/2011/08/lock-on_protest_at_alliance_pa.html. Accessed 21 August 2013.

75 Cunningham interview.

76 'Republicans protest at Alliance HQ', www.u.tv, 11 August 2011. Available at: www.u.tv/News/Republicans-take-over-Alliance-HQ/211617ef-491a-44b1-bbcf-042f336fb1d4. Accessed 12 August 2011.

77 Madden, Anne, 'Trio charged over jail protest', *Belfast Telegraph*, 12 August 2011. Available at: www.belfasttelegraph.co.uk/news/local-national/northern-ireland/trio-charged-over-jail-protest-at-alliances-hq-28645725.html. Accessed 12 August 2011.

78 Cunningham interview.

79 See: 'Alliance HQ targeted in "dirty protest"', *UTV News*, 16 December 2011. Available at: www.u.tv/News/Alliance-HQ-targeted-in-dirty-protest/3f289fb1-aa5c-4d89-921c-b7ab6e3c40c5. Accessed 17 December 2011.

80 'Dirty protest at Justice Minister's HQ', *Irish Republican News*, 5 October 2012. Available at: www.republican-news.org/current/news/2012/10/dirty_protest_at_justice_minis.html. Accessed 6 October 2012.

81 'Dirty protest at Justice Minister's HQ'.

82 Devenport, Mark, 'Talking to dissident republicans – is it the next step?', *BBC News Online*, 8 January 2012. Available at: http://www.bbc.co.uk/news/uk-northern-ireland-16462230. Accessed 9 January 2012.

83 Healey, Catherine, 'Republican prisoners complain of living in "Victorian" conditions', *journal.ie*, 15 November 2015. Available at: www.thejournal.ie/portlaoise-prison-victorian-conditions-e-block-slopping-out-2442350-Nov2015/. Accessed 15 November 2015.

84 McKinney, Seamus, 'Leading republican Tony Taylor returned to prison after licence revoked', *Irish News*, 12 March 2016. Available at: www.irishnews.com/news/2016/03/12/news/leading-republican-tony-taylor-returned-to-prison-after-licence-revoked-447862/. Accessed 13 March 2016.

85 'Candlelight vigil held in support of the Free Tony Taylor campaign', derrynow. com, 14 December 2016. Available at: www.derrynow.com/news/candlelight-vigil-held-in-support-of-the-free-tony-taylor-campaign/134195. Accessed 15 December 2016. See also: '"White line picket" for Tony Taylor', *Derry Journal*, 23 September 2016. Available at: www.derryjournal.com/news/white-line-picket-for-tony-taylor-1–7593909. Accessed 15 December 2016.

86 'On the first anniversary of his arrest, Sinn Fein again call for the release of Derry republican Tony Taylor', *Derry Now*, 10 March 2017. Available at: www.derrynow.com/news/first-anniversary-arrest-sinn-fein-call-release-derry-republican-tony-taylor/149908. Accessed 10 March 2017.

87 'Direct Action carried out against Israeli goods, Belfast', *Indymedia Ireland*, 16 November 2012. Available at: www.indymedia.ie/article/102737?author_name=RNU+PRO&. Accessed 16 November 2012.

88 'Anti G8 walkabout Belfast', *Indymedia Ireland*, 14 June 2013. Available at: www.indymedia.ie/article/103788?userlanguage=ga&save_prefs=true. Accessed 14 June 2013.

89 'PSNI attack peaceful G8 protest in Belfast', *Indymedia Ireland*, 17 June 2013. Available at: www.indymedia.ie/article/103796?author_name=RNU+PRO&. Accessed 18 June 2013.

90 'RNU New Year statement 2014', *Indymedia Ireland*, 31 December 2013. Available at: www.indymedia.ie/article/104392?author_name=RNU+PRO&. Accessed 31 December 2013.

91 'RNU New Year statement 2014'.

92 'Three arrested after water meter protest at Father Murray Park', *Dundalk Democrat*, 9 October 2014. Available at: www.dundalkdemocrat.ie/news/local-news/56185/Three-arrested-after-water-meter-protest.html. Accessed 20 March 2017.

93 'RNU Dundalk protest at local filling station', *Talk of the Town*, 9 February 2015. Available at: www.talkofthetown.ie/rnu-dundalk-protest-at-local-filling-station/. Accessed 20 March 2017.

94 Cunningham interview.

95 Cunningham interview.

96 'End landlord extortionism', republicanunity.org. Available at: www.republicanunity.org/campaigns-3/end-landlord-extortionism/. Accessed 10 January 2012.

Epilogue: Brexit, the border and nationalism's bounceback

We are in a new era, in this election we have seen a seismic change and realignment of politics here.[1]

The countercultural alternative

When Gerry Adams told supporters at the Louth count centre in the hours after the 2016 Irish general election that a tremor had gone through Irish politics, he had no idea how tumultuous the rest of 2016 and early 2017 were going to be for the party and, ultimately, for Northern Ireland in particular. Sinn Féin's stellar performance in the Dáil elections had been nearly twenty years in the making, and the fifty candidates that had stood in the forty constituencies did so with a greater degree of confidence than they had ever had. Taking more than 13 per cent of the vote in not just a crowded polity, but the extra crowded left space, established it as the coming force in the state, and this despite what the party had described as a 'media war' against it. The party emphasized its outsider, revolutionary bona fides by illustrating how business and political elites had turned on it as it, 'faced a media dirty war during the Dáil general election as the Establishment rounded on the only serious threat to the Golden Circles and the elites of Irish Society'.[2] Much has been made in this book, and many others elsewhere, about how the party had moved from the margins of the mainstream to sitting in government in Northern Ireland, and how it had moved from the furthest peripheries of Republic of Ireland politics to being seen as a credible option for many among the electorate. However, not even Adams could have predicted how far the party's standings would surge in a little more than twelve months, starting with the Irish general election in late February 2016 and ending with the Assembly election of March 2017.

In the Republic of Ireland, the party had been increasing its vote in creditable increments since 1997, when it captured a 2.5 per cent share and finished in sixth place on votes cast, but took only one seat,

Caoimhghín Ó Caoláin in Cavan-Monaghan. In 2002, this jumped to 6.5 per cent and five seats, notably in Dublin South West and Kerry North. In 2007 the party experienced a slight increase in vote but lost a seat, with perhaps the sense that the party was losing momentum as it fought on several fronts. However, just as financial and political opportunity was to present itself in 2016 and 2017 on both sides of the border, the Celtic Tiger collapse had previously proved to be a catalyst in Sinn Féin's fortunes and those of the parties and organizations across the left space.

In the four years between the 2007 poll and the 2011 election, the country had been through a period of national self-doubt and recrimination caused by the full ramifications of the calamity of the banking collapse. There had already been a prelude to this in the early part of the decade, and the left space grew with dissatisfaction with the constant lurches from one government to another with none of them doing anything to address the root causes of financial corruption and cronyism seemingly ingrained in the state. Fianna Fáil, which was returned to power in coalition with the Progressive Democrats and Green Party in 2007, would pay the price for the bailout of the banks and the years of corruption tribunals when its vote collapsed at the 2011 election. As the EU, the Central Bank and the IMF imposed severe austerity measures on a nation which had been forced to bail out banks which had gambled on a housing boom that was, to mix construction metaphors, built on shifting sand, house prices rocketed as poverty and homelessness were on a steep upward curve. As the property boom collapsed, leaving negative equity for many home owners – and, more significantly, thousands of empty homes, ghost estates, newly developed office and retail space lying vacant, and the spectre of Nama bailing out the banks and their toxic loans – Sinn Féin was in a natural position to fight for the disenfranchised. Untainted with any link to the crisis, having never been in government, it seized the opportunity to campaign as the leading party of the left. Joanne Spain said:

> Nama is the crime of the century and may well be the source of the next decade's tribunals. I don't write this to be sensationalist. The inconsistencies, the blatant falsities, the sheer brass-necked hypocrisy of the Nama legislation scares the living daylights out of me. I can put it no simpler than this – each man, woman and child in this State is being robbed by this Government to pay for the balls-up of the banks and developers.[3]

The collapse had been charted by journalists and economists in the national media and online, with David McWilliams and Conor McCabe among the most important writers. McCabe, a socialist economist who had large presence on the Internet, blogs and social media, illustrated the sheer scale of the housing bubble when he noted that there were more than

302,600 empty homes in Ireland, excluding holiday homes.[4] Six years prior to McCabe's post, Sinn Féin had already shown its concern when an *An Phoblacht* editorial lambasted the coalition, saying, 'the hundreds of boarded up council homes must be made habitable again. The failure of this government to tackle the housing crisis makes the need for radical solutions all the more glaring.'[5] Nine years later, while profiling the work of the Peter McVerry Trust, a homeless charity, it noted that the numbers of people without a home had increased by 100 per cent.[6]

Sinn Féin's social justice campaigning, which was more pronounced in the Republic of Ireland in opposition than it was in government in Stormont, took it to the centre of the anti-establishment left that raged against the inequalities caused by financial collapse and recession, austerity measures that were seeing thousands of jobs cut across the state, and the increasing imposition of neo-liberal economics in a state witnessing the ever-growing influence of global conglomerates like Apple and their tax avoidance measures.

In 2011, amid the media circus surrounding Gerry Adams's successful candidacy in Louth, the party did credibly again, taking nearly 10 per cent of the vote and gaining nine seats, taking the total to fourteen. The party could now clearly be asserted to be laying credible foundations in the Republic of Ireland. Using its now customary language of being at the centre of radical change, Declan Kearney wrote: 'The tectonic plates of popular opinion have fundamentally shifted. We need to be at the centre of this continuing political realignment. There is an opportunity to build national and democratic politics from the platform of real world campaigns on social and economic change in the South.'[7]

In the face of public fury at the austerity measures imposed by the EU troika, Sinn Féin's historic inclination towards internationalism saw it find radical left bedfellows, including Syriza, the left-wing party that had swept to power in Greece in 2015 on an anti-austerity platform, and its counterpart in Spain, Podemos. For the party, these radical expressions against neo-liberalism and austerity chimed with the times in Ireland. Illustrated with a photograph of Sinn Féin activists leading an anti-water charges rally, Peadar Kirby, although counselling against an immediate left-wing breakthrough in Europe, wrote: 'SYRIZA in Greece, Podemos in Spain, the Scottish National Party breakthrough in Scotland and now the colourful victory of the marriage equality referendum in Ireland show the eruption of grassroots discontent and aspiration within the political system.'[8]

Syriza had become an increasingly powerful influence in Sinn Féin thinking in the Republic of Ireland, especially among those central in the party's policy-making centre in Leinster House and some of those who wrote for *An Phoblacht*. In 2012, the party's glossy magazine *IRIS* had

profiled influential left-wing economist Yanis Varoufakis, who became the
Greek finance minister in 2015 after his party had risen to power, and it
had built emotional links between his life under military rule in Greece
in the 1970s and the Irish republican experience.[9] It was easy to see how
his story of his father being dragged away by military police and imprisoned in a concentration camp would chime with a publication that still
made much of the prison experiences of Irish republicans. He told *IRIS*:
'Mrs Merkel and the powers that be are saying we have to continue down
the road of austerity and this is making the problem worse.'[10] *An Phoblacht*
covered Greece and Tsipras on a number of occasions after Syriza started
its rise to power.

In March 2014, months prior to Syriza winning the Greek election, its
leader Alexis Tsipras toured Dublin for two days, meeting with left-wing
political activists, trade unionists and senior Sinn Féin figures. Interviewed by Ó'Broin, he outlined his candidacy to become European Commission president, and his platform illustrated striking ideological
commonalities with Sinn Féin: he was anti-austerity, supportive of opening
democracy in the EU and giving authority back to the parliaments, and
pro-solidarity. He noted, 'We want a Europe of solidarity and not the neo-
liberal Europe.'[11] Harry McGee asserted in the *Irish Times* that the Ó'Broin
interview could have 'come straight out of a fanzine', also noting that,
'other left-wing parties don't believe Sinn Féin is a true party of the left'.
He did counter accusations that the party was left *arriviste*: 'that said, it
is definitely left-leaning and has led the anti-austerity charge in Ireland'.[12]

This is the central point with which to understand Sinn Féin's recent
growth in the Republic of Ireland: it was not merely opportunist. Its ideological fealty to the Greek and Spanish radical left was genuinely at the
heart of its modern anti-establishment, radical left roots. These instincts
were inevitably tempered in Stormont under the power-sharing agreement, perhaps proving that it was a party better designed for highly active
ideological opposition as opposed to the compromises required by being
in government. The party, as the primary arbiter of republicanism in the
modern era, could also have been accused of becoming too ideologically
broad to be genuinely radical, leading it to become opportunist in pursuit
of power.[13] The twin forces of British counter-diplomacy and the highly
choreographed nature of both the Peace Process and the administration
of power in Stormont meant that there was little room for the party to
express its central, radical core. In a sense, the economic, financial and
political crisis in the Republic of Ireland from 2008 onwards allowed it
some degree of liberation, to allow it to be itself, or what it had always
wanted to be. That said, there were opportunities that presented themselves that the party also ruthlessly used.

At the 2016 general election for the Dáil, Sinn Féin had established itself as the third party in the state, and took twenty-three seats with 13.8 per cent of the vote. It was also winning seats in areas it had not previously: Carlow-Kilkenny, Offaly, Waterford and Wicklow, areas where Fianna Fáil would have expected to put on a stronger showing. The party was growing beyond the urban and suburban heartlands of Dublin, and had done so not simply because it fought a strong election and caught the zeitgeist, but because it had invested in public activism, both at a national level and in building strong local campaigning structures. The party was keen to emphasize links to the glorious republican past in the centenary year of the 1916 Rising, and the *An Phoblacht* cover line was 'Radical rising', pictured above portraits of the seven signatories of the Proclamation.[14]

At the macro-political level, and to borrow Ó Caoláin's quote used in chapter two, Sinn Féin was the voice of an idea. That idea was greater degrees of social justice, and it was encapsulated in the water protests. When the decision was taken in 2009 to prepare the way for water taxes in Ireland, it was met with almost immediate opposition, although the plan was initially ruled out because of the projected cost of installing the meters. However, in 2010 one of the conditions of a loan from EU/IMF was the introduction of water charges and metres, sparking nationwide protests which would eventually turn into the Right2Water and Right2Change campaigns. The latter of these recommended one hundred left candidates for the 2016 general election, including all fifty from Sinn Féin.[15]

The water campaign marches attracted thousands of protestors, angered not just at the cost of water and the imposition of meters, but also with the involvement of the private sector. The campaign also sparked moments of civil disobedience as residents stopped workers installing meters in homes, with five people jailed in Dublin in February 2015 for contempt of court after they obstructed and threatened workers.[16] The *Irish Examiner* reported that Gardaí had arrested 188 people at water protests during 2014–2015, some for damage and assault, but the majority for public order offences.[17]

It would be wrong to say that Sinn Féin cynically jumped on the protests as a means simply to gather support, but it did make the most of them. Although the left wingers, Alliance Against Austerity and People Before Profit were central to the establishment of Right2Water and Right2Change, along with trade unions, Sinn Féin was a highly visible and loud presence in Dublin, particularly at a March 2015 rally which organizers claimed attracted more than 80,000 protestors (an estimate contested by police).[18] Protests around water charges were a suitable fit for the party, especially within the progressive left element of its equality agenda. The December 2014 edition of *An Phoblacht* led with the headline, 'We want our water', while Ó'Broin, writing in the Another View column, correctly identified that this was an important moment for democracy in the Republic of Ireland: 'the mass mobilizations against the water charges show a new engagement with politics', and, 'a party that offers a real alternative to the corrupt and incompetent politics of the centre right may end up in power sooner than it thinks'.[19] Although Sinn Féin did not take power, his analysis was highly prescient.

In the valedictory edition of *An Phoblacht* in March 2016 after the election, Eoin Ó Murchú outlined a blueprint for the near future of Irish politics which saw the construction of a popular coalition of left parties, with Sinn Féin at the heart of it.[20] He called for the reform of the Labour Party to recapture the Connollyite roots of the movement and champion the cause of workers, in a much wider left alliance than already existed in the state.

The decline of Labour had been rapid by any definition. Having benefited greatly from deep public dissatisfaction with Fianna Fáil in 2011 when nearly doubling its total seats to thirty-seven, by 2016 the party had haemorrhaged votes. It lost thirty seats, and saw a 13 per cent decline in votes as it plummeted to fourth place overall. Sinn Féin benefited from Labour becoming the target of public anger at the years of economic hardship that were the advent to the subsequent recovery. The *Financial Times* noted, 'Labour took the brunt of the Irish public's dissatisfaction with five years of austerity under the Fine Gael/Labour coalition, suffering the same fate as the Liberal Democrats in last year's UK election. And like Mr Kenny's Fine Gael, it got no credit for the subsequent economic recovery in Ireland.'[21]

The RTE exit polling data showed that the water charges issue was the most important for only 10 per cent of the population, but was much more important for those that voted for Sinn Féin.[22] The party also attracted many more people in the under thirty-five age bracket: for people this age, with no memory of the worst atrocities of the Troubles or PIRA violence, the party did not have the whiff of cordite attached to it. Rather, it was an energetic, progressive party of the left which was able to acquit itself well in the public space and which had young representatives who could present themselves well on TV.

Having learned the lessons of the Troubles years and marginalization from the media, Sinn Féin also emphasized dynamic interaction with the media, especially TV and radio. The party's finance spokesman, Pearse Doherty, and Ó'Broin were regular guests on the influential *Tonight with Vincent Brown* current affairs TV programme, much beloved of those in Irish political social media circles. Ó'Broin noted that appearances on the programme are valuable for spreading the message beyond the usual constituency and for gathering social media followers.[23] Hedges asserted that while the transformation in media consumption habits has been detrimental to the fortunes of the newspaper, television and radio have been kinder and the party has a number of 'quality performers' appearing on TV, both North and South.[24]

Almost a year to the day after the breakthrough 2016 election result, Sinn Féin's popularity appeared to be being sustained, with Red C/RTE polls seeing public support surging to 19 per cent in the Republic of Ireland, although polls in Ireland have been unreliable in the past.[25] In a further development the party also appeared to suggest that it was changing its stance on joining a coalition government in the Republic of Ireland, something it had ruled out prior to mid 2017.[26].

No smoke without fire: RHI and Brexit

In the Northern Assembly, Sinn Féin's 2017 election in comparison to its 2016 experience was a case of that most clichéd of journalistic terms: mixed fortunes and mixed emotions. In 2016 it was, like the other major parties, facing up to percentages of the vote share that had slowed or were showing signs of being in decline. Sinn Féin recorded the worst deficit of the top six parties, with a near 3 per cent drop in vote share and the loss of one seat.

Away from those that voted along sectarian lines in constituencies where there was something at stake to vote for, in other parts of Northern Ireland a declining turnout was testament to those that were either turned off by the tribalism or by an Assembly that had been dogged by successive corruption scandals. Finola Meredith noted in the *Guardian*, 'Lulled to tedium by the flawed but relatively stable setup at Stormont, it seems that many people in Northern Ireland can only be bothered to vote when it's a rabid tussle between orange and green.'[27] In an Assembly with relatively little democratic or financial independence from Westminster, the apathy arose from the sense that nothing ever got done other than sectarian squabbling. The headline on a column by *Newsletter* writer Alex Kane summarized how a sector of the electorate felt: 'The real crisis at Stormont is that nothing ever changes.'[28] Drained by scandals surrounding the overpaying of millions of pounds for repairs of public housing involving the DUP,[29] followed by a further scandal where a senior elected official and party were apparently accused of being paid for involvement in the sale of Nama's loans in Northern Ireland,[30] both the subject of high-profile television documentaries, a section of the electorate was turning its back on Northern Irish politics. This was readily apparent in the decline in voter turnout in every Northern Ireland Assembly election since its inception in 1998, where nearly 70 per cent of those eligible for a ballot voted. By the 2016 election that number was down to less than 55 per cent, and this was christened the 'AWOL electorate'.[31] However, two issues – Brexit and the RHI Cash for Ash scandal – would arrest that slump almost immediately.

In the first instance the Brexit vote in England and Wales and the decision to leave the European Union caused shockwaves among Catholic Nationalist voters in Northern Ireland who had voted overwhelmingly to stay, as had the overall electorate with 56–44 per cent to remain. Sinn Féin, which had in the past been diametrically opposed to the extension of the European Union in the Republic of Ireland, saw 85 per cent of its electorate vote to remain.[32] Maillot noted that the party had travelled from outright opposition to the EU to being critically engaged.[33] The party's MEP for Dublin, Lynn Boylan told the *Irish Times*: 'the way we look at it: Sinn Féin is Eurocritical.'[34] However, Sinn Féin's strong electorate in the borderlands, which benefited enormously from the opening up of the border and huge investment in transport and infrastructure, will have accounted for much of the remain vote. Allied to the border communities, those living in the Catholic urban hinterlands of the cities and towns saw the benefit of several tranches of EU Peace money aimed at delivering the Peace Process and facilitating reconciliation among previously at-conflict communities.

As the urban working class in depressed post-industrial England and Wales voted overwhelmingly to leave the EU because it was purported that they had never seen any of the financial benefits of Britain's membership, that was categorically not the case in Northern Ireland. As ever the identity binaries came into play, with those who considered themselves to be British or from Ulster, mostly from the Protestant/unionist community (but not universally so), voted by a margin of between 60 and 70 per cent to leave, based largely on fears of a further erosion of British sovereignty.[35] The DUP, since the days of Ian Paisley, had been fanatical anti-Europeans, and Paisley's rants against the Union were a precursor or template for those of Nigel Farage and UKIP two decades later.

On the other hand, Martin McGuinness said, 'There will be no good Brexit. It will be bad for our people, bad for our economy, and bad for our services. It will further entrench partition and is fundamentally undemocratic.'[36] December's edition of *An Phoblacht* was even more strident in its bold front-cover declarations: 'Brexit changes everything/Towards a United Ireland/Time to talk unity.'[37] In the same edition, Ó'Muilleoir argued for the financial reasons why a reunified Ireland remaining within the EU was on the agenda for the party: 'partition has been an economic cul-de-sac for Ireland – north and south. Ireland can no longer afford to be partitioned.'[38]

Uncertainty over the return to a hard border, with the much hated security posts that once dotted its length, was of huge concern to the economy of towns like Newry and Enniskillen which had been rejuvenated by the freedom of movement that was a result of EU law and the Peace Process. In the early months of 2017, a group called Border Communities Against Brexit met with Sinn Féin politicians, and had previously erected a series of fake border crossings to raise awareness of what might happen in the future.[39] Gerry Adams noted, 'I want to commend the work of the Border Communities group. The issue of Brexit is probably the most important and difficult challenge facing the citizens of this island in recent decades.'[40] The anti-Brexit front was pan-nationalist, with 95 per cent of SDLP supporters voting to remain. SDLP leader, Colum Eastwood joined Michelle O'Neill, the new leader of Sinn Féin in the Northern Ireland Assembly after the resignation of Martin McGuinness in January 2017, at a protest at Stormont on the day the British government triggered Article 50.[41]

The debates on Scottish independence in 2014, and those after Brexit, had seen those surrounding a Border Poll for Northern Ireland re-emerge. After the Scottish independence referendum it was reported that the majority of people in Ireland welcomed a vote on the issue, but a majority would still vote against Irish reunification.[42] Sinn Féin returned to the economic benefits of holding a border poll referendum with the ultimate aim of reunification. The party's Northern Ireland minister for agriculture and rural development, Michelle Gildernew told its ard fheis, 'We would all be better off with a single economic unit on the island of Ireland rather than two competing economies – one single fully functioning health care system rather than two failing ones, one education system providing our children with the future that they deserve.'[43] Whether this was Sinn Féin opportunism or an opportunity that presented itself to re-emphasize the core values that had underscored policy for a united Ireland, Brexit was tailor-made for the party to make valuable ground as its opponents in unionism had no place to hide. Political journalist John Manley captured Sinn Féin's position: 'The uncertainty and upheaval that Brexit is expected to bring can only help a party that has cross-border harmonisation as a core belief, while over the coming months and years the DUP's anti-European dogmatism is bound to grate with its professed pro-business bent.'[44]

Brexit and the border poll paradoxically served both to compound the profound political alienation of dissenting republicans while also validating the long-term position on Irish sovereignty. Both éirígí and Republican Sinn Féin maintained long-standing opposition to the European Union based on issues of a dilution of Irish sovereignty and the advance of neoliberal economics that they saw it brought. RSF president Des Dalton partly echoed Sinn Féin's policy on Brexit on the basis that it might trigger debates on independence in Ireland and further afield, but welcomed the decision saying:

> It strikes a blow against the modern imperialism of the undemocratic EU superstate and will encourage further resistance across Europe. Secondly, it exposes the old imperialism and lack of democracy that lies at the heart of the so-called United Kingdom. It will hopefully unleash forces that will hasten its end. We would view the likelihood of a new referendum on Scottish Independence as a progressive step.[45]

However, this position put the party at odds with the overwhelming sentiment of the Catholic and nationalist support on either side of the border.

éirígí, with its very recent high-profile flirtation with mainstream media notoriety during the Lisbon referenda period of 2008–2009, remained rooted in a rejection of the EU's threat to socialist values and Irish independence,: 'the Irish people's needs are best served by full independence and control of our own destiny. Partition interferes with the right of the Irish people to control our own destiny – but there is also a massive democratic deficit at the heart of the European Union'[46] Both parties found themselves among strange bedfellows: UKIP, the fundamentalist Northern Ireland unionists of the DUP and the Traditional Unionist Voice, sections of the Conservative Party including Boris Johnson and Michael Gove, as well as, if one British newspaper is to be believed, the British Queen herself.[47] Leeson noted that referenda often throw up unlikely bedfellows and defended the party's position:

> We wouldn't see ourselves as aligned with Nigel Farage and the like, though we are both advocating the same thing. Referenda can be peculiar in that you can have people from opposite ends of the political spectrum calling for the same vote but in such circumstances you can't choose your bedfellows.[48]

Perhaps the greatest irony is that Brexit delivered the debate on the border and sovereignty that dissenters had steadfastly clung to for decades, as others believed that a solution to partition would come magically through some kind of evolution of the so-called post-nationalist era. The EU had partly been predicated upon building a structure designed to deal with flare-ups of nationalism which had been at the root cause of continent-wide conflict throughout the nineteenth and early to mid twentieth centuries, and to nullify the potential for warfare. The civil wars in the former Yugoslavia in the 1990s had galvanized this. However, with Scottish independence, Brexit and its outplaying in Northern Ireland, Catalonia, and upsurges of right-wing sentiment in Hungary, the Netherlands and France, debates about what the nation is, of sovereignty and self-determination were back on the agenda. Quoted in the pro-remain

New European newspaper, republican analyst Kevin Bean identified that, either by accident, design or sheer endurance, dissenters were at the centre of a major political question for the first time in decades: 'The old phrase of a stopped clock telling the right time twice a day has resonance in debates about Ireland and republican dissidents for whom the border has never been off the agenda.'[49] Brexit may have re-opened debates on existential questions about the Irish border, but it was a political scandal and its attendant opening up of sectarian and political schisms in Northern Ireland that may prove to be the fitting endnote to this book.

At the outset of this story, Sinn Féin had made the momentous journey from the junior partner to PIRA to fully constitutional political party fighting elections on all fronts. However, it was the second force in nationalist politics in Northern Ireland and a distant sixth place in the Republic of Ireland's national elections. While it had won two Westminster seats at the 1997 election (equalling the SDLP) with Gerry Adams regaining Belfast West and Martin McGuinness taking Mid-Ulster, it was 64,000 votes behind its nationalist rivals. It had to wait until 2004 to gain its first MEP when Bairbre De Brún was elected. Unionist control of Stormont was still assured as first the Ulster Unionist David Trimble and then Ian Paisley of the DUP became First Minister.

Sinn Féin remained an uneasy partner in government with the DUP when the parties came to power after the 2003 Assembly elections (although the Assembly was suspended until 2007). Although much has been made of the unlikely close bond that was built between the former Protestant firebrand Paisley and ex-PIRA commander Martin McGuinness during their time as the 'Chuckle Brothers' when first and deputy first ministers, in reality there had been little thawing of sectarian/political relations between the parties.[50] Both parties could be accused of holding their noses while administering the business of the Assembly, but had little public respect for one another. This engendered an administration that appeared to lapse from one crisis to another and was predicated on the kind of puerile and populist publicity-generating cultural point-scoring encapsulated by DUP MLA Gregory Campbell when he mocked Sinn Féin members' use of the Irish language in the Assembly chamber.[51] There was a growing sense of factional dysfunction in the administration which was allied with the mounting instances of the DUP being linked to financial scandals. The biggest of these scandals would provide Sinn Féin with the opportunity to record perhaps the most momentous election result in Northern Ireland since its establishment in 1921.

The Renewable Heating Initiative, a seemingly innocuous scheme that was designed to provide businesses with a subsidy to use renewable wood pellet fuel, would detonate a sequence of events that recalibrated Northern

Irish politics and take Sinn Féin to within touching distance of power. The scheme, initially overseen by the DUP's environment minister, paid businesses £1.60 for every pound they invested in renewable heating burners, effectively rewarding them for heating, in some instances, empty properties such as barns and sheds. It was also exploited by the Northern Ireland farming industry, and, in particular, poultry farmers, with the implication that the state was subsidizing private businesses. Although it had originally been budgeted for £25m, an upsurge in take-up, allegedly from DUP-supporting businesses, meant that, despite whistleblowers alerting the media to the scheme's maladministration, it was on target to cost £500m.[52]

The public fall-out was calamitous for both the DUP and Arlene Foster, who had become First Minister in 2015 on the resignation of Peter Robinson. The story dominated the news agenda for several weeks, as public belief in the Assembly being riven by corruption and cronyism was compounded. As Foster refused to resign over the scandal, Sinn Féin pushed the matter to its logical conclusion and collapsed the Assembly when Martin McGuinness, suffering from terminal illness, resigned as First Minister, triggering a second election in less than a year. What resulted was an election that reconfirmed the sectarian divides of Northern Ireland and re-energized a Catholic/nationalist/republican vote like never before.

In the face of the crisis, and a considerable upsurge in public outcry at the sheer scale of the corruption, Foster and the DUP doubled down on developing an 'us-versus-them' election strategy which demonized Sinn Féin, and Gerry Adams particularly, as the bogey man for the unionist community, without publicly apologizing for the scandal of perceived misuse of public funds. Despite this, her approval ratings plummeted, with her rating lower than any other leader, and her party seeing its lead cut completely.[53] As Sinn Féin also campaigned for the implementation of an Irish-language act, enshrined in the St Andrews Agreement, the DUP said that they would oppose it. Foster told a DUP campaign launch that there would be no Irish-language act, seeing it as a concession to republicans: 'If you feed a crocodile it will keep coming back for more.'[54] The statement had a nakedly sectarian effect and rebounded against the DUP and can, with some justification, be seen as a catalyst for the highest turnout of Catholic voters in Northern Ireland for some time. Despite a recent history of diminished turnouts linked to a lack of confidence in Stormont, the 2017 election turnout was 65 per cent, the highest since the 1998 post-GFA poll.

The crocodile statement had the alarmist effect on the DUP vote that Foster intended, and it returned to the voting booths in mass numbers. In the face of what might have been a career-ending scandal in most other places, the DUP vote only dropped by 1 per cent, but it lost ten seats, down to twenty-eight. But it ended the unionist majority in Stormont which had endured since the state was established. The Sinn Féin vote, galvanized by the spectacle of an unrepentant unionist First Minister advocating an openly divisive strategy, increased by 4 per cent, taking twenty-seven seats. Rather than being the sole arbiters of their own fortune, Sinn Féin had been dealt a winning hand by an opponent. Gerry Moriarty, evoking the image of the crocodile, said that nationalism had felt like it had been poked in the stomach and snapped back. He wrote, 'In this election everything went right for Sinn Féin. It portrayed Arlene Foster as the ogre; she responded by casting Gerry Adams as the bogey man. The bogey man won.'[55] Most importantly, by dropping below thirty seats, the DUP lost the petition of concern on legislation, affecting a power of veto. It was also the end of the unionist majority in a Parliament and a building which had for so long been the symbol of unionist domination of Northern Ireland. *An Phoblacht* was characteristically verbose, describing 'the once monolithic unionist citadel tumbles to the earth'.[56]

If the recalibrated aims of the republican armed struggle had become transformed into the advocacy for nationalist civil rights and parity of esteem, then the 2017 Northern Ireland election had to be seen as the last but one step before ultimate success. The subsequent *An Phoblacht* editorial may correctly have stated that 'unionism has been shaken to its core by an election result that has rocked the foundations of its former citadel of Stormont'[57], but the ultimate message of the 2017 Assembly election was that it was not the armed conflict that republicanism still memorializes in the pages of its magazines and newspapers and in its commemorative street theatre, that delivered civil rights or parity of esteem, but the long-term engagement in constitutional politics on both sides of the border.

Notes

1 Hedges, John, 'On the one road', *An Phoblacht*, March 2016.
2 Moloney, Mark, 'The media war against Sinn Féin', *An Phoblacht*, March 2016.
3 Spain, Joanne, 'Nama crime of the century', *An Phoblacht*, 20 August 2009.
4 McCabe, Conor, 'Irish housing, 1981–2006: take a bow to the new revolution', *Irish Left Review*, 27 June 2010. Available at: www.irishleftreview.org/2010/06/27/irish-housing-1981–2006-bow-revolution/. Accessed 28 June 2010.
5 'Homeless rise shames Coalition', *An Phoblacht/Republican News*, 27 May 2004.
6 Moloney, Mark, 'Homelessness – "out of control"', *An Phoblacht*, 29 September 2013. Available at: www.anphoblacht.com/contents/23420. Accessed 20 October 2013.
7 Kearney, Declan, 'What next for Sinn Féin?', *An Phoblacht*, 4 March 2011.
8 Kirby, Peadar, 'We need a new vision of the future', *An Phoblacht*, July 2015.

9 Smyth, Robbie, 'No silver bullet will cure all of the problems of capitalism', *IRIS*, January–March 2012. Available at: www.issuu.com/anphoblacht/docs/iris25/1?e=4548481/4617068. Accessed 24 March 2017.

10 Smyth, 'No silver bullet will cure all of the problems of capitalism'.

11 Ó'Broin, Eoin, 'Radical and realistic', *An Phoblacht*, April 2014.

12 McGee, Harry, 'Greece deal: implications for Syriza's Irish political support-ers', *Irish Times*, 13 July 2015. Available at: www.irishtimes.com/news/world/europe/greece-deal-implications-for-syriza-s-irish-political-supporters-1.2283323. Accessed 24 March 2017.

13 Bean, *New Politics of Sinn Féin*, p. 142.

14 *An Phoblacht*, March 2016.

15 See: *Right2Change.ie*. Available at: http://www.right2change.ie/election-2016. Accessed 25 March 2017.

16 'Five anti-water protesters jailed for contempt of court', *Irish Times*, 19 Febru-ary 2015. Available at: www.irishtimes.com/news/crime-and-law/courts/high-court/five-anti-water-protesters-jailed-for-contempt-of-court-1.2109666. Accessed 25 March 2017.

17 O'Keeffee, C., '188 water protestors arrested in 12 months', *Irish Examiner*, 9 October 2015. Available at: www.irishexaminer.com/ireland/188-water-protesters-arrested-in-12-months-358356.html. Accessed 25 March 2017.

18 Carty, E. and McCormack, C., 'Thousands of people line streets of capital for national Right 2 Water campaign', *Irish Independent*, 21 March 2015. Avail-ableat:www.independent.ie/irish-news/water/irish-water-crisis/thousands-of-people-line-streets-of-capital-for-national-right-2-water-campaign-31084118.html. Accessed 25 March 2017.

19 Ó'Broin, Eoin, 'Next election could be a game changer', *An Phoblacht*, Decem-ber 2014.

20 Ó Murchú, Eoin, 'Let's build a new future on what has been achieved', *An Phoblacht*, March 2016.

21 Boland, Vincent, 'Irish Labour Party head Burton to resign', *Financial Times*, 10 May 2016. Available at: https://www.ft.com/content/864a42c8-f6dc-3907-8ba0-d4be3d21487d?mhq5j=e1 Accessed 12 May 2016.

22 Little, Conor, 'The Irish general election of February 2016: towards a new politics or an early election?', *West European Politics*, vol. 40, no. 2, 2016, pp. 479–488.

23 Ó'Broin interview.

24 Hedges interview.

25 'Support for Sinn Féin surges, opinion poll suggests', *RTE News*, 25 February 2017. Available at: www.rte.ie/news/2017/0225/855413-red-c-poll/. Accessed 23 March 2017.

26 Leahy, Pat, 'Sinn Féin's changed coalition stance is the big political move of 2017', *Irish Times*, 15 July 2017. Available at: https://www.irishtimes.com/opinion/sinn-f%C3%A9in-s-changed-coalition-stance-is-the-big-political-move-of-2017-1.3155190. Accessed 16 July 2017.

27 Meredith, Finola, 'Northern Ireland's positive apathy', *Guardian*, 7 May 2011. Available at: www.theguardian.com/commentisfree/2011/may/07/northern-ireland-assembly-elections-2011. Accessed 23 March 2017.

28 Kane, Alex, 'The real crisis at Stormont is nothing ever changes', *Newsletter*, 18 June 2015. Available at: www.newsletter.co.uk/news/opinion/the-real-crisis-of-stormont-is-that-nothing-ever-changes-1–6784489. Accessed 18 March 2017.

29 McCaffrey, Barry, 'The DUP's full role in Red Sky row revealed', *the detail.tv*, 12 September 2012. Available at: www.thedetail.tv/articles/the-dup-s-full-role-in-red-sky-row-revealed. Accessed 25 March 2017.

30 Sheehan, Maeve, and Quinlan, Ronald, 'Namagate: the extraordinary story of money, power and politics', *Belfast Telegraph*, 12 July 2015. Available at: www.belfasttelegraph.co.uk/news/northern-ireland/namagate-the-extraordinary-story-of-money-power-and-politics-31370595.html. Accessed 23 March 2017.

31 McDonald, Henry, 'DUP braced to lose seats in Northern Ireland assembly elections', *Guardian*, 27 February 2017. Available at: www.theguardian.com/politics/2017/feb/27/dup-braced-to-lose-seats-in-northern-ireland-assembly-elections. Accessed 28 February 2017.

32 Garry, John, *The EU Referendum Vote in Northern Ireland: Implications for our Understanding of Citizens' Political Views and Behaviour*, 2017. Available at: www.qub.ac.uk/home/EUReferendum/Brexitfilestore/Filetoupload, 728121,en.pdf. Accessed 24 March 2017.

33 Maillot, Agnès, 'Sinn Féin's approach to the EU: still more "critical" than "engaged"?', *Irish Political Studies* vol. 24, no. 4, 2009, pp. 559–574.

34 Lord, Miriam, 'The Sinn Féin candidate who is making a name for herself', *Irish Times*, 22 May 2014. Available at: www.irishtimes.com/news/politics/the-sinn-f%C3%A9in-candidate-who-is-making-a-name-for-herself-1.1804406. Accessed 24 March 2017.

35 Garry, *The EU Referendum Vote*.

36 'Stop Westminster Tories driving us off Brexit cliff', *An Phoblacht*, November 2016.

37 *An Phoblacht*, December 2016.

38 Ó'Muilleoir, Máirtín, 'A united Ireland makes economic sense', *An Phoblacht*, December 2016.

39 Monaghan, J., 'Mock customs posts set up along border during protests against Brexit checkpoints', *Irish News*, 20 February 2017. Available at: www.irishnews.com/news/2017/02/20/news/mock-customs-posts-set-up-along-border-during-protests-against-brexit-checkpoints-937035/. Accessed 20 February 2017.

40 'Adams meets "Border Communities Against Brexit" group in Dáil', *sinnfein. ie*, 12 January 2017. Available at: www.sinnfein.ie/contents/43022. Accessed 13 January 2017.

41 Young, David, 'Anti-Brexit campaigners march on Stormont amid concerns of "hard" Irish border', *Newsletter*, 29 March 2017. Available at: www.newsletter.co.uk/news/politics/anti-brexit-campaigners-march-on-stormont-amid-concerns-of-hard-irish-border-1–7890803. Accessed 29 March 2017.

42 Clarke, Liam, 'Northern Ireland says "yes" to a border poll ... but a firm "no" to united Ireland', *Belfast Telegraph*, 29 September 2014. Available at: http://www.belfasttelegraph.co.uk/news/northern-ireland/northern-ireland-

says-yes-to-a-border-poll-but-a-firm-no-to-united-ireland-30622987.html. Accessed 29 March 2017.

43 Moriarty, G., 'Sinn Féin calls for border poll on a united Ireland', *Irish Times*, 7 March 2017. Available at: http://www.irishtimes.com/news/ireland/irish-news/sinn-f%C3%A9in-calls-for-border-poll-on-a-united-ireland-1.2130814. Accessed 29 March 2017.

44 Manley, John, 'Sinn Féin surge will make life uncomfortable for the DUP', *Irish News*, 4 March 2017. Available at: http://www.irishnews.com/paywall/tsb/irishnews/irishnews/irishnews//news/2017/03/04/news/analysis-sinn-fe-in-surge-will-make-life-uncomfortable-for-the-dup-951882/content.html. Accessed 29 March 2017.

45 'British EU Referendum result weakens old and new imperialisms', republicansinnfein.org, 24 June 2016. Available at: https://republicansinnfein.org/2016/06/24/british-eu-referendum-result-weakens-old-and-new-imperialisms/. Accessed 29 March 2017.

46 Moriarty, Gerry, 'Éirígí backs Brexit with Northern Ireland poster campaign', *Irish Times*, 30 May 2016. Available at: http://www.irishtimes.com/news/politics/%C3%A9ir%C3%ADg%C3%AD-backs-brexit-with-northern-ireland-poster-campaign-1.2666248. Accessed 29 March 2017.

47 Mason, Rowena, 'Laura Kuenssberg says source told her the Queen backed Brexit', *Guardian*, 26 December 2016. Available at: https://www.theguardian.com/politics/2016/dec/26/queen-did-back-brexit-run-up-to-referendum-laura-kuenssberg. Accessed 29 March 2017.

48 Quoted in Manley, John, 'EU referendum throws up odd couplings', *Irish News*, 17 June 2016. Available at: http://www.irishnews.com/news/2016/06/17/news/eu-referendum-throws-up-odd-couplings-566169/. Accessed 18 June 2016.

49 Hoey, Paddy, 'Troubled times could trigger a return to arms', *New European*, 21 October 2016.

50 McDonald, Henry, 'Ian Paisley: from Northern Irish ayatollah to Chuckle Brother', *Guardian*, 12 September 2014. Available at: https://www.theguardian.com/politics/2014/sep/12/ian-paisley-northern-irish-ayatollah-chuckle-brother-martin-mcguinness. Accessed 29 March 2017.

51 '"Curry my yoghurt": Gregory Campbell, DUP, barred from speaking for day', *BBC News Online*, 4 November 2014. Available at: http://www.bbc.co.uk/news/uk-northern-ireland-29895593. Accessed 29 March 2017.

52 'Q&A: what is the Renewable Heat Incentive (RHI) scheme?', *BBC News Online*, 13 December 2016. Available at: http://www.bbc.co.uk/news/uk-northern-ireland-38307628. Accessed 29 March 2017.

53 Bell, Jonathan, 'Poll: Arlene Foster rating plummets – DUP and Sinn Fein neck-and-neck', *Belfast Telegraph*, 1 February 2017. Available at: http://www.belfasttelegraph.co.uk/news/northern-ireland-assembly-election/poll-arlene-foster-rating-plummets-dup-and-sinn-fein-neckandneck-35415176.html. Accessed 29 March 2017.

54 'DUP will never agree to Irish Language act, says Foster', *BBC News Online*, 6 February 2017. Available at: http://www.bbc.co.uk/news/uk-northern-ireland-38881559. Accessed 29 March 2017.

55 Moriarty, Gerry, 'NI Assembly: nationalism felt it was poked in the stomach and it snarled back', *Irish Times*, 5 March 2017. Available at: http://www.irishtimes.com/news/ireland/irish-news/ni-assembly-nationalism-felt-it-was-poked-in-the-stomach-and-it-snarled-back-1.2998485. Accessed 29 March 2017.

56 Kirby, Peadar, 'A tale of two elections', *An Phoblacht*, March 2017.

57 'An Phoblacht editorial', March 2017 – sharing power, equality and integrity', *An Phoblacht*, March 2017. Available at: http://www.anphoblacht.com/contents/26703. Accessed 28 March 2017.

Select bibliography

Primary sources

Interviews

Cunningham, Ciarán: PRO Republican Network for Unity. Interviewed Belfast, 8 January 2012.

Dalton, Des: President of Republican Sinn Féin. Interviewed Dublin, 20 May 2011.

Fealty, Mick: editor of Sluggerotoole.com, writer for the *Blanket* and the *Guardian*. Interviewed by Skype, 8 June 2011.

Garibaldy: blogger at *Cedar Lounge Revolution*. Interviewed by Skype, 25 November 2012.

Hartley, Tom: former manager *Republican News*, former Sinn Féin Lord Mayor of Belfast. Interviewed Liverpool, 3 May 2012.

Hedges, John: editor of *An Phoblacht*. Interviewed Dublin, 26 November 2016.

MacCionnaith, Breandán: General Secretary of éirígí. Interviewed by phone, 9 April 2009.

Mackel, Pádraig: PRO for éirígí. Interviewed by phone, 15 April 2010.

McGregor, Mark: former Sinn Féin member and party administrator, writer for Sluggerotoole.com. Interviewed Crumlin, 3 January 2010.

McIntyre, Anthony: former republican prisoner, senior writer on the *Blanket* and *Fourthwrite*, editorial board of the *Other View*. Interviewed by Skype, 12 December 2010.

McIntyre, Carrie: editor of the *Blanket* and writer for *Fourthwrite*. Interviewed by Skype, 12 December 2010.

McKearney, Tommy: former republican prisoner. Editor of *Fourthwrite* and writer for the *Blanket*, editorial board of the *Other View*. Interviewed by phone, 20 November 2009.

Morrison, Danny: former editor, An *Phoblacht/Republican News* and writer for *Andersonstown News* and *Daily Ireland*. Interviewed by Skype, 5 November 2011.

Ó'Broin, Eoin: *An Phoblacht* columnist, Sinn Féin TD for Dublin Mid-West. Interviewed by phone, 2 June 2012.

O'Doherty, Malachi: former editor *Fortnight*, writer for the *Blanket*, *Irish Times*, *Belfast Telegraph* and broadcaster. Interviewed Liverpool, 21 March 2011.

Ó'Donghaile, Deaglán: writer and academic and contributor to the *Blanket*. Interviewed Liverpool, 4 February 2010.

Ruddy, Gerry: Former editor of *Starry Plough*. Interviewed Belfast, 3 June 2016.

World by Storm: blogger at *Cedar Lounge Revolution*. Interviewed by Skype, 20 September 2012.

Archives

Belfast Central Library, newspaper collection

Linen Hall Library, Belfast, Northern Ireland Political Collection/Tom Hartley Collection/republican boxes/Peace Process boxes/miscellaneous boxes

Manchester Central Library, newspaper collection

Newspapers, online sources and party publications

Andersonstown News
The Atlantic
BBC News Online
Belfast Telegraph
The *Blanket*
Cedar Lounge Revolution
Christian Science Monitor
The *Citizen*
Congress '86
Daily Ireland
Daily Mail
Daily Mirror
Daily Telegraph
Derry Journal
Derry32csm.com
The detail.tv
Dublin Opinion.com
Dundalk Democrat
éirígí.org (website has fallen out of use)
1169andcounting
Fortnight
Forum Magazine
Fourthwrite
An Glór Gafa
Greenleft Weekly
Guardian and *Observer*
Hibernian
Independent/Independent on Sunday
Indymedia.ie
Irelandclick.com
IRIS
Iris Bheag

Irish Independent/Sunday Independent
Irish Left Archive
Irish Left Review
Irish News
Irish Post
Irish Republican Bulletin Board
Irish Republican News
Irish Times
Irsp.ie
Longkesh.info
Look Left
michellmalkin.com
Mute Magazine
New European
New Republican Forum
New Scientist
New York Times
New Yorker
Newsletter
Nuzhound.com
Ograshinnfein.blogspot.co.uk
Other View
Parliamentary Brief
Pensive Quill
An Phoblacht
An Phoblacht/Republican News
Politics.ie
The *Republic*
Republicanunity.org (website has fallen out of use)
Right2Change.ie
RTE news online
Saoirse
Saoirse32.wordpress.com
Searchlight
Sinn Féin Keep Left
Sluggerotoole.com
solidarity-us.org
Sovereign Nation
Starry Plough
Sunday Business Post
Sunday Times
Sunday Tribune
32csm.net (website has fallen out of use)
Talkof thetown.ie
thefivedemands.org

Time
u.tv
Vacuum Magazine
Vimeo.com
Washington Post
Westtyronesinnfein.com
Wired.com
Youtube.com

Publications

Adams, Gerry, *The Politics of Irish Freedom* (Dingle: Brandon, 1986).

—— 'To cherish a just and lasting peace', *Fordham International Law Journal* vol. 22 (1998): 1177–1195.

Allen, Robert C. (ed.), *Channels of Discourse, Reassembled: Television and Contemporary Criticism* (Abingdon: Routledge, 1992).

Altheide, David L., and Snow, Robert P., 'Toward a theory of mediation', *Communication Yearbook* 11 (1988): 194–223.

Anderson, Benedict, *Imagined Communities: Reflections on the Origin and Spread of Nationalism*, 2nd edition (New York: Verso Books, 2006).

Arthur, Paul, 'The media and politics in Northern Ireland', in Seaton, Jean, and Pimlott, Ben (eds), *The Media in British Politics* (Aldershot: Gower, 1997): 200–214.

Atton, Chris, 'A reassessment of the alternative press', *Media, Culture and Society* vol. 21, no. 1 (1999): 51–76.

—— *Alternative Media* (London: Sage, 2002).

—— 'News cultures and new social movements: radical journalism and the mainstream media', *Journalism Studies* vol. 3, no. 4 (2002): 491–505.

—— *An Alternative Internet* (Edinburgh: Edinburgh University Press, 2004).

—— *Alternative Journalism* (London: Sage, 2008).

Aughey, Arthur, and Morrow, Duncan (eds), *Northern Ireland Politics* (Longman: London, 1996).

Bairner, Alan, 'The media', in Aughey, Arthur, and Morrow, Duncan (eds), *Northern Ireland Politics* (Harlow: Longman, 1996): 173–180.

Baker, Stephen, 'The alternative press in Northern Ireland and the political process', *Journalism Studies* vol. 6, no. 3 (2005): 375–386.

Bates, Thomas R., 'Gramsci and the theory of hegemony', *Journal of the History of Ideas* vol. 36, no. 2 (1975): 351–366.

Bean, Kevin, 'The first draft of history', *Irish Studies Review* vol. 4, no. 13 (1995): 40–42.

—— 'The new departure? Recent developments in Republican strategy and ideology', *Irish Studies Review* vol. 3, no. 10 (1995): 2–6.

—— 'Defining republicanism: shifting discourses of new nationalism and post-republicanism', in Elliott, Marianne (ed.), *The Long Road to Peace in Northern Ireland* (Liverpool: Liverpool University Press, 2002): 129–142.

—— *The New Politics of Sinn Féin* (Liverpool: Liverpool University Press, 2007).

—— 'Civil society, the state and conflict transformation in the nationalist community', in Power, Maria (ed.), *Building Peace in Northern Ireland* (Liverpool: Liverpool University Press, 2011).

—— ' "New dissidents are but old provisionals writ large"? The dynamics of dissident republicanism in the new Northern Ireland', *Political Quarterly*, vol. 83, no. 2 (2012): 210–218.

—— and Hayes, Mark (eds), *Republican Voices* (Monaghan: Seesyu Press, 2001).

—— 'Sinn Féin and the New Republicanism in Ireland: electoral progress, political stasis, and ideological failure', *Radical History Review* (Spring 2009): 126–142.

Bell, J. Bowyer, *The Secret Army: A History of the IRA, 1916–1970* (London: Blond, 1970).

—— *The IRA, 1968–2000: Analysis of a Secret Army* (Vol. 7. Abingdon: Frank Cass Publishers, 2000).

Benhabib, Seyla, 'Models of public space: Hannah Arendt, the liberal tradition, and Jürgen Habermas', in Calhoun, Craig (ed.), *Habermas and the Public Sphere* (Cambridge, MA: MIT Press, 1992): 73–98.

Bennett, Tony, Curran, James, and Woollacott, Janet (eds), *Culture, Society and the Media* (London: Methuen, 1982).

Bennett, W. Lance, and Entman, Robert M. (eds), *Mediated Politics: Communication in the Future of Democracy* (Cambridge: Cambridge University Press, 2001).

Berry, David, and Theobald, John (eds), *Radical Mass Media Criticism: A Cultural Genealogy* (Montreal: Black Rose Books, 2006).

Bew, John, Frampton, Martyn, and Gurruchaga, Inigo, *Talking to Terrorists* (New York: Columbia University Press, 2009).

Bheacháin, Caoilfhionn Ní, ' "The mosquito press": anti-imperialist rhetoric in republican journalism, 1926–39', *Éire-Ireland*, vol. 42 no. 1 (2007): 256–289.

Bishop, Patrick, and Mallie, Eamonn, *The Provisional IRA* (London: Corgi, 1988).

Bowman-Grieve, Lorraine, 'Irish republicanism and the Internet: support for new wave dissidents', *Perspectives on Terrorism*, vol. 4 no. 2 (2010): 22–34.

—— and Conway, Maura, 'Exploring the form and function of dissident Irish Republican online discourses', *Media, War and Conflict* vol. 5, no. 1 (2012): 71–85.

Buttigieg, Joseph A., 'Gramsci on civil society', *Boundary 2* vol. 22, no. 3 (1995): 1–32.

Calhoun, Craig (ed.), *Habermas and the Public Sphere* (Cambridge, MA: MIT Press, 1992).

Carey, John, *Communication as Culture* (London: Routledge, 1992).

Carson, Niall, and Hoey, Paddy, 'The Bell and the Blanket: journals of Irish republican dissent', *New Hibernia Review* vol. 16, no. 1 (2012): 75–93.

Castells, Manuel, 'Communication, power and counter-power in the network society', *International Journal of Communication* vol. 1, no. 1 (2007): 236–266.

—— 'The new public sphere: global civil society, communication networks, and global governance', *ANNALS of the American Academy of Political and Social Science* vol. 616, no. 1 (2008): 78–93.

—— *The Power of Identity: The Information Age: Economy, Society, and Culture Volume II*, 2nd edition (London: Blackwell, 2009).

—— *The Rise of the Network Society: The Information Age: Economy, Society, and Culture Volume 1*, 2nd edition (London: Blackwell, 2010).

—— *Networks of Outrage and Hope: Social Movements in the Internet Age* (London: Polity, 2012).

Chadwick, Andrew, and Howard, Philip N. (eds), *Handbook of Internet Politics* (Abingdon: Routledge, 2009).

Chomsky, Noam, and Herman, Edward S., *Manufacturing Consent: The Political Economy of the Mass Media* (London: Random House, 2010).

Cohen, Jean L., and Arato, Andrew, *Civil Society and Political Theory* (Cambridge, MA: MIT Press, 1994).

Connolly, James, *Selected Writings* (London: Pluto Press, 1988).

Conway, Brian, 'Moving through time and space: performing bodies in Derry, Northern Ireland', *Journal of Historical Sociology*, vol. 20, no. 1–2 (2007). 102–125.

Coogan, Tim Pat, *On the Blanket: The H Block Story* (Dublin: Ward River, 1980).

—— *The Troubles: Ireland's Ordeal, 1966–1995, and the Search for Peace* (London: Hutchinson, 1995).

—— *Ireland in the Twentieth Century* (London: Arrow Books, 2009).

Couldry, Nick, *Inside Culture* (London: Sage, 2000).

—— and Curran, James (eds), *Contesting Media Power: Alternative Media in a Networked World* (Lanham: Rowman & Littlefield, 2003).

Crossley, Nick, and Roberts, John (eds), *After Habermas: New Perspectives on the Public Sphere* (Oxford: Blackwell, 2004).

Cunningham, Stuart, 'Popular media as public "sphericules" for diasporic communities', *International Journal of Cultural Studies*, vol. 4, no. 2 (2001): 131–147.

Curran, James, 'Rethinking the media as a public sphere', in Dahlgren, Peter, and Sparks, Colin (eds), *Communication and Citizenship: Journalism and the Public Sphere* (London: Routledge, 1991): 27–57.

—— 'Rethinking media and democracy', *Mass Media and Society* vol. 3, no. 1 (2000): 120–154.

—— *Media and Power* (London: Routledge, 2002).

—— and Seaton, Jean, *Power Without Responsibility: The Press, Broadcasting and the Internet in Britain*, 7th edition (London: Routledge, 2009).

Curran, James, Fenton, Natalie, and Freeman, Des, *Misunderstanding the Internet* (Abingdon: Routledge, 2012).

Currie, P.M., and Taylor, Max, *Dissident Irish Republicanism* (London: Continuum, 2011).

Curtis, Liz, *Nothing But the Same Old Story: The Roots of Anti-Irish Racism* (London: Information on Ireland, 1984).

—— *Interference on the Airwaves: Ireland, the Media and the Broadcasting Ban* (London: NUJ, 1993).

—— *Ireland: The Propaganda War*, 2nd edition (Belfast: Sasta, 1998).

Dahlberg, Lincoln, 'The Internet and democratic discourse: exploring the prospects of online deliberative forums extending the public sphere', *Information, Communication and Society* vol. 4, no. 4 (2001): 615–633.

—— and Siapera, Eugenia (eds), *Radical Democracy and the Internet* (London: Palgrave, 2007).

Dahlgren, Peter, *Television and the Public Sphere: Citizenship, Democracy and the Media* (London: Sage, 2000).

—— 'The Internet and the democratization of civic culture', *Political Communication* vol. 17, no. 4 (2000): 335–340.

—— 'The public sphere and the net: structure, space, and communication', in Bennett, W. Lance, and Entman, Robert M. (eds), *Mediated Politics: Communication in the Future of Democracy* (Cambridge: Cambridge University Press, 2001): 33–55.

—— 'The Internet, public spheres, and political communication: dispersion and deliberation', *Political Communication* vol. 22, no. 2 (2005): 147–162.

—— and Sparks, Colin, *Communication and Citizenship: Journalism and the Public Sphere in the New Media Age* (London: Routledge, 1991).

Davis, Richard, 'Have the Northern Ireland ceasefires of 1994 ended "zero sum game" and mirrored thinking?', in O'Day, Alan (ed.), *Political Violence in Northern Ireland: Conflict and Conflict Resolution* (Westport, CT: Praeger, 1997): 33–44.

De Jong, Wilma, Shaw, Martin, and Stammers, Neil (eds), *Global Activism, Global Media* (London: Pluto Press, 2005).

Dery, Mark, *Culture Jamming: Hacking, Slashing, and Sniping in the Empire of the Signs. Open Magazine* Pamphlet Series, New York, 1993.

Deuze, Mark, 'Participation, remediation, bricolage: considering principal components of a digital culture', *Information Society* vol. 22, no. 2 (2006): 63–75.

—— 'Journalism, citizenship, digital culture', in Papacharissi, Zizi (ed.), *Journalism and Citizenship* (London: Routledge, 2009): 15–27.

Dixon, Paul, 'Political skills or lying and manipulation? The choreography of the Northern Ireland Peace Process', *Political Studies* vol. 50, no. 4 (2002): 725–741.

—— 'Performing the Northern Ireland Peace Process on the world stage', *Political Science Quarterly* vol. 121, no. 1 (2006): 61–91.

—— *Northern Ireland: the Politics of War and Peace*, 2nd edition (Basingstoke: Palgrave Macmillan, 2008).

—— and O'Kane, Eamonn, *Northern Ireland Since 1969* (Harlow: Longman, 2011).

Downey, John, and Fenton, Natalie, 'New media, counter publicity and the public sphere', *New Media and Society* vol. 5, no. 2 (2003): 185–202.

—— 'Participation and/or deliberation? The Internet as a tool for achieving radical democratic aims', in Dahlberg, Lincoln, and Siapera, Eugenia (eds), *Radical Democracy and the Internet* (London: Palgrave Macmillan, 2007): 108–127.

Downing, John, *Radical Media: Rebellious Communication and Social Movements* (London: Sage, 2000).

Durham, Gigi, and Kellner, Douglas (eds), *Media and Cultural Studies: Keyworks Vol. 2* (London: Blackwell, 2005).

Eagleton-Pierce, Matthew, 'The internet and the Seattle WTO protests', *Peace Review* vol. 13, no. 3 (2001): 331–337.

Edwards, Aaron, 'When terrorism as strategy fails: dissident Irish republicans and the threat to British security', *Studies in Conflict and Terrorism* vol. 34, no. 4 (2011): 318–336.

—— and Bloomer, Stephen (eds), *Transforming the Peace Process in Northern Ireland* (Dublin: Irish Academic Press, 2008).

Eldridge, John (ed.), *Getting the Message: News, Truth and Power* (London: Routledge, 1993).

—— *Glasgow Media Group Reader Vol. 1: News Content, Language and Visuals* (London: Routledge, 1995).

Elliott, Marianne, *The Long Road to Peace in Northern Ireland* (Liverpool: Liverpool University Press, 2007).

English, Richard, *Armed Struggle: The History of the IRA* (London: Macmillan, 2002).

—— *Irish Freedom: A History of Nationalism in Ireland* (London: Macmillan, 2007).

Evans, Jocelyn, and Tonge, Jonathan, 'Menace without mandate? Is there any sympathy for dissident Irish Republicanism in Northern Ireland?', *Terrorism and Political Violence* vol. 24, no. 1 (2011): 61–78.

Fawcett, Liz, 'Who's setting the post-devolution agenda in Northern Ireland?', *Harvard International Journal of Press/Politics* vol. 7, no. 4 (2002): 14–33.

—— 'Why peace journalism isn't news', *Journalism Studies* vol. 3, no. 2 (2002): 213–223.

Fealty, Mick, ' "Slugger O'Toole": the new media as track two diplomacy', in Popiolkowski, Joseph J., and Cull, Nicholas J. (eds), *Public Diplomacy, Cultural Interventions and the Peace Process in Northern Ireland: Track Two to Peace?* (Los Angeles: Figueroa Press, 2009): 89–98.

Feeney, Brian, 'The peace process: who defines the news – the media or government press offices?', in Kiberd, Damien (ed.), *Media in Ireland: The Search for Diversity* (Dublin: Four Courts, 1997): 41–58.

—— *Sinn Féin: A Hundred Turbulent Years* (Dublin: O'Brien Press, 2002).

Fiske, John, 'British cultural studies and television', in Allen, Robert C. (ed.), *Channels of Discourse, Reassembled: Television and Contemporary Criticism* (Abingdon: Routledge, 1992): 214–245.

—— *Understanding Popular Culture*, 2nd edition (Abingdon: Routledge, 2011).

Frampton, Martyn, *Legion of the Rearguard: Dissident Irish Republicanism* (Dublin: Irish Academic Press, 2011).

Fraser, Nancy, 'Rethinking the public sphere: a contribution to the critique of actually existing democracy', in Calhoun, Craig (ed.), *Habermas and the Public Sphere* (Cambridge, MA: MIT Press, 1993): 56–80.

Fukuyama, Francis, *The End of History and the Last Man* (New York: Avalon Books, 1992).

Ganter, Granville, 'Counterpublics book review', *St. John's University Humanities Review* vol. 1, no. 1 (March 2003). Available at: http://facpub.stjohns.edu/~ganterg/sjureview/vol1-1/publics.html.

Gestrich, Andreas, 'The public sphere and the Habermas debate', *German History* vol. 24, no. 3 (2006): 414–415.

Gilmor, Dan, *We the Media* (Sebastopol: O'Reilly Media, 2004).

Gitlin, Todd, 'Public sphere or public sphericules?', in Liebes, Tamar, and Curran, James (eds), *Media, Ritual, and Identity* (London: Routledge, 1998): 168–174.

Gramsci, Antonio, *Selections from the Prison Notebooks* (London: Lawrence & Wishart Ltd, 2005).

Habermas Jürgen, *Structural Transformation of the Public Sphere* (London: Polity Press, 1989).

—— 'Further reflections on the public sphere', in Calhoun, Craig (ed.), *Habermas and the Public Sphere* (Cambridge, MA: MIT Press, 1992): 421–461.

—— 'Political communication in media society: does democracy still enjoy an epistemic dimension? The impact of normative theory on empirical research', *Communication Theory* vol. 16, no. 4 (2007): 411–426.

Habermas Jürgen, Lennox, Sara, and Lennox, Frank, 'The public sphere: an encyclopedia article (1964)', *New German Critique* vol. 3 (1974): 49–55.

Hall, Michael (ed.), 'Republicanism in transition: (1) The need for a debate', *Island Pamphlets* No. 96 (Newtownabbey: Island Publications, 2011).

—— 'Republicanism in transition: (2) Beginning a debate', *Island Pamphlets* No. 97 (Newtownabbey: Island Publications, 2011).

—— 'Republicanism in transition: (3) Irish Republicanism today', *Island Pamphlets* No. 98 (Newtownabbey: Island Publications, 2011).

—— 'Republicanism in transition: (4) The question of "armed struggle" ', *Island Pamphlets* No. 99 (Newtownabbey: Island Publications, 2011).

—— 'Republicanism in transition: (5) An engagement with Loyalists', *Island Pamphlets No. 100* (Newtownabbey: Island Publications, 2011).

Hall, Stuart, 'Notes on deconstructing "the popular" ', in Storey, John (ed.), *Cultural Theory and Popular Culture: A Reader* (Harlow: Pearson, 1998): 442–453.

—— 'Encoding/decoding', in Durham, Gigi, and Kellner, Durham (eds), *Media and Cultural Studies: Keyworks Vol. 2* (London: Blackwell, 2005): 163–173.

Hanley, Brian, and Millar, Scott, *The Lost Revolution: The Story of the Official IRA and the Workers' Party* (Dublin: Penguin, 2009).

Hauser, Gerard R., 'Prisoners of conscience and the counterpublic sphere of prison writing: the stones that start the avalanche', in Asen, Robert, and Brouwer, Daniel C. (eds), *Counterpublics and the State* (Albany, NY: SUNY Press, 2001): 35–58.

Hill, Kevin A., and Hughes, John E., *Cyberpolitics: Citizen Activism in the Age of the Internet* (Lanham, MD: Rowman and Littlefield, 1998).

Hjarvard, Stig, 'The mediatization of society', *Nordicom Review*, vol. 29, no. 2 (2008): 105–134.

Holland, Jack, and McDonald, Henry, *INLA: Deadly Divisions* (Dublin: Poolbeg Press Ltd, 2010).

Honohan, Iseult (ed.), *Republicanism in Ireland: Confronting Theories and Traditions* (Manchester: Manchester University Press, 2008).

Jarvis, Jeff, *Public Parts* (New York: Simon & Schuster, 2011).

Kahn, Richard, and Kellner, Douglas, 'Internet subcultures and oppositional politics', in Muggleton, David, and Weinzel, Rupert (eds), *The Post-subcultures Reader* (Oxford: Berg, 2003): 299–314.

—— 'Oppositional politics and the Internet', *Cultural Politics* vol. 1, no. 1 (2005): 75–100.

Katz, Elihu, and Lazarsfeld, Paul, *Personal Influence: The Part Played by People in the Flow of Mass Communications*, 2nd edition (New Brunswick, NJ: Transaction Publications, 2005).

Katz, Elihu, Blumler, Jay G., and Gurevitch, Michael, 'Uses and gratifications research', *Public Opinion Quarterly* vol. 37, no. 4 (1973): 509–523.

Kavanagh, Patrick, *Collected Poems* (London: Penguin, 2005).

Kellner, Douglas, 'Globalisation, technopolitics and revolution', in Foran, John (ed.), *The Future of Revolutions: Rethinking Political and Social Change in the Age of Globalization* (London: Zed Books, 2003): 14–34.

Kiberd, Damien (ed.), *Media in Ireland Vol. 1: The Search for Diversity* (Dublin: Four Courts, 1997).

—— (ed.), *Media in Ireland Vol. 2: The Search for Ethical Journalism* (Dublin: Four Courts, 1999).

—— (ed.), *Media in Ireland Vol. 3: Issues in Broadcasting* (Dublin: Four Courts, 2002).

Killen, John, *The Unkindest Cut: A Cartoon History of Ulster, 1900–2000* (Belfast: Blackstaff Press, 2000).

Klein, Naomi, *No Logo*, 3rd edition (London: Picador, 2010).

Krotz, Friedrich, 'Mediatization: a concept with which to grasp media and societal change', in Lundby, Knut (ed.), *Mediatization: Concepts, Changes, Consequences* (Oxford: Peter Lang, 2009): 21–40.

Lago, Rita, 'Interviewing Sinn Féin under the new political environment: a comparative analysis of interviews with Sinn Féin on British television', *Media, Culture and Society* vol. 20, no. 4 (1998): 677–685.

Legg, Marie-Louise, *Newspapers and Nationalism: The Irish Provincial Press, 1850–1892* (Dublin: Four Courts Press, 1999).

Liebes, Tamar, and Curran, James (eds), *Media, Ritual, and Identity* (London: Routledge, 1998).

Lievrouw, Leah A., *Alternative and Activist New Media* (Cambridge: Polity, 2011).

Lloyd, David, 'Regarding Ireland in a post-colonial frame', *Cultural Studies* vol. 15, no. 1 (2001): 12–32.

Lundby, Knut (ed.), *Mediatization: Concepts, Changes, Consequences* (New York: Peter Lang, 2009).

Lyons, F.S.L., *Ireland Since the Famine* (Fontana: London, 1973).

Maillot, Agnés, *New Sinn Féin: Irish Republicanism in the Twenty-first Century* (Abingdon: Routledge, 2005).

—— 'Sinn Féin's approach to the EU: still more "critical" than "engaged"?', *Irish Political Studies* vol. 24, no. 4 (2009): 559–574.

Mallie, Eamonn, and McKittrick, David, *The Fight for Peace: The Secret Story Behind the Irish Peace Process* (London: Heinemann, 1996).

—— *Endgame in Ireland* (London: Hodder & Stoughton, 2001).

Mazzoleni, Gianpietro, and Schulz, Winifried, 'Mediatization of politics: a challenge for democracy?', *Political Communication*, vol. 16, no. 3 (1999): 247–261.

McDonald, Henry, *Gunsmoke and Mirrors: How Sinn Féin Dressed up Defeat as Victory* (Dublin: Gill & Macmillan, 2008).

McGarry, Fearghal (ed.), *Republicanism in Modern Ireland* (Dublin: University College Dublin Press, 2003).

McGovern, Mark, 'Irish republicanism and the potential pitfalls of pluralism', *Capital and Class* vol. 24, no. 2 (2000): 133–161.

McGuigan, Jim, *Culture and the Public Sphere* (London: Routledge, 2002).

—— and Allan, Stuart, 'Mediating politics: Jürgen Habermas and the public sphere', in Berry, David, and Theobald, John (eds), *Radical Mass Media Criticism: A Cultural Genealogy* (Montreal: Black Rose Books, 2006): 90–108.

McIntyre, Anthony, 'Modern Irish republicanism: the product of British state strategies', *Irish Political Studies* vol. 10 (1995): 97–122.

—— *Good Friday: The Death of Irish Republicanism* (New York: Ausubo Press, 2008).

McKearney, Tommy, *The Provisional IRA: From Insurrection to Parliament* (London: Pluto Press, 2011).

McKeown, Laurence, *Out of Time: Irish Republican Prisoners 1970–2000* (Belfast: Beyond the Pale Publications, 2001).

McKittrick, David, and McVea, David, *Making Sense of the Troubles* (London: Penguin, 2001).

McLaughlin, Greg, and Miller, David, 'The media politics of the Irish peace process', *Harvard International Journal of Press/Politics* vol. 1, no. 4 (1996):116–134.

McLaughlin, Greg, and Baker, Stephen J., 'House training the paramilitaries: the media and the propaganda of peace', in Coulter, Colin and Murray, Michael, *Northern Ireland After the Troubles: A Society in Transition* (Manchester: Manchester University Press, 2008): 253–271.

—— *The Propaganda of Peace: The Role of Media and Culture in the Northern Ireland Peace Process* (Bristol: Intellect Books, 2010).

McNair, Brian, *Introduction to Political Communication*, 5th edition (London: Routledge, 2011).

Meikle, Graham, *Future Active: Media Activism and the Internet* (London: Pluto Press, 2002).

Melucci, Alberto, *Challenging Codes: Collective Action in the Information Age* (Cambridge: Cambridge University Press, 1996).

Miller, David, 'The history behind a mistake', *British Journalism Review* vol. 1, no. 2 (1990): 34–43.

—— 'The media on the rock: the media and the Gibraltar killings', in Rolston, Bill, *The Media and Northern Ireland: Covering the Troubles* (Basingstoke: Macmillan, 1991): 69–98.

—— 'Contesting political violence: terrorism, propaganda and the media', *Linen Hall Review* vol. 9, no. 1 (1992): 37–39.

—— 'The Beeb at bay', *British Journalism Review*, vol. 4, no. 1 (1993): 20–26.

—— 'The Northern Ireland Information Service and the media: aims, strategy, tactics', in Philo, Greg, *Getting the Message: Audience Research in the Glasgow University Media Group* (London: Routledge, 1993): 73–103.

—— 'Official sources and "primary definition": the case of Northern Ireland', *Media, Culture and Society* vol. 15, no. 3 (1993): 385–406.

—— 'Why the public needs to know', *Index on Censorship* vol. 22, no. 8/9 (1993): 5–6.

—— *Don't Mention the War: Northern Ireland, Propaganda and the Media* (London: Pluto Press, 1994).

—— *The Glasgow Media Group Reader Vol. II: Industry, Economy, War and Politics* (Abingdon: Routledge, 1995).

—— 'The media, propaganda and the Northern Ireland peace process', in Kiberd, Damien (ed.), *Media in Ireland Vol. 3: Issues in Broadcasting* (Dublin: Four Courts, 2002): 114–129.

Miller, Rory (ed.), *Ireland and the Middle East: Trade, Society and Peace* (Dublin: Irish Academic Press, 2007).

Moloney, Ed, 'Closing down the airwaves: the story of the broadcasting ban', in Rolston, Bill (ed.), *The Media and Northern Ireland* (Basingstoke: Macmillan, 1991): 8–50.

—— *A Secret History of the IRA* (London: Penguin, 2002).

—— *Voices From the Grave* (London: Faber & Faber, 2010).

Morozov, Evgeny, *The Net Delusion: How Not to Liberate the World* (London: Penguin, 2011).

Mouffe, Chantal, 'Deliberative democracy or agonistic pluralism?', *Social Research* vol. 66, no. 3 (1999): 745–758.

Muggleton, David, and Weinzerl, Rupert (eds) *The Post-subcultures Reader* (Oxford: Berg, 2003).

Murray, Gerard, and Tonge, Jonathan, *Sinn Féin and the SDLP* (London: Hurst & Company, 2005).

Nagle, John, 'Potemkin village: neo-liberalism and peace-building in Northern Ireland?', *Ethnopolitics* vol. 8 no. 2 (2009): 173–190.

Nixon, Paul, Rawal, Rajash, and Mercea, Dan (eds), *Chasing the Promise of Internet Politics* (London: Routledge, 2013).

Ó'Muilleoir, Máirtín, *Belfast's Dome of Delight: City Hall Politics 1981–2000* (Belfast: Beyond the Pale Publications, 1999).

Oates, Sarah, Owen, Diana, and Gibson, Rachel K. (eds), *The Internet and Politics: Citizens, Voters and Activists* (London: Routledge, 2006).

O'Brien, Brendan, *The Long War: The IRA and Sinn Féin* (Dublin: O'Brien, 1993).

O'Brien, Gillian, ' "Spirit, impartiality and independence": the Northern Star, 1792–1797', *Eighteenth-Century Ireland/Iris an dá chultúr* vol. 13 (1998): 7–23.

Ó'Broin, Eoin, *Sinn Féin and the Politics of Left Republicanism* (London: Pluto, 2009).

O'Connor, Fionnuala, *In Search of a State: Catholics in Northern Ireland* (Belfast: Blackstaff, 1993).

O'Day, Alan (ed.), *Political Violence in Northern Ireland: Conflict and Conflict Resolution* (Westport, CT: Praeger Publishing, 1997).

O'Doherty, Malachi, *The Trouble with Guns: Republican Strategy and the Provisional IRA* (Belfast: Blackstaff Press, 1998).

—— *The Telling Year: Belfast 1972* (Dublin: Gill & Macmillan, 2007).

O'Kane, Eamonn, 'Anglo-Irish relations and the Northern Ireland peace process: from exclusion to inclusion', *Contemporary British History* vol. 18, no. 1 (2004): 78–99.

O'Leary, Brendan, and McGarry, John, *The Politics of Antagonism: Understanding Northern Ireland* (London: Athlone Press, 1993).

O'Rawe, Richard, *Blanketmen* (Dundrum: New Island, 2005).

—— *Afterlives* (Dublin: Lilliput Press, 2010).

Papacharissi, Zizi, 'The virtual sphere: the Internet as a public sphere', *New Media and Society* vol. 4, no. 1 (2002): 9–27.

Patterson, Henry, *The Politics of Illusion: A Political History of the IRA* (London: Serif, 1997).

Pearse, Pádraic, *Collected Works of Padraic H. Pearse* (Dublin: Phoenix Publishing Co., 1924).

Philo, Greg, *Getting the Message: Audience Research in the Glasgow University Media Group* (London: Routledge, 1993).

—— *The Glasgow Media Group Reader, Vol. II: Industry, Economy, War and Politics* (London: Routledge, 1995).

Platon, Sara, and Deuze, Mark, 'Indymedia journalism: a radical way of making, selecting and sharing news?', *Journalism* vol. 4, no. 3 (2003): 336–355.

Popiolkowski, Joseph J., and Cull, Nicholas J. (eds), *Public Diplomacy, Cultural Interventions and the Peace Process in Northern Ireland: Track Two to Peace?* (Los Angeles: Figueroa Press, 2009).

Rafter, Kevin, *Sinn Féin 1905–2005: In the Shadow of Gunmen* (Dublin: Gill & Macmillan, 2005).

Reilly, Paul, 'Ourselves alone (but making connections): the social media strategies of Sinn Fein', in Nixon, Paul, Rawal, Rajash, and Mercea, Dan (eds), *Politics and the Internet in Comparative Context: Views from the Cloud* (London: Routledge, 2013).

Rheingold, Howard, *The Virtual Community: Homesteading on the Electronic Frontier* (London: MIT Press, 2000).

Rolston, Bill, 'News fit to print: Belfast's daily newspapers', in Rolston, Bill (ed.), *The Media and Northern Ireland: Covering the Troubles* (London: Macmillan, 1991): 152–186.

—— and Miller, David, *War and Words: The Northern Ireland Media Reader* (Belfast: Beyond the Pale Publications, 1996).

Ross, F. Stuart, *Smashing H-Block: The Rise and Fall of the Popular Campaign Against Criminalization, 1976–1982* (Liverpool: Liverpool University Press, 2011).

Routledge, Paul, 'Critical geopolitics and terrains of resistance', *Political Geography*, vol. 15, nos. 6–7 (1996): 509–531.

Ryan, Mark, *War and Peace in Ireland* (London: Pluto Press, 1994).

Sanders, Andrew, *Inside the IRA: Dissident Republicans and the Battle for Legitimacy* (Edinburgh: Edinburgh University Press, 2011).

Schlesinger, Philip, *Media, State and Nation: Political Violence and Collective Identities* (London: Sage, 1991).

—— and Sparks, Colin (eds), *Culture and Power: A Media, Culture and Society Reader* (London: Sage, 1992).

Shirky, Clay, *Here Comes Everybody* (London: Penguin, 2008).

Shirlow, Peter, and McGovern, Mark, 'Language, discourse and dialogue: Sinn Féin and the Irish peace process', *Political Geography*, vol. 17, no. 2 (1998): 171–186.

Siggins, Lorna, *Once Upon a Time in the West: The Corrib Gas Controversy* (London: Transworld, 2010).

Smyth, Jim, 'On the road to God knows where: understanding Irish Republicanism', *Capital and Class* vol. 29, no. 2 (2005): 135–158.

Sparre, Kirsten, 'Megaphone diplomacy in the Northern Irish peace process', *Harvard Journal of Press/Politics* vol. 6, no. 1 (2001): 88–104.

Spencer, Graham, 'Pushing for peace: the Irish government, television news and the Northern Ireland Peace Process', *European Journal of Communication* vol. 18, no. 1 (2003): 55–80.

—— 'The impact of television news on the Northern Ireland peace negotiations', *Media, Culture and Society*, vol. 26, no. 5 (2004): 603–623.

—— *The Media and Peace: From Vietnam to the 'War on Terror'* (London: Palgrave Macmillan, 2005).

—— 'Sinn Féin and the media in Northern Ireland: the new terrain of policy articulation', *Irish Political Studies* vol. 21, no. 3 (2006): 355–382.

Strinati, Dominic, *An Introduction to Theories of Popular Culture* (London: Routledge, 2004).

Strömbäck, Jesper, 'Four phases of mediatization: an analysis of the mediatization of politics', *Harvard Journal of Press/Politics* vol. 13, no. 3 (2008): 228–246.

Stryker, Sheldon, Owens, Timothy J., and White, Robert W. (eds), *Self, Identity, and Social Movements* (Minneapolis: University of Minnesota Press, 2000).

Sunstein, Cass, *Republic 2.0* (Princeton, NJ: Princeton University Press, 2009).

Taylor, Peter, *Provos: The IRA and Sinn Fein* (London: Bloomsbury, 1997).

Todd, Jennifer, 'Social transformation, collective categories, and identity change', *Theory and Society* vol. 34, no. 4 (2005): 429–463.

Tonge, Jonathan, *Northern Ireland: Conflict and Change* (Harlow, Pearson Education, 2002).

—— 'Sinn Féin and "new republicanism" in Belfast', *Space and Polity*, vol. 10, no. 2 (2006): 135–147.

—— 'The political agenda of Sinn Fein: change without change?', in Stanyer, J., and Stoker, G. (eds), *Political Studies Association Annual Conference* (Jordanstown, Belfast: Political Studies Association, 1997): 750–760.

Van De Donk, Wim, Loader, Brian D., Nixon, Paul G., and Rucht, Dieter (eds), *Cyberprotest: New Media, Citizens and Social Movements* (London: Routledge, 2004).

Voitchovsky, Sarah, Maître, Bertrand, and Nolan, Brian, 'Wage inequality in Ireland's "Celtic Tiger" boom', *Economic and Social Review* vol. 43, no. 1 (2012): 99–133.

Wade, Karen, Greene, Derek, Lee, Conrad, Archambault, Daniel, and Cunningham, Pádraig, 'Identifying representative textual sources in blog networks' International AAAI Conference on Web and Social Media, Fifth International AAAI Conference on Weblogs and Social Media, 2011, Barcelona, Catalonia, Spain, 17–21 July.

Warner, Michael, *Publics and Counter Publics* (Cambridge, MA: MIT Press, 2002).

White, Robert W., and Fraser, Michael R., 'Personal and collective identities and long-term social movement activism: Republican Sinn Féin', in Stryker, Sheldon, Owens, Timothy J., and White, Robert W. (eds), *Self, Identity, and Social Movements* (Minneapolis, MN: University of Minnesota Press, 2000).

Whiting, Sophie, ' "The discourse of defence": "dissident" Irish republican newspapers and the "propaganda war" ', *Terrorism and Political Violence* vol. 24, no. 3 (2012): 483–503.

—— *Spoiling the Peace? The Threat of Dissident Republicans to Peace in Northern Ireland* (Manchester: Manchester University Press, 2015).

Williams, Raymond, *Keywords: A Vocabulary of Culture and Society* (Oxford: Oxford University Press, 1983).

Wilson, Robin, and Fawcett, Liz, 'The media election: coverage of the 2003 Northern Ireland Assembly poll', Democratic Dialogue. Available at: http://cain.ulst.ac.uk/dd/papers/index.html.

Wolfsfeld, Gadi, *Media and the Path to Peace* (Cambridge: Cambridge University Press, 2004).

—— *Making Sense of Media and Politics* (Abingdon: Routledge, 2011).

Index

Lightning Source UK Ltd.
Milton Keynes UK
UKHW021228071019

351156UK00004B/416/P